ADVANCED METHODS
of *Music Therapy Practice*

Analytical Music Therapy,
The Bonny Method of Guided Imagery and Music,
Nordoff-Robbins Music Therapy,
and Vocal Psychotherapy

NICKI S. COHEN

Jessica Kingsley *Publishers*
London and Philadelphia

On page 75, the photograph of Mary Priestley is used with kind permission of John Priestley. On page 95, the photograph of Helen Bonny is used with the kind permission of her family. On page 129, the photograph of Paul Nordoff and Clive Robbins, copyright © 2017 Nordoff-Robbins Center for Music Therapy, is used with kind permission of Dr. Kenneth Aigen. On page 149, the photograph of Diane Austin is used with kind permission of Diane Austin. On page 189, the image "Two Trees II", copyright © Thomas Wood 2017, is used with kind permission of Thomas Wood.

First published in 2018
by Jessica Kingsley Publishers
73 Collier Street
London N1 9BE, UK
and
400 Market Street, Suite 400
Philadelphia, PA 19106, USA

www.jkp.com

Copyright © Nicki S. Cohen 2018

Front cover image source: Shutterstock®.

All rights reserved. No part of this publication may be reproduced in any material form (including photocopying, storing in any medium by electronic means or transmitting) without the written permission of the copyright owner except in accordance with the provisions of the law or under terms of a licence issued in the UK by the Copyright Licensing Agency Ltd. www.cla.co.uk or in overseas territories by the relevant reproduction rights organisation, for details see www.ifrro.org. Applications for the copyright owner's written permission to reproduce any part of this publication should be addressed to the publisher.

Warning: The doing of an unauthorised act in relation to a copyright work may result in both a civil claim for damages and criminal prosecution.

Library of Congress Cataloging in Publication Data
A CIP catalog record for this book is available from the Library of Congress

British Library Cataloguing in Publication Data
A CIP catalogue record for this book is available from the British Library

ISBN 978 1 84905 776 9
eISBN 978 1 78450 008 5

Printed and bound in Great Britain

"Nicki Cohen has identified relevant advanced methods in music therapy as she reaches outside the 'box' of early traditional practice. She provides an accessible treatise introducing us to the founders on a personal level, and the methods on historical and theoretical levels. As the profession of music therapy continues to mature, the timeliness of this book is perfect. A welcome addition as the profession looks seriously to advanced practice and its implication in the broader health care milieu."

—*Jim Borling, Professor of Music, Program Director for Music Therapy, Fellow, Association for Music and Imagery (FAMI), Radford University, USA*

"I found Nicki Cohen's descriptions and analyses of four advanced music therapy methods to be enlightening and fascinating. She presents a range of information on the methods, including answers to a series of questions that were asked and answered by people who studied and worked directly with the founders of the methods or, in the case of Vocal Psychotherapy, by the founder (Diane Austin). She draws the reader into each approach with a deeper understanding of its practice."

—*Barbara L. Wheeler, PhD, MT-BC, Professor Emeritus, Montclair State University, New Jersey of related interest*

Guided Imagery & Music (GIM) and Music Imagery Methods for Individual and Group Therapy
Edited by Denise Grocke and Torben Moe
ISBN 978 1 84905 483 6
eISBN 978 0 85700 877 0

The Music of Being
Music Therapy, Winnicott and the School of Object Relations
Alison Levinge
ISBN 978 1 84905 576 5
eISBN 978 1 78450 019 1

The Music in Music Therapy
Psychodynamic Music Therapy in Europe: Clinical, Theoretical and Research Approaches
Edited by Jos De Backer and Julie Sutton
ISBN 978 1 84905 353 2
eISBN 978 0 85700 712 4

Basic Anatomy and Physiology for the Music Therapist
Daniel J. Schneck
ISBN 978 1 84905 756 1
eISBN 978 0 85700 992 0

Music Therapy with Families
Therapeutic Approaches and Theoretical Perspectives
Edited by Stine Lindahl Jacobsen and Grace Thompson
ISBN 978 1 84905 630 4
eISBN 978 1 78450 105 1

The scratch of the bow in the empty air

For Helen

ACKNOWLEDGEMENTS

I would like to thank the following people who assisted me through the completion of this book:

- Lisa Clark, who first encouraged this project in the crowded bookstall of a conference; Rachel Menzies, who helped me clean up Section II; and Elen Griffiths, who saw this project through to its completion.
- Pamela Youngblood, who fought to get me a faculty leave so that I could write this book.
- My beeping, fidgety finches that kept me entertained as I wrote.
- Bruce Bond, my husband, my beshert. Thank you for the soup and crackers you brought me at night on a tray when I skipped dinner.

Also, countless thanks to those wise and generous experts who graciously allowed me to interview them: Ken Aigen, Gary Ansdell, Diane Austin, Leslie Bunt, Barbara Hesser, Inge Nygaard Pedersen, John Priestley, Allison Reynolds, Benedikte Scheiby, Sierra Stearns, and Alan Turry.

CONTENTS

Preface 11
List of Acronyms 17

SECTION I

1. Music Therapy in the United States:
   An Historic Overview 21
2. Music Therapy in the United Kingdom:
   An Historic Overview 45
3. Music Therapy Method 57

SECTION II

4. Mary Priestley and Analytical Music Therapy 75
5. The Bonny Method of Guided Imagery and Music . 95
6. Nordoff-Robbins Music Therapy 129
7. Diane Austin and Vocal Psychotherapy 149

SECTION III

8. Questions 167
9. The Two Trees 189

   Appendices 195
   Bibliography 233
   Subject Index 242
   Author Index 247

PREFACE

My life has always been centered on music. Ever since my decision to pursue the practice of music therapy in 1971, I have never wavered from identifying myself as a music therapist. After completing my undergraduate training in 1977, I worked for two years in a state home for adults with developmental disabilities. That two-year period almost annihilated me. I was only 22 years old. I was horrified by the conditions under which the residents lived, and was even more aghast at the apathy towards those conditions reflected by the professionals who worked at the home. My music therapy clinic was a single room with cement floors, no windows, plastic seats, and a consistently faint smell of urine. The institution mandated that our treatments be based on operantly defined behaviors. Although I tried to keep my personal life vital, the numbness that had been creeping into my being started to impact my life outside of work. I called in sick more than I've ever done before or since. Although I was very fond of the adult residents with whom I worked, I felt robotic, negative, and my music therapy sessions felt stale and repetitive.

With a leap of faith, I left my full-time job in 1980 to pursue a private practice in music therapy. I worked six to seven days a week. Most of my clients were adolescents diagnosed with mental retardation or autism who were living in residential homes. I served these homes for seven years. I remember once suggesting to my supervisors that we discontinue some of the clients who had been receiving music therapy sessions, as they did not seem to be making therapeutic progress on their objectives. The employers disagreed and would not allow me to reduce my work. They claimed that the clients obviously enjoyed and got a lot from their music therapy sessions. I questioned why that wasn't enough for me, and I found myself growing weary of the routes back and forth to the different group homes. I still felt stuck inside a box that I had somehow constructed, and pined for something outside the box. I was searching for meaning and sensed that it was somewhere within the parameters of music therapy practice. Perhaps I needed to learn more about music therapy at an advanced level and to understand theories other than behaviorism to finally comprehend what music therapy is or what it could be.

It was with great energy and motivation that I entered a doctoral program in 1987 at a large university specializing in music therapy research. I enjoyed every moment of being a graduate student and teaching fellow. I felt sharp, aware, and never brighter than during those three years. Ironically, it did not occur to me until much later that during my time at the university I did not work with any clients save in my dissertation research. This research took me in a new direction, beyond operant conditioning and into the medical model and neurological rehabilitation. By bringing my love and knowledge of singing into new music therapy techniques, I could assist persons with neurogenic communication disorders with their speech. The outcomes from the singing and rhythmic treatments were promising, and I continued to conduct research in this area for years, to publish research articles, and to present at professional conferences.

It wasn't until 1992, when I became employed as a Music Therapy professor at a university, that I was challenged again to seek the full potential of music therapy. The standard definitions of music therapy found in the textbooks were useful but did not articulate what it was in the field that I was craving. For example, I never felt my definitions of music therapy were congruent with the experience for which I hungered. It was as though I had moved right past it without ever really knowing it. That was just it. Boom. I was still in a self-constructed box, and the meaningful potential of music therapy, of life, and of my full power, still beckoned outside of the box. True, the box was more extravagant now. But it was a box, nevertheless, and I was still inside it.

In 1995, I took another leap of faith and signed up for a five-day Level One training course in Guided Imagery and Music (GIM) through the Bonny Foundation. I remember rationalizing that it would be good for me to attend this class so that I could speak about GIM more clearly in my classes. I drove from Texas to a spiritual retreat center in Wichita, Kansas (KS). I remember receiving the key for my small dorm room, and as I started to unlock it, two older women arrived at the door next to mine. They turned out to be Helen Bonny and Roseanne Kasayka, the teachers of the course, and witnesses to my first stage of spiritual transformation through the GIM method.

It is now 2017 and 22 years later. I completed my training with the Bonny Foundation and became a Fellow of the Association for Music and Imagery in 2001. Helen Bonny was my mentor and one of the most influential persons in my life. We remained close until her death in 2010. I completed my requirements to become a primary trainer in the Bonny Method of Guided Imagery and Music in 2016 and now I can teach others this profound method. My life has forever been changed since that first day of class in Wichita, KS. I now fully understand the power and meaning of music therapy. This has made me a better teacher, therapist, citizen, and person.

BOOK RATIONALE AND OUTLINE

Since this story seems to have a happy ending, you might be wondering why I am writing this book. The reason is because it took me almost 30 years to discover the unleashed power of music therapy. I wonder how many younger music therapists give up and pursue other professions. I question why my long-term involvement in the music therapy profession did not contribute to my understanding of music therapy. And finally, I wonder why it took training in an advanced music therapy method that had developed outside of the parameters of the profession or academia to bring me to a comprehension of the full potential of music therapy.

This book is my attempt to answer the questions posed above. I chose four advanced methods of music therapy that take at least two years of training to complete, require the minimum of a Master's degree to study, and whose practices are comprehensive and psychodynamic in nature: Analytical Music Therapy, the Bonny Method of Guided Imagery and Music, Nordoff-Robbins Music Therapy, and Vocal Psychotherapy. In most cases, these methods are taught outside of the general parameters of any Music Therapy academic degree requirements.

Section I of the book contains general information about the development of the music therapy profession in the United States (US) and the United Kingdom (UK), and my rationale for the choice of the term "method" to describe each of these practices. The reasons for my choosing the two countries is as follows: (1) two of the methods were born in the US (i.e., Bonny Method and Vocal Psychotherapy) and two were born in the UK (i.e., Nordoff-Robbins Music Therapy and Analytical Musical Therapy); (2) both countries share the same language, functions of music, and therapeutic orientations; and (3) the music therapy profession developed in both places at approximately the same time. Section II of the book presents the historical development, current training and practice, techniques, and a literature review for each of the four methods. Section III of the book resulted from a series of interviews with 11 experts in the four methods. I selected one representative from the US and one from the UK per method. All interviews contained an identical set of 17 questions. The majority of the experts were trainers in one of the methods; most were academicians; and all had been music therapists for over 30 years. A few of the experts provided a more generalized perspective regarding the development of the four methods and their relationships to the professional development of music therapy. Using a generic form of qualitative inquiry, I presented case studies, both cross cases and within, and using the NVivo software program, analyzed the transcribed responses from the experts to the following seven questions:

1. What is it about this method that still resonates with you?

2. What has the advanced method taught you about music therapy?

3. Has your relationship with this advanced method changed over the years? If so, how?

4. Do you believe that the founders of this advanced method intended to create a new music therapy approach?

5. Did there seem to be changes in the professional music therapy associations' attitudes towards the method over time?

6. Do you consider this method to be a part of music therapy practice? Why or why not? Has your viewpoint on this changed over time?

7. Overall, what do you foresee for the future of this advanced method?

DISCLAIMERS

In the process of writing this book, I ran into some challenges; they tended to represent culturally based differences in vocabulary between the US and the UK. I discovered a major discrepancy between the two countries regarding the usage and perception of the terms *advanced*, *post-graduate*, and *method*. The second challenge resulted from my choice of the experts interviewed in this book. Many individuals meet the criteria to be an expert in one of the four methods. Since my methodology in Section III was qualitative in nature, I hand-picked a sample of experts who met the criteria and who represented, to me, cross-cultural, informed, and insightful perspectives regarding the four methods. That being said, I extend my apologies to anyone I may have offended by not including them in this project. The final challenge was due to my choice of the term *method* to describe the four advanced practices. Chapter Three of this book provides a rationale for my choice of this word. I fully accept that others may disagree with my choice, and I hope they can look past this term to appreciate the remaining content of this book.

LIST OF ACRONYMS

AAMT	American Association for Music Therapy
ACMT	Advanced Certified Music Therapist
AMI	Association for Music and Imagery
AMT	Analytical Music Therapy
AMTA	American Music Therapy Association
APMT	Association of Professional Music Therapists
AVPT	Austin Vocal Psychotherapist
BAMT	British Association for Music Therapy
BMGIM	Bonny Method of Guided Imagery and Music
BC	Board Certified
BSMT	British Society for Music Therapy
CBMT	Certification Board for Music Therapists
CMT	Certified Music Therapist
CNS	central nervous system
CPSM	Council for the Professions Supplementary to Medicine
EAMI	European Association for Music and Imagery
GIM	Guided Imagery and Music (Bonny Method of)
HCPC	Health and Care Professions Council
HPC	Health Professions Council
KSAs	knowledge, skills, and abilities
LOP	Levels of Practice

LSD	lysergic acid diethylamide
MBSR	mindfulness-based stress reduction
MENC	Music Educators National Conference
MPRC	Maryland Psychiatric Research Center
MT-BC	Music Therapist-Board Certified
MTNA	Music Teachers National Association
NAMT	National Association for Music Therapy
NASM	National Association of Schools of Music
NCHCA	National Commission on Health Certifying Agencies
NIMH	National Institute of Mental Health
NHS	National Health Service
NMC	National Music Council
NOCA	National Organization for Competency Assurance
NRMT	Nordoff-Robbins Music Therapy
NR-MT	Nordoff-Robbins Music Therapy
PSMA	Professionals Supplementary to Medicine Act
RMT	Registered Music Therapist
TC	therapeutic community
UFMT	Urban Federation of Music Therapists
VP	Vocal Psychotherapy

SECTION I

CHAPTER ONE

MUSIC THERAPY IN THE UNITED STATES

A Historic Overview

My goal for this chapter is to explore the history of music therapy in the United States (US). According to Bunt and Stige, "The United States was the first country to develop music therapy into a modern profession and discipline" (2014, p.5). Through this chapter, current music therapy practice and future perspectives can be understood within the context of past events. I plan to answer the following questions:

1. How did the music therapy profession develop in the United States?

2. What is the nature of music therapy education and training in the United States, and from where did it evolve?

3. What professional music therapy associations emerged in the United States, and what discrete roles did they serve?

MUSIC THERAPY IN THE UNITED STATES BEFORE 1900

Even though music was part of the prevailing theories of treatment of diseases prior to the 19th century (Boxberger 1963), the modern period in history (circa 1789–1914) produced the smallest amounts of literature concerning the therapeutic aspects of music (Horden 2000). During the 18th century, literature written about therapeutic music was based solely on anecdotal rather than scientific evidence (Davis, Gfeller and Thaut 1999). In the late 18th century, a few treatises began to appear concerning the medicinal value of music. Interest in this topic grew at a slow but steady pace. In 1789, an unsigned article entitled "Music Physically Considered" appeared in the *Columbian Magazine*. This was the first known publication about music therapy literature in the US (Heller 1987). Interestingly, the article introduced basic ideas that are still germane to current music therapy practice, such as the stimulative and pleasure-evoking aspects of music, the need for a knowledgeable and skilled practitioner when applying music as therapy, and the nebulous effects of music on the emotions. In 1796, an article called "Remarkable Cure of a Fever by Music: An Attested Fact" appeared in the *New York Weekly Magazine* (Davis *et al.* 1999). Also by an anonymous author, this publication summarized a music teacher's recovery from illness after listening to live music.

In the 19th century, physicians began to consider psychosomatic factors in the etiology and treatment of diseases (Boxberger 1963). Few documents about therapeutic music were published, and most centered on music as an adjunct to medical treatment (Davis 1987). Said publications appeared primarily as medical dissertations or in medical journals, and advocated music as an alternative, more holistic approach to medical treatment. However, the majority of physicians in the 19th century remained opposed to the holistic viewpoint, which espoused that medicine was also a social science (Boxberger 1963). In addition, the fact that most of the authors worked independently of each other and wrote specifically for a medical audience hampered the distribution of these writings to the lay public. It was not until the last quarter of the 19th century that articles about the therapeutic benefits of music began to appear in more public forms of literature (Davis 1987).

Some of the authors writing about therapeutic music during the first decade of the 19th century were protégées of Dr. Benjamin Rush (1746–1813), a physician and professor at the University of

Pennsylvania, who advocated for music in the treatment of mental illness (Davis *et al.* 1999). Rush was better known as one of the signers of the Declaration of Independence and as the "Father of American Psychiatry" (Horden 2000, p.323). Edwin Atlee and Samuel Matthews were two medical students who studied with Rush, and both wrote their dissertations on the medicinal value of music. Atlee's work, produced in 1804, discussed the ability of music to arouse and influence emotions, while Matthews' dissertation, composed in 1806, advocated the value of music to treat diseases of the body and mind (as cited in Davis 1987). Matthews suggested that music should match the mood of the patient. Although their works were brief and slight in content, both authors are to be remembered for recommending a unique approach to medicine at the turn of the 19th century, one which emphasized music as a way of treating more than just the physical body.

In 1817, a Quaker community built the Friends Asylum, one of the earliest hospitals in the US devoted exclusively to the humane care and treatment of persons with mental illnesses. Located near Philadelphia, Pennsylvania (PA), this facility was constructed to address Benjamin Rush's concerns about the ongoing, horrific treatment of patients with mental illnesses (Horden 2000; van Atta 1980), and music was one of the therapies offered. In fact, during the first half of the 19th century, similar institutions for patients with mental ill health and schools for students with visual and hearing impairments began to hire music instructors. One of the best known of these instructors was Lowell Mason, who taught vocal and piano music at the Perkins School for the Blind in Boston, Massachusetts (MA) from 1832 to 1837. Mason's work was not considered by the school to be therapeutic in nature, but rather as a form of "intellectual gratification" (Horden 2000, p.324). Mason went on to develop a public school music curriculum for the city of Boston, and became known as the "Father of Music Education" (Birge 1966, p.37).

Other music teachers focused on music education with deaf students. For example, William Wolcott Turner and Ely Bartlett created a music curriculum at the American Asylum for the Deaf in Hartford, Connecticut (CT) during the 1840s. These two teachers co-authored an article entitled "Music Among the Deaf and Dumb," which was published in the *American Annals of the Deaf and Dumb* (Darrow and Heller 1985).

The second half of the 19th century witnessed an increase in the number of publications about the therapeutic values of music. Noteworthy among these was an article by James Whittaker that appeared in the *Cincinnati Clinic* in 1874. Whittaker, a physician, presented a novel perspective by claiming that patients' responses to music were linked not only to physiological factors but also to psychological and socio-cultural influences (Davis *et al.* 1999). Another landmark article was published in 1878 in the *Virginia Medical Monthly*. Edited by Landon Edwards, this piece described a series of experiments at New York City's Blackwell's Island facility for patients with mental ill health. The research involved the provision of live music played by professional musicians. While the psychiatric patients listened to the music, physicians took physiological measurements to determine if the music had facilitated any physical changes (Davis *et al.* 1999). Although the findings were inconclusive, Edwards remains recognized for his support of music to decrease distress in psychiatric patients.

The Blackwell's Island article described the therapeutic practice of bringing performing musicians into the hospital. This trend indicated a shift away from strictly custodial care to a more humane model of treatment for patients with mental ill health. Another article reflecting this trend was written by George Blumer and published in the *American Journal of Insanity* in 1892 (as cited in Davis 1987). Blumer was a physician and director of the Utica State Hospital in New York. As he believed that music was part of a morally responsible treatment for mental illness, he hired musicians to perform for the patients.

At the end of the 19th century, neurologist James Leonard Corning conducted a scientific study on the application of "vibrative music techniques" as a treatment for mental illness (Davis *et al.* 1999, p.23). Published in the *Medical Record* in 1899, this was the first scientifically controlled attempt to treat mental illness through music, and served as a headlight for the scientific inquiry that was to follow in the 20th century.

TURN OF THE 20TH CENTURY TO 1940

One of the technological highlights at the turn of the 20th century was Thomas Edison's invention of the phonograph. This new musical phenomenon, introduced in 1877, forever changed the way in which human beings experienced music. Prior to this invention, all music had to be encountered via live performances. Music occurred in direct time and was a social and interactive event that happened in specific performance settings. Following the invention of the phonograph, music could, for the first time, be experienced in private or non-performance settings.

The invention of the phonograph also brought about a renewed interest in the therapeutic influences of music and set the stage for the growing appeal of music in medical settings. After the first commercially available disc recordings went on sale in 1896 (Taylor 1981), physicians began bringing phonographs into hospitals to explore the impact of recorded music on medical patients. The first publication about this new practice was printed in 1914, when Dr. Evan O'Neill Kane published a letter in the *Journal of the American Medical Association* about his use of a phonograph in the operating room to calm or distract surgical patients from the "horror of the situation" (as cited in Taylor 1981, p.63).

It was not until the turn of the century that women began to make major contributions towards the development of the music therapy profession (Horden 2000). In fact, the early pioneers of music therapy in the 20th century were primarily women. Eva Vescelius founded the National Therapeutic Society of New York City in 1903, and served as its president until her death in 1917 (Schmidt Peters 1987). She offered the first course in music therapy, called "Musicotherapy," and began publication of a journal, *Music and Health*, in 1913. Vescelius believed that the purpose of music was "to return a sick person's discordant vibrations to harmonious ones" (as cited in Davis *et al.* 1999, p.24).

Margaret Anderton was the first person to teach Music Therapy at a university. In 1919, she taught a one-semester, undergraduate-level course at Columbia University in New York (de l'Etoile 2000). The class offered practical training and was attended by musicians who wished to work in hospitals as therapists. Anderton professed that the sounds of certain instruments had healing effects for psychological conditions, especially the sound of wind instruments constructed of wood (Taylor 1981). Isa Maud Ilsen co-taught the course. Ilsen was a Norwegian immigrant, nurse, hospital administrator, and music director who founded the National Association for Music in Hospitals in 1926 (Schmidt Peters 1987). She was the director of hospital music for the American Red Cross in World War I reconstruction hospitals. Considering music to be an adjunct to medical treatment, Ilsen warned that music should never interfere with hospital procedures (Boxberger 1963). She strongly believed in the power of rhythm, but discouraged the use of jazz music, which she considered to be inappropriate for medical patients (Davis *et al.* 1999). Ilsen's attitudes towards jazz may have been reflective of the opinions during the era when jazz music was considered improper and jazz musicians were associated with undesirable segments of society (Merriam 1964). Ilsen recommended classical music for treatment, but she also mentioned the importance of the patients' cultural backgrounds and musical preferences in her choices of music.

Harriet Ayer Seymour wrote a guide for aspiring music therapists in 1920 entitled, *What Music Can Do for You*. She was known for conducting experiments on the effects of certain types of music on physical and mental disorders, and for writing the first Music Therapy textbook, *An Instruction Guide in the Use of Practice of Musical Therapy* (as cited in Davis *et al.* 1999). In this text, Seymour recommended the same therapeutic treatment for all patients, which was the live performance of light classical and folk music by musicians under the guidance of a lead therapist. Seymour defined music therapy as the combination of music and positive thought, or "musical meditation" (p.25).

Esther Gatewood, PhD, a contemporary of Anderton and Seymour, believed in the neurological principle that two separate sensory stimuli entering the central nervous system (CNS) tended to neutralize each other, with only the stronger, more dominant stimulus entering into consciousness (Taylor 1981). To wit,

Gatewood believed that music and pain were two separate sensory stimuli, and that music could function as an *audio-distracter* to neutralize the effects of the pain. Gatewood's theory foreshadows the well-known *Gate Theory of Pain Control*, which purports that musical stimuli can help close the neural gate that carries pain signals to the brain, therefore decreasing the perception of pain experienced by the patient (Melzack and Wall 1982). Gatewood recommended using patient-preferred music. Akin to Samuel Matthews' statement made more than a hundred years earlier, Gatewood believed that the professional should match the patient's mood and then gradually change the music to alter the patient's temperament. This technique would later be referred to as "The Iso Principle" (Davis *et al.* 1999, p.20).

During the first half of the 20th century, published literature about music in hospitals focused primarily on the *anesthetic* and *analgesic* effects of music (Taylor 1981). Facilities such as Duke University Hospital in Durham, North Carolina (NC) began playing radio music in the operating arenas and patient rooms via earphones or wall speakers (Taylor 1981). Dr. E. F. Erdman recommended the "silent gramophone," a Western electric music reproducer with headphones, as a means of calming patients during surgery (Davis and Gfeller 2008; Taylor 1981). Dentist E. S. Best believed that the noise of dental equipment aggravated his patients' pain responses, and utilized music during dental procedures to decrease the impact of the noise (Taylor 1981).

Following World War I, psychiatry was considered the primary therapeutic modality. US military personnel with psycho-pathological and physical war-related conditions began filling military and psychiatric hospitals (Hillman Boxill 1985). In an attempt to meet the needs of these veterans, *milieu therapy* came into practice. It involved the collaboration of therapies to improve patients' lives. Music provided a supportive function in the patients' psychotherapy, as did other adjunctive therapies such as occupational therapy, recreation therapy, physical therapy, bibliotherapy, manual arts therapy, and corrective therapy (Michel and Pinson 2005). Professional musicians, known as *hospital musicians*, were brought into institutions to conduct instrumental and choral groups and to teach music lessons (Hillman Boxill 1985).

Wilem van de Wall was one such musician who helped to clarify the difference between a hospital musician and a music therapist. Van de Wall was a professional harpist with the Metropolitan Opera and the New York Symphony (Schmidt Peters 1987). He established Music Therapy programs in mental hospitals and prisons during the period between the two World Wars. His book, *Music in Institutions* (1936), is based on his experiences developing Music Therapy programs in hospitals. Van de Wall lectured on music and health at Columbia University from 1925–1932, and was appointed chairperson of the Committee for the Use of Music in Hospitals in 1944.

Ira M. Altshuler, a contemporary of van de Wall, was a psychiatrist and composer who founded a music program at a general hospital in Michigan (Schmidt Peters 1987). He lectured and wrote about what he called "musical therapy" during the late 1930s through the 1950s (Altshuler 1945). He was credited with coining the term "Iso Maneuver" to describe the practice of matching music to the psychiatric patient's mood or level of functioning (Altshuler 1941, 1945). This was 20 years after the introduction of this concept by Esther Gatewood.

An increasing number of medical specialists advocated empirical research to justify the beneficial properties of music to their peers. Dr. Kenneth Pickrell and associates, for example, conducted a project in 1944 on the application of music throughout all phases of surgery (as cited in Taylor 1981). The researchers chose music with "sweet orchestrations" rather than marches, hymns, or spirituals (p.69). Physicians discovered that music was helpful in masking previously unidentified hospital noises that had exacerbated patient anxiety. In a similar study, researchers at the University of Chicago examined the application of music with 200 surgical patients, and concluded that: (1) music was beneficial both prior to and during surgery, and (2) the music helped to reduce the amount of sedative medication usually required (Taylor 1981).

THE NEED FOR TRAINING STANDARDS

During the decade of the 1940s, music service organizations (e.g., Musicians Emergency Fund, Hospitalized Veterans Music Service, Sigma Alpha Iota) provided musicians to Veterans Administration facilities and state institutions; however, the musicians were mostly unpaid, part-time workers who lacked any professional training. At the same time, hospitals in the US began to adopt a more holistic attitude towards treatment, one that recognized that medicine was also a social science (Boxberger 1963) and that a number of possible therapeutic modalities existed, instead of only psychiatry. Medical administrators began to accept that music could do more than entertain or distract, and music services started to serve more of a therapeutic function in the hospitals (Hillman Boxill 1985). This was not an easy task for the hospital musicians, however. According to Ainlay (1948, as cited in Bunt and Stige 2014), both musicians and physicians in the 1940s–1950s seemed to lack an understanding of music's value apart from its general cultural function. Not only did the fledgling profession of hospital music attempt to free itself from identification as just another recreational pastime, but also from the stigma brought on by previous practices in music therapy where music was considered more "mystical than scientific" (Boxberger 1963, p.39), or the belief that listening to music could bring nothing but positive responses, when music could actually be contraindicative in certain situations (Bunt and Stige 2014). This shift in resolve spearheaded the development of more standardized Music Therapy training programs. Although the term *music therapy* had been used informally since the 1920s to refer to the music services provided in the hospitals, no professional music therapy association or standardized training existed until 1950.

Also during the 1940s, professional music organizations (i.e., Music Teachers National Association, Music Educators National Conference, and National Music Council) began forming committees and holding conferences to investigate the therapeutic potential of music (Boxberger 1963). In 1946, the Music Teachers National Association (MTNA) created a Committee on Music in Therapy, and the Music Educators National Conference (MENC) formed the Special Committee on Functional Music (de l'Etoile 2000; Schmidt Peters 1987). The MENC Committee recommended that musical performances at hospitals be differentiated from music therapy services, and that steps be taken to license music therapists. The National Music Council (NMC) formed the Committee on Music in Hospitals, which was chaired by Howard Hanson, president of the organization and an eminent composer. Ironically, the first Committee membership lacked representation from hospital musicians. This problem was rectified in 1947, however, when Ray Green was asked to assume the position of chairperson. One of many benefits of Green's leadership was the publication of the *Hospital Music Newsletter*, which first appeared as part of the *Bulletin of the National Music Council Early Educational Programs* (Boxberger 1963).

Although the first course in Music Therapy was offered as early as 1919 at Columbia University, an official curriculum leading to a degree in Music Therapy was not established in the US until 1944. It was then that Roy Underwood developed the first Bachelor's degree in Music Therapy at Michigan State University in East Lansing, Michigan (MI). Dr. Ira Altshuler collaborated with Underwood to create the first university-affiliated internship program at Wayne County Hospital in Eloise, MI (de l'Etoile 2000). In 1946, Donald Michel developed a Music Therapy internship at the Winter Veteran's Administration Hospital in Topeka, KS. Michel worked with the students of E. Thayer Gaston (1901–1971), chairman of the Music Education Department at the University of Kansas (KU) (Davis *et al.* 1999). Gaston also collaborated with Dr. Karl Menninger of the Menninger Clinic in Topeka, KS, a facility that specialized in psychoanalytic treatment, to establish the second internship site. In 1946, KU began offering graduate-level courses in Music Therapy, and in 1948, it approved the first graduate Music Therapy degree program in the US. The academic requirements for this degree included the completion of a six-month internship. Other academic programs established in the 1940s were the College of the Pacific (1947), Alverno College (1948), and Chicago Musical College (de l'Etoile 2000).

PROFESSIONAL ASSOCIATIONS
National Association for Music Therapy

The need to make music more applicable to modern medicine initiated the drive toward a national organization (Boxberger 1963). During the Music Teachers National Association (MTNA) annual meeting in Cleveland, Ohio (OH) in February 1950, a special committee was formed to develop a national organization of music therapists. Ray Green was elected to chair this committee. In June 1950, the first organizational meeting of the National Association for Music Therapy (NAMT) was held in New York City (Hillman Boxill 1985). Green was elected president, and the constituents adopted a constitution, set goals, created membership categories, and formed a standing committee for research (Davis *et al.* 1999). In December 1950, the first NAMT Conference was held in collaboration with the MTNA Conference in Washington, DC.

During its first decade, NAMT witnessed substantial growth, both in its organizational structure and in the professional status of music therapists. It established a central office in Lawrence, KS, formed regional chapters, adopted an insignia, and became incorporated (Boxberger 1963). In addition, the NAMT leadership solidified relationships with other professional organizations and published two documents: an annual yearbook called the *Book of Proceedings*, and the *Bulletin of the National Association for Music Therapy*, which was printed on a tri-quarterly basis. Professional registration policies and procedures were created, resulting in the granting of the title "Registered Music Therapist" (RMT), beginning in 1956, to individuals who had successfully completed a Music Therapy academic training program. The purpose of this designation was to provide assurance to the public that music therapists had met specified educational and clinical standards (Davis *et al.* 1999).

Due to a growth in the number of university courses and degree programs offered, NAMT membership approved the first standardized Music Therapy curriculum in 1952 (de l'Etoile 2000). This undergraduate curriculum was course-based, and the content varied greatly according to the expertise of the educators. In 1959,

Charles Braswell, a Music Therapy educator and active NAMT member, recommended that the purpose of the curriculum should be to train students in musical competencies and the ability to work with others (as cited in de l'Etoile 2000). Braswell also encouraged the development of strong research skills. He published an outline of recommended courses, which became the template for many university program curricula in the years to come.

NAMT helped to coordinate the presentation and publication of information about music therapy. The number of published studies increased, as did the areas of clinical impact, especially concerning medical treatment (Taylor 1981). NAMT began to look for ways to disseminate the most current research results. In 1964, the *Journal of Music Therapy* began publication under the editorship of William Sears, with the set goal of sharing scholarly findings about music therapy with a larger professional audience. NAMT moved its office from Lawrence, KS to Washington, DC in 1982 (Frederick Tims, personal communication, February 6, 2007) to increase NAMT's visibility and legislative impact. During the same year, NAMT began publishing *Music Therapy Perspectives*, a second, more practice-oriented periodical (AMTA 2015). The 50 years following the founding of NAMT contained three pivotal events: (1) the establishment of the American Association for Music Therapy (AAMT); (2) the creation of the Certification Board for Music Therapists (CBMT); and (3) the unification of NAMT and AAMT into the American Music Therapy Association (AMTA).

American Association for Music Therapy

The Urban Federation of Music Therapists (UFMT) was established in 1971 to meet the unique needs of music therapists working with an emerging diversity of client populations, techniques, and treatment philosophies, especially those working in large urban centers, such as New York City (Hillman Boxill 1985). Members of UFMT shared two major criticisms of NAMT: (1) the narrow focus that NAMT held towards Music Therapy education and training, and (2) the concern that NAMT was becoming too bureaucratic, and the needs of its individual members were becoming neglected (Dena Coldron, personal communication, March 21, 1998). UFMT's headquarters were located at New York University, the site of the first approved academic degree by UFMT in 1973. The goals of the new organization centered on research, information sharing, and the certification of music therapists. The inaugural board of directors included a president, vice-president, secretary, and treasurer. Robert Cumming, then editor of *Music Journal*, was elected as the first president. In 1975, UFMT changed its name to the American Association for Music Therapy (AAMT) because of the belief that identifying an association primarily with urban settings was limiting in scope (Dena Coldron, personal communication, March 21, 1998).

Once founded, AAMT's organizational infrastructure grew quickly. An organizational chart was implemented that delineated the particular Standing Committees of Registration/Certification, Membership, Education and Training, Public Relations, Professional Organizations, Program, Newsletter, Journal, Fundraising, and Clinical Facilities (Dena Coldron personal communication, March 21, 1998). In 1978, two academic programs in Philadelphia, Temple University and Hahnemann Medical College became AAMT-approved. Over the next 20 years, other Music Therapy programs followed suit, including the College of St. Mary of the Woods, Molloy College, Lesley College, the Naropa Institute, and Incarnate Word College (Dena Coldron, personal communication, March 21, 1998).

In the 1980s and 1990s, AAMT experienced massive organizational changes. It began publication of the professional journal *Music Therapy* in 1981 (Schmidt Peters 1987) and the *International Newsletter of Music Therapy* in 1983 (Dena Coldron, personal communication, March 21, 1998). One year later, the newsletter changed its name to *Tuning In*. From 1982 to 1995, the AAMT Board of Directors switched from the practice of using outside managerial firms to self-management. Between 1988 and 1995, it experienced numerous shifts in leadership and in the location of its headquarters.

From its inception until its dissolution in 1998, AAMT tended to maintain a smaller number of members than NAMT, although some music therapists chose to belong to both associations. AAMT endorsed its own training programs and granted the first professional designation, the "Certified Music Therapist" (CMT), in 1982. The advanced certification, or "Advanced Certified Music Therapist" (ACMT), was added in 1989 (Dena Coldron, personal communication, March 21, 1998). Although AAMT lasted only 27 years, it strongly influenced the development of Music Therapy education and practice in the US. It permitted flexibility and autonomy to its members by adopting clinical and educational techniques not always in keeping with current clinical practices. In addition, key documents resulted from AAMT member efforts, including the first list of professional Music Therapy competencies. Written by Bruscia, Hesser, and Hillman Boxill (1981), this document served as the forerunner for NAMT's *Professional Competencies* (1996). And when AAMT unified with NAMT in 1998 to form the American Music Therapy Association (AMTA), many of the original AAMT practices and philosophies were integrated into the new association's standards.

Certification Board for Music Therapists

Due to increasing demands for objectivity and credibility in healthcare practice by employers and state agencies, the Certification Board for Music Therapists (CBMT) was established in 1984 (Schmidt Peters 1987; Joy Schneck, personal communication, May 5, 2006). CBMT serves as an independent certification and recertification agency for music therapists in the US (CBMT 2001; Michel and Pinson 2005). The first certification exam was administered at the NAMT Annual Music Therapy Conference on November 16, 1985 (Schmidt Peters 1987). The test items were based on the *Examination Content Outline*, a list of professional knowledge, skills, and abilities (KSAs) resulting from the first Job/Practice Analysis conducted in 1983 (CBMT 1985). It clearly defined the scope of what CBMT certified an individual to do (Joy Schneck, personal communication, May 5, 2006). Any person who passed the exam thereby received the credential "Board Certified" (BC).

The certification process, which occurs in five-year cycles, is based on the guidelines of the National Commission on Health Certifying Agencies (NCHCA) and the National Organization for Competency Assurance (NOCA). The first certification cycle, from 1988–1992, included 3097 music therapists; 2626 were granted transitional certification and 471 passed the exam during 1985–1987 (Joy Schneck, personal communication, May 5, 2006). In the decade following the inception of CBMT, practicing music therapists could keep both their professional designations (i.e., RMT, CMT, ACMT) and also assume the MT-BC (Music Therapist-Board Certified) credential. While CBMT's certification program served the distinct purpose of evaluating Music Therapy education and training and constructing an objective examination to insure competence, NAMT and AAMT continued to award and administer their own designations, and CBMT had little say regarding how these designations were awarded, used, or maintained (Joy Schneck, personal communication, May 5, 2006). Varying combinations of Music Therapy designations and credentials ensued (i.e., RMT, CMT, ACMT, RMT-BC, CMT-BC, ACMT-BC, MT-BC), which proved to be very confusing to the governmental organizations and consumers the music therapists were marketing themselves to.

Unification: American Music Therapy Association

From 1971 to 1998, the NAMT, AAMT and CBMT attempted to represent the profession, but were often at cross-purposes. With the sweeping changes in the healthcare field during the 1990s, including the influx of managed care regulations, state licensure legislation, and growing competition from other therapeutic providers for healthcare dollars, representatives from the two associations, in consultation with CBMT, began to have a dialogue about the possibilities of unifying. What eventually ensued was the formation of the American Music Therapy Association (AMTA) in 1998.

An immense amount of deliberation and compromise preceded this unification. Transitional committees, such as the Implementation Task Force and the Commission on Education and Training, hammered out association policies. The Executive Director of NAMT, Dr. Andrea Farbman, was retained as the Executive Director of AMTA, and the NAMT office, located in Silver Spring, Maryland (MD), became the location for the new association. New educational and clinical standards were developed to reflect the ideologies and practices of both organizations. One of the more difficult decisions centered on the future of NAMT and AAMT professional publications. A period of intense deliberations by representatives from both groups ensued. What resulted was a continuation of the NAMT periodicals, *Journal of Music Therapy* and *Music Therapy Perspectives*, while the AAMT journal, *Music Therapy*, ceased publication. Association newsletters were combined and renamed *Music Therapy Matters*. Over time, a new organizational structure evolved to represent the tenets of the new organization.

AMTA AND CBMT: POST-UNIFICATION

At present, two major associations represent the profession of Music Therapy in the US: the American Music Therapy Association (AMTA) and the Certification Board for Music Therapists (CBMT). Each serves a unique role. While AMTA sets and oversees the standards for the academic and clinical training of music therapists, CBMT functions as the sole credentialing body.

American Music Therapy Association

AMTA is "committed to the advancement of education, training, professional standards, credentials, and research in support of the music therapy profession" (AMTA 2014). More specifically, AMTA serves to disseminate information concerning how music can be used for the betterment of public health and welfare (AMTA 2016a rev.). In 2014, AMTA had approximately 3800 members (Jane Creagan, personal communication, June 23, 2014). Although a great deal of business is conducted at the Annual Conference held each November, the national office staff and volunteer membership work continuously to address the ongoing needs of the music therapists and music therapy recipients. At present, AMTA's employees include an executive director; separate directors for Communications and Conferences, Membership Services and Information Systems, Government Relations, and Professional Programs; and other support staff.

Official documents
Since unification in 1998, AMTA has adopted or produced a number of official documents, including the AMTA *Bylaws* (rev. 2016a), *Code of Ethics* (rev. 2014), *Professional Competencies* (rev. 2013), *Scope of Music Therapy Practice* (AMTA and CBMT 2015), *Standards for Education and Clinical Training* (AMTA rev. 2015a), and *Standards of Clinical Practice* (AMTA rev. 2015b).

The *Bylaws* are the major guidelines regarding AMTA's organizational structure and administration. The *Code of Ethics* is a regulatory code of professional conduct regarding music therapists' relationships with clients, peers, employers, research participants, and the public. The *Standards of Clinical Practice* define clinical music therapy practice, both in general and with specific client populations. These describe the music therapy treatment process from client assessment to termination. Finally, the *Advanced Competencies* (AMTA 2016b) form the basis of the evaluation criteria for graduate Music Therapy academic programs.

Since 2006, AMTA has introduced five new advisories: *Advisory on Levels of Practice* (2006); *Advisory on Specialized Training* (2007a); *Advisory on Acronyms* (2007b); *Master's Level Entry: Core Considerations* (2010); and *Master's Level Entry: Moving Forward* (2011). All five were written by a representative group of AMTA members called the AMTA Education and Training Advisory Board. The *Levels of Practice* (LOP) document, submitted in 2006, defined professional and advanced professional levels of practice, delineated between the two levels, and recommended ways in which music therapists could progress to advanced levels of practice. Each level of practice was divided into the following four areas: Professional Growth, Musical Development, Personal Growth and Development, and Clinical Experience. It was written to meet the needs of an increasing number of music therapists in the 21st century whose employers requested LOP guidelines due to increased demands for accountability by external monitoring/accrediting agencies. This publication also provided a standardized definition of music therapy practice at both the professional and advanced levels. It helped to clarify both the complexity and parameters of music therapy practice, an essential task due to an increase in US states' counseling licensure boards' attempts to curtail or limit music therapy practice. It also provided the foundation for the writing of the *Advanced Competencies* (rev. 2016b), published a year later.

General education and training
One of the major functions of AMTA is to approve all Music Therapy academic programs and clinical training sites. Although the academic and clinical criteria are standardized, Music Therapy education and training depend on each student's unique circumstances. For instance, "traditional" students enter a Music Therapy degree program immediately after graduating from high school, and take a minimum of four years of courses to complete their Music Therapy training. Undergraduate transfer students are required to take all required Music Therapy courses plus any required courses that they have not previously taken. Equivalency students enter their training with a Bachelor's degree in music. Depending on the program, these students either pursue a second Bachelor's degree or the undergraduate coursework required to sit for the board certification exam. Master's-equivalency students, who are graduate students completing their undergraduate Music Therapy equivalency while concurrently pursuing a Master's degree, typically take three to four years to complete all of their academic requirements. Students who are already board-certified music therapists can opt to pursue a Master's or doctoral degree in Music Therapy.

All AMTA-approved Music Therapy academic programs must be reviewed and re-accredited every ten years by the National Association of Schools of Music (NASM), the major accrediting body for academic music degree programs in the US. In order for NASM to grant accreditation to a music program, specific criteria must be met. For example, all Music Therapy curricula must contain courses such as music theory, ear training, music history, music ensembles, keyboard training, and applied music instruction. In addition to the NASM regulations, other entities, such as the state government or the academic institution, may mandate additional coursework.

Despite the external course requirements that contribute to a Music Therapy degree plan, the integration of all the Music Therapy student's skills usually occurs within the Music Therapy course sequence. The Music Therapy curriculum serves to introduce, develop, and assimilate the multiple skills needed to practice Music Therapy successfully. For that reason, faculty members teaching undergraduate core Music Therapy courses must meet certain standards, such as the appropriate professional credential or designation in Music Therapy, the minimum of a Master's degree in Music Therapy or a related area, and at least three years of full-time clinical Music Therapy practice. Faculty who teach graduate Music Therapy courses must hold a doctoral degree, have the appropriate professional credential or designation in Music Therapy, and have accrued at least five years of full-time clinical Music Therapy experience (AMTA rev. 2015a).

AMTA competencies

The AMTA curriculum is presently competency-based, which means that rather than requiring particular courses, AMTA mandates that students demonstrate specific competencies by the end of their formal training. To understand how the competency-based curricular model evolved, it is best to go back to 1981. Until this time, the NAMT educational standards were course-based, meaning that specific courses were required (e.g., music therapy practicum, music psychology), but their content was not, resulting in a lack of standardization across programs. The AAMT competencies, adopted in 1981, were the first attempt to standardize what skills music therapists in the US were expected to demonstrate upon entrance into the field. The AAMT document served as the forerunner for the NAMT *Educational Competencies*, which were first published in 1993. The latter document was later renamed *Professional Competencies* (AMTA rev. 2013) in 1996 (Jane Creagan, personal communication, January 2007). NAMT continued to require a course-based curriculum, however, until unification with AAMT in 1998. As the music therapy profession matured, the number of competencies increased. Since 1998, all AMTA-approved Music Therapy undergraduate curricula have been competency-based.

Internship

Internship plays an integral role in every Music Therapy student's education, and must be completed before the candidate can sit for the Music Therapy board certification exam. The internship follows the completion of the student's Music Therapy undergraduate-level coursework, but precedes the awarding of the Bachelor or Master's degree. The intensive and comprehensive nature of the internship allows for the development, refinement, and integration of the fundamental clinical and musical skills previously taught through classroom and laboratory simulations.

All Music Therapy students are required to complete a total of 1200 clinical training hours (AMTA rev. 2015a). At present, a student can apply either for an internship that has been officially approved by AMTA, called a *roster internship*, or one that has been established between an academic program and a local clinical site, called a *university-affiliated internship* (AMTA rev. 2015a). The *internship supervisor*, who is a board-certified music therapist with at least two years of full-time clinical experience in music therapy (AMTA rev. 2015a), is primarily responsible for ongoing intern supervision. In order to qualify as an intern supervisor, a supervisor must complete the required continuing education training and have sufficient experience working in an internship setting.

Levels of education

In the US, over 70 undergraduate degree programs currently exist, along with 30 Master's degree programs and eight doctoral programs (Jane Creagan, personal communication, January 2017). At present, individuals are eligible to practice music therapy in the US after completing the required Music Therapy coursework at an AMTA-approved academic program and passing the CBMT board certification exam. However, since its inception in the US, the music therapy profession has grappled with just how much education and training is necessary for professional practice. The advent of new areas such as emerging client populations, expanding technologies, new research paradigms, changing governmental relations issues, massive challenges in healthcare management, and cutting-edge therapeutic techniques may make it impossible in the future for music therapists to practice with just an undergraduate degree. Some argue that even today, many related therapeutic professions, such as occupational therapy, physical therapy, art therapy, dance therapy, and speech-language pathology, require the minimum of a Master's degree to practice. The disciplines of physical therapy and clinical psychology already require a doctorate. In preparation for possible changes, the AMTA *LOP* document (2006) states that in the future, at least a Master's degree in music therapy is necessary to practice at an advanced level of practice.

Certification Board for Music Therapists

As stated previously in this chapter, the certification process, which occurs in five-year cycles, is based on the guidelines of the National Commission on Health Certifying Agencies (NCHCA) and the National Organization for Competency Assurance (NOCA). Due to the continued efforts of the CBMT employees, Executive Board, and membership, the "MT-BC" credential received trademark status in 2006 (Joy Schneck, personal communication, January 23, 2006).

To maintain the MT-BC credential, the *certificants*, or board-certified music therapists, must either accrue 100 hours of continuing education credits or retake the exam during the fourth year of the cycle. According to the *NOCA Standards for the Accreditation of Certification Programs, Standard #20*, a recertification program must measure or enhance the continued competence of the certificants (NOCA 2004). However, since its inception, the CBMT Board of Directors also wanted to ensure that recertification was attainable in a manner affordable to the music therapist (Joy Schneck, personal communication, May 5, 2006). Although 100 hours of continuing education certainly enhances the certificants' competence, it can be costly to attain. Since the exam is updated every five years to measure current practice, passing the exam demonstrates that the practitioner has remained current with professional practice and has maintained the necessary competence. Along with overseeing the credentialing process, CBMT provides guidelines and approval for Music Therapy continuing education courses. Although the majority of the courses are offered at national and regional Music Therapy conferences, an increasing number of local continuing education workshops and online course modules are becoming available, which means that music therapists who are not able to attend Music Therapy conferences are still able to acquire continuing education credits.

SUMMARY

Although music has been used for healing and medicinal purposes since antiquity, the development of the music therapy profession in the US primarily occurred during the 20th century. The first half of the century witnessed changes in mental healthcare practices, from the psychoanalytic to the milieu therapy model. During the first 50 years, corresponding changes occurred in music therapy practice—specifically in the hospitals—and the nation witnessed the development of the first Music Therapy courses and degree programs. The National Association for Music Therapy (NAMT) was founded in 1950, and its early goals included the development and expansion of music therapy clinical practice, the education of the lay public and medical community about music therapy, and the standardization of Music Therapy educational and training programs. The American Association for Music Therapy (AAMT) was founded in 1971, followed by the establishment of the Certification Board for Music Therapists (CBMT) in 1984. Finally, the AAMT and NAMT unified in 1998 to become the American Music Therapy Association (AMTA).

The music therapy profession has experienced a miraculous growth spurt since its formal inception in 1950. However, the road has been quite rocky at times for music therapists. Both state and federal governmental agencies have attempted to limit the practice of music therapy, and third party reimbursement agencies have been slow to recognize music therapy as a reimbursable service. Recently, many music therapists have worked together successfully at the state level to achieve licensure, which would allow the clients in that state to receive music therapy.

As chapters in Section II contain information on music therapists from the US and UK who were the founders of the advanced methods that form the basis of this book, these influential individuals were not discussed at any length in this chapter.

Chapter Two

MUSIC THERAPY IN THE UNITED KINGDOM
A Historic Overview

My goal for this chapter is to describe the evolution of the music therapy profession in the United Kingdom (UK) to the present day. It follows a similar trajectory as the preceding chapter, with the exception of a major divergence occurring between the UK and the United States (US) in the 20th century regarding educational practices. I plan to answer the following questions:

1. How did the music therapy profession develop in the United Kingdom?

2. What is the nature of education and training in the United Kingdom, and from where did it evolve?

3. What professional music therapy associations emerged in the United Kingdom, and what discrete roles did they serve?

4. What were the similarities and differences between the development of music therapy training and recognition in the United States and the United Kingdom?

MUSIC THERAPY IN HANDEL'S ENGLAND

The earliest reference to music and medicine in England was found in *Medicina Musica, or, a Mechanical Essay on the Effects of*

Singing, Musick, and Dancing on Human Bodies, a 125-page essay published in 1729. The author, Richard Browne, was a physician who attended medical school at the University of Leiden in the Netherlands (Gibbons and Heller 1985). On September 30, 1676, he was licensed by the Royal College of Physicians. Little is known about Richard Browne except for this one publication. Due to its publication date, this treatise was probably published posthumously by another source.

Gibbons and Heller (1985) discussed the historical significance of Browne's manuscript in an article entitled "Music Therapy in Handel's England." To give the reader a sense of the London environment at the time the treatise was published, London contained fewer than one million people, King George II was in his second year of reign, and John Gay's *Beggar's Opera* was very popular with Londoners (p.59). In addition, George Frederic Handel, who had arrived in London 17 years earlier, was in mid-career and had not yet written the *Messiah* (p.59).

Browne based his scientific sources on the well-known medical and scientific authors of his day: Archibald Pitcairne, Hermann Boerhaave, Giorgio Baglivi, Lorenzo Bellini, and Marcello Malpighi (p.60). In his treatise, Browne referred to some of the myths about the curative powers of music that are still popular today (i.e., that accelerating music cures the effects of a tarantula bite, that David's harp cured Saul's madness) (p.60).

Despite his more popular references to the curative power of music, Browne's *Medicina Musica* was a significant document in the history of music therapy.

For one, it was the first treatise in the English language to assert that:

> (1) success in music does not depend on proficiency attainable only by practiced musicians but rather on success at appropriate ability and function levels; (2) music can change and evoke moods; (3) music can give rise to extra musical associations; (4) emotions can cause psychosomatic disorders; (5) stimulative and sedative music can have differing effects on individuals; (6) music can

influence physiological processes; (7) music may be harmful in treating some health conditions; (8) music has a wide variety of therapeutic applications; and, (9) music may be used in preventive health care. (Gibbons and Heller 1985, p.72)

Although Browne could not have envisioned some applications now common in music therapy practice, his contributions and foresight in the field of music therapy were amazingly accurate.

THE 19TH CENTURY

Akin to the US, a sparse amount of publications regarding music and medicine appeared in the UK during the 18th and 19th centuries. The scientific revolution swept through the 19th century, creating an intense interest in the scientific method and confirming the efficacy of approaches via research methodology. In the medical community, a general awareness of the poor conditions patients faced in hospitals was growing; how by improving the conditions, the patients recovered better; and how physicians needed to treat the social and psychological aspects of illness in addition to the physical body (Tyler 2000). This shift in perception from a purely medical model to one of encouraging scientific research, promoting health, and encouraging recovery was also occurring in the US.

Also during the 19th century, community music groups and municipal societies became a popular form of socialization. The music ensembles included brass bands, orchestras, and choral societies. These music groups eventually found their way into the large, chronic care hospitals. In fact, in 1879, Sir Edward Elgar, a famous British composer and conductor, was appointed Bandmaster of the Worcester County Lunatic Asylum Band (Tyler 2000).

The combination of the popularity of the large musical groups and the emphasis on scientific research created prime conditions for the formation of the Guild of St. Cecilia. To comprehend the impact of the Guild, it is important to learn about its founder, Canon Frederick Kill Harford (1832–1906). Harford was a musician, composer, hymn-writer, and a Minor Canon at Westminster Abbey (Tyler 2000). Harford believed strongly that music could be an effective form of treatment for certain medical conditions. He published essays in both medical and music journals, such as *The Lancet* and *The Magazine of Music*. Harford wrote about how the use of soothing, sacred music helped an elderly, sick woman to sleep (Tyler 2000), and how the sedative nature of music could reduce pain and anxiety in medical patients. He appealed to physicians to study the positive impact of music on medical patients.

In 1891, after his published appeal, Harford scheduled a rehearsal for musicians who were interested in playing in hospitals. Due to the number who showed up, Harford formed the Guild of St. Cecilia. The Guild's sound originally consisted of muted violins, harps, and female voices (Bunt and Stige 2014; Tyler 2000). It was similar to the National Therapeutic Society of New York, established in the US by Eva Vescelius in 1903 (Bunt and Stige 2014). Unlike the hospital volunteers in the US, the Guild was a professional society that charged fees to perform in London hospitals. One unusual condition established by Harford was that patients should not visually witness the musicians. For that reason, the Guild members either played behind a screen or in adjacent rooms to the patients (Bunt and Stige 2014; Tyler 2000).

Towards the end of the century, the phonograph began to be used in medical settings, specifically dentistry, obstetrics, and gynecology, to determine its impact on anesthesia and post-surgical recovery. Just like Dr. Evan O'Neill Kane had used the newly introduced phonograph in US operating rooms to help distract or calm patients, technology made its way across the ocean to assist the Guild in the form of the telephone. Due to his strong belief that music should be heard but not seen, Harford experimented by having the Guild members perform into the telephone and hospital patients listen to the music on the other end of the line. Harford wrote up his findings from this endeavor, but they were met with great skepticism from the medical press (Davis 1988).

The Guild of St. Cecilia was highly innovative and a forerunner for later applications of music in medicine. Although leading medical reformers of the day, such as Florence Nightingale, strongly supported the Guild (Bunt and Stige 2014), it was not without its problems. Due to Harford's poor health, criticism from the medical community and press, the seemingly temporary effects from the music, and a lack of funding, the Guild discontinued in 1906 following Harford's death (Bunt and Stige 2014; Tyler 2000). Regardless, Harford was a forerunner in the early years of the music therapy profession in the UK, and will be remembered for the following propositions regarding music and medicine: (1) music was effective for patients in physical or emotional distress; (2) music could be used as an adjunctive treatment to enhance medical care; (3) for music to work in medical treatment, cooperation was necessary between medical and musical professionals; and (4) research was imperative to establish the credibility of music in medicine (Tyler 2000, p.378). Amazingly, these propositions are still regarded as valid today, even though the Guild was discontinued in 1906.

THE 20TH CENTURY: THE FORMATIVE YEARS

In the early 20th century, music was used in medical settings based on the following precepts: (1) by entering the nervous system, music could neutralize other stimuli such as pain and fear, thus assisting medical procedures; and (2) music positively impacted the mood of patients, bringing feelings of comfort and pleasure and counteracting feelings of boredom and anxiety (Tyler 2000, p.379). Similar to the hospital musicians in the US at this time, early 20th-century music in hospital practices fell into two distinct treatment models: (1) recreational: music functioned as a therapeutic form of entertainment—all of the group ensembles and performing musicians in hospitals were examples of this; and (2) medical: music functioned as part of medical treatment (Tyler 2000, p.379).

Although the earliest formalized music therapy effort undoubtedly took place in the US after World War II (Wigram, Pedersen, and Bonde 2002), the UK quickly followed suit. The first professional music therapy society was founded in 1958 as the Society for Music Therapy and Remedial Music (Charboneau,

Gordon, and Green 2008). Juliette Alvin (1897–1982), original founder of the Society (Goodman 2011), was a professional cellist and pioneer of music therapy for children with autism. This early professional society collaborated with the Guildhall School of Music and Drama (Guildhall for short), a music conservatory in London, to offer short courses on Music Therapy during the 1960s. These short courses began to attract students. In 1967, a one-year, post-graduate Music Therapy program was offered at Guildhall, with Juliette Alvin as director (Bunt 2015), and with the first graduates in 1968.

Before 1970, children with disabilities spent many years in hospital without receiving public education, and were considered "ineducable" (Tyler 2000). Musicians and music teachers working in hospitals found enormous potential in these children. *Music in the Wards* was a report written in 1970 by Juliette Alvin that summarized the value of music teaching in Queen Mary's Hospital for Children, Carshalton (Alvin 1970 as cited in Tyler 2000). In 1970, the *Education (Handicapped Children) Act* was passed five years before a similar law in the US. This provided all children with disabilities in the UK with a public education, which increased the need for the music teachers who wished to work with them. The approval of Guildhall as a vocational training course by the Department of Education and Science in England allowed Music Therapy students to apply for financial aid from their local education authorities to help cover their tuition and living expenses (Bunt 2015).

In 1967, the Society for Music Therapy and Remedial Music changed its name to the British Society for Music Therapy (BSMT) (Bunt and Stige 2014). The BSMT began publishing the *British Journal of Music Therapy*. In 1976, a group of BSMT members broke away and formed their own group, the Association of Professional Music Therapists (APMT) (Bunt 2015). Although smaller in number, the APMT functioned as a professional organization and its members sought to improve standards for education and registration for music therapists. Angela Fenwick was the first chairperson of the APMT (Bunt and Stige 2014). Akin to the National Association for

Music Therapy in the US, geographical subdivisions existed within the APMT (Goodman 2011).

In 1980, the inaugural Research Fellowship in Music Therapy was awarded to Leslie Bunt by the Music Therapy Charity in collaboration with the Music Department of City University, London (Bunt 2015). Dr. Malcolm Troup, who remained a strong advocate for music therapy, was Head of the Music Department at City University. In fact, he had been Director of Music of the Guildhall School of Music and Drama during the period that Juliette Alvin was directing the first Music Therapy courses there.

Growth in courses

From 1967 until 1981, three Music Therapy courses were concurrently operating in London. As stated previously, the first Music Therapy academic program was initiated at Guildhall in 1967. Seven years later, in 1974, the Goldie Leigh Hospital in South London offered the first courses that were taught by Paul Nordoff and Clive Robbins, music therapy pioneers who were developing their legendary method called Creative Music Therapy (Nordoff-Robbins Music Therapy is examined later in this book). In 1981, Elaine Streeter, an original member of the first Nordoff-Robbins trainees at the Goldie Leigh Hospital, set up a new course in Nordoff-Robbins Music Therapy at Southlands College, Roehampton (Bunt 2015). Streeter had completed the first Master's thesis in Music Therapy at the University of York in 1979 (Bunt 2015).

Unlike the US, where, by the late 1950s, Music Therapy training took place solely in university settings, Music Therapy training in the UK from 1967 until 2006 took place both in university settings and at separate centers run by charitable organizations. For example, in 1991, a Nordoff-Robbins Centre opened in North London. This served as a hub for meetings of the BSMT, APMT, and music therapists from all UK training courses. In 1995, this Nordoff-Robbins Centre initiated the first two-year full-time Master's-level training.

A mandate by the Health Professions Council (HPC) in 2006 stated that arts therapy education, which included music therapy, had to be conducted at a Master's level. Akin to the US, a number of academic Music Therapy programs opened, closed, or were assimilated into other programs during the turn of the 21st century. At the time of the writing this text, seven academic Music Therapy programs exist in the UK: Guildhall School of Music and Drama, London; Nordoff-Robbins validated by City University, London; Nordoff-Robbins in Queen Margaret University, Edinburgh; University of Roehampton, London; University of the West of England, Bristol; Anglia Ruskin University, Cambridge; and University of South Wales, Newport (Bunt 2015).

Music therapy as a career

At first glance, the history of music therapy appears less rocky in the UK than in the US. Part of the reason is that state and federal governments in the US are constantly enacting new legislation regarding what therapeutic methodologies are and are not allowed. In recent years, music therapists in the US have worked together at state level to gain licensure, which protects music therapists in that state from litigious action by other professionals, and also confirms that music therapy is beneficial to the clients served. Many other therapeutic organizations (e.g., counseling associations) in the US have tried to prevent music therapists from practicing in their state, and in some states (i.e., New York), music therapists must have Master's degrees and licensure to practice.

In the UK, music therapists also had to struggle for recognition. To understand this, it is important to return to 1960 when, under the *Professionals Supplementary to Medicine Act* (PSMA), an Arts Therapists Board was created. This development greatly increased recognition and support for the arts therapies in the UK, although it did not necessarily create jobs. In 1982, the music therapy profession was awarded the first Career and Grading Structure by the Whitney Council of the Department of Health and Social Security (Bunt 2015, p.10), another landmark event. Almost 40 years after the

PSMA was passed, the music therapy profession was awarded State Registration along with drama and art therapy, and was recognized as part of the Council for Professions Supplementary to Medicine (CPSM). All of the professions under the CPSM umbrella are regulated under an act of Parliament, and each has its own professional association, in accordance with European Standards (Bunt and Hoskyns 2002). The CPSM extended the 1960 PSMA to allow arts therapists, along with occupational therapists and physiotherapists, to provide treatment in healthcare facilities. When State Registration was enacted, music therapists were awarded the designation "state-registered arts therapists" (Bunt 2015, p.12), which strongly improved their professional standing and job opportunities. Arts therapists then received State Registration in 2002 by the HPC, which was renamed the Health and Care Professions Council (HCPC) in 2012 (Bunt 2015, p.2). This registration was paramount to the success of music therapy, as registration is compulsory to be employed through the National Health Service (NHS) and Social Services in the UK (Goodman 2011). Music therapists in the UK are currently credentialed as "HCPC-registered music therapists."

From 1976 until 2008, the two music therapy associations in the UK co-existed and represented a united front. They co-sponsored a World Music Therapy Conference in Oxford in 2002 (Bunt and Hoskyns 2002; Goodman 2011), and newly qualified professionals from all over the world came together to share ideas and visions for the future of music therapy. In 2008, the two British associations, one a public charitable body and one a professional organization (Bunt 2015) began to move towards unification; and in 2011, the BSMT and APMT officially joined to become the British Association for Music Therapy (BAMT).

Training and education

The HCPC *Standards of Education and Training Guidance* manual (HCPC 2017) is divided into the following sections: Programme Admissions, Programme Management and Resources, Curriculum,

Practice Placements, and Assessment. All professionals registered through the HCPC must adhere to these standards and all arts therapies training programs must teach these standards. This forms the basis of healthcare professional training in the UK. In addition, the HCPC has published the *Standards of Conduct, Performance and Ethics* (2016) and discipline-specific standards (i.e., *Standards of Proficiency: Arts Therapists*) (2013). In the later manual are the standards not only for all arts therapists, but also specific proficiencies for drama and music therapists. These form the basis of the specific proficiencies that are taught in Music Therapy training programs in the UK.

All Music Therapy academic programs must be approved by the HCPC in order for the students to receive registration. A typical Music Therapy academic degree program for full-time students takes two years to complete. Both the Nordoff-Robbins and Guildhall School of Music and Drama require intensive, full-time training. Graduate Music Therapy students may also work while attending classes on a part-time basis. Students are usually expected to enter the program with well-honed musical skills and a Bachelor's degree. If the student is lacking in certain pre-requisite skills, the university may require that the student take remedial courses or training prior to beginning the course of study.

An example of a Music Therapy academic program in the UK is at the University of the West of England in Bristol. A visit to the campus (in 2015) informed this author of the following three-year training format:

- Seven required class modules are taught over three years.

- In years one and two, each class is taught for one entire day a week, followed by one day of clinical placements and one half-day per week for reflection, private study, and personal or musical growth.

- The third and final year involves fewer and longer class sessions.

- Some of the training is conducted via distance learning, and various written assignments are required.

Once the courses are completed and the Master's degree in Music Therapy is awarded, the music therapist can apply for and receive registration from the HCPC.

SUMMARY

Thus far, Chapters One and Two of this text focused on the history of music therapy in the United States and the United Kingdom. Although these two countries can boast of being the first to develop standardized music therapy education and practice, they differ regarding the venue of training, terms used, the academic level at which music therapy is taught, and how music therapy practice is standardized.

As chapters in Section II contain information on music therapists from the US and UK who were the founders of the advanced methods that form the basis of this book, these influential individuals were not discussed at any length in this chapter.

CHAPTER THREE

MUSIC THERAPY METHOD

In Act II, Scene II of the tragedy, *Romeo and Juliet* by William Shakespeare, Juliet, a Capulet, claims, "A rose by any other name would smell as sweet" when challenged by the fact that Romeo is from the house of Montague (*The Riverside Shakespeare* 1974, p.1068). For the sake of clarity, I have linked this rose with one word, *method*, as the term to describe advanced music therapy practice. Historically, many words have been used synonymously in music therapy literature to describe clinical practice (e.g., theory, model, method, approach, strategy, technique). Some authors have provided rationales for why they chose certain terms over others (Bruscia 1998, 2014; Darrow 2008). I propose that *method* is most suitable to the topic of advanced music therapy practice in the context of the first quarter of the 21st century. To clarify my premise, I plan to address the following questions in this chapter:

1. What are current definitions for the terms "theory," "model," and "method"?

2. Have the meanings of these terms changed over time?

3. What criteria did I employ to delimit this book to advanced music therapy methods?

4. Why did I choose the four advanced methods featured in this book?

5. What specific content will this book contain?

In the process of searching for operative definitions for music therapy practice, I discovered that not only did music therapy texts contain a variety of terms used synonymously to represent the same meaning, but so did many sources external to music therapy practice. Functioning as a microcosm of a larger system, music therapy authors therefore also tend to mirror a lack of linguistic conformity when discussing clinical practice. Bruscia agrees when he states, "In the literature, one often finds that the terms 'method,' 'approach,' 'model,' 'procedure,' and 'technique' are used interchangeably, as if they all mean the same thing" (2014, p.407). However, when I reviewed *theory*, *model*, and *method*, in this precise order, I discovered that they do seem to flow in a logical fashion from a more general, abstract level (i.e., theory) through a more tangible representation of the abstraction (i.e., model), and finally to a structured, orderly process for bringing into action the original theory (i.e., method). In an attempt to represent this relationship, Table 3.1 contains definitions of these three terms. I plan to discuss each of the three terms in detail, starting with a general discussion of each, and how they apply to music therapy practice.

Table 3.1: Definitions of theory, model, and method

Term	Definition
Theory	• A conception or mental scheme (*Online Etymology Dictionary* 2014b) • A plausible or scientifically acceptable general principle or body of principles offered to explain natural phenomena (*Merriam Webster* 2014c) • A coherent group of general propositions used as principles of explanation for a class of phenomena (*Dictionary.com* 2014b) • A particular conception or view of something to be done or of the method of doing it (*Dictionary.com* 2014b)

Model	• A simplified representation of a system or phenomenon... with any hypotheses required to describe the system or explain the phenomenon (*Dictionary.com* 2014a)
	• Something (as a similar object or a construct) used to help visualize or explore something else that cannot be directly observed or experimented on (*Merriam Webster* 2014b)
	• A representation, generally in miniature, to show the construction or appearance of something (*Dictionary.com* 2014a)
Method	• A way of doing something...orderliness, regularity (*Online Etymology Dictionary* 2014a)
	• A way, technique, or process of or for doing something (*Merriam Webster* 2014a)

THEORY

The word *theory* tends to be naturally vague in meaning. Hammersley (2004, p.1123) defines it as "normative principles that provide a general guide for practice, without supplying detailed instructions." To wit, the meaning of the word theory is clarified more by what it is not than by what it is. Hammersley continues that theory contrasts with practice in the following areas: (1) theory refers to general principles rather than what is actually done; (2) theory is speculative and not empirical in nature; and (3) theories are not evidence-based, but exist along a continuum between broad frameworks of belief.

Stam (2010a) tends to agree with Hammersley's third explanation presented above. Stam links the function of theory to the desire to define a genuine problem (e.g., social, scientific) with logical terms in order to clarify the innovative features of the phenomenon being described (Stam 2010a, p.1498). Historically, scientists attempted to represent theories via empirical examples. However, they discovered that even observations are theory-laden, since people tend to approach the world with their own theoretical and culture-influenced world-views (Stam 2010a, p.1499). Therefore, a contemporary definition of theory has to include the perceptions of its creator.

One of the clearest examples of a theory I could find is Maibom's definition of *Theory Theory* (2010). According to Maibom, Theory Theory is based on people's attempts to understand each other via their actions. This theory explains the actions of others in terms of the psychological properties that a culture ascribes to those actions. To clarify further, Theory Theory proposes a way of discerning internal psychological states by associating them with individuals' observable actions.

Music therapy theories

Hanson-Abromeit (2015, p.28) defines theory in music therapy as "the foundation in which to design intentional interventions." In its younger years, the profession of music therapy in the US and UK did not claim any indigenous theories, per se, although Gaston (1968) and Sears (1968) made strong statements about the therapeutic properties of music. One of the first publications to reference the relationship between existing theories and music therapy practice was Even Ruud's *Music Therapy and its Relationship to Current Treatment Theories* (1980). Although Ruud did not propose a dedicated music therapy theory, he did relate music therapy practice to four of the most prevalent treatment theories of the time: behavioral, psychoanalytic, humanistic/existentialist, and the medical model. Bunt and Stige (2014) refer to this as the period that music therapists borrowed from other disciplines to underpin our practice. Also in 1980, Watts published an article in the *Journal of Music Therapy* about three sociological theories of aging and their relationship to music therapy practice. In these cases, music therapy was presented as an adjunct modality that was capable of aligning with external theories.

During the late 1980s, Carolyn Kenny, a music therapist, described rich music therapy processes in her books, *Field of Play* and *Mythic Artery* (Kenny 2012). Her publications were about more than just music therapy; Kenny wove the knowledge of anthropology and indigenous content into her writing; she introduced music therapists to a unique, collaborative perspective that was emerging in the profession; and she provided a foundation upon which later music therapy theories could emerge.

In 2002, Bruscia introduced "five forces of thought in music therapy" (pp.xxii–xiii). The five forces were akin to popular theories of practice in the social sciences. Although two of these theories (i.e., behavioral and humanistic) were the same as Ruud's (1980), three (i.e., psychodynamic, transpersonal, and culture-centered) represented bold new paradigms regarding the role of the spirit, mind, psyche, music, therapeutic relationship, and consciousness via music therapy processes.

Indigenous theories

Indigenous theories of music therapy now exist (Bruscia 2014). Bruscia's book *Readings on Music Therapy Theory* (2012) features theories that have emerged since 2000. Endemic theories have begun to enter the profession's consciousness. In one example, *Culture-Centered Music Therapy*, Stige (2002) introduces community music therapy (aimed in part at cultural change in the community), ecological music therapy (focusing on communication at micro- and mesosystem levels), and individual music psychotherapy (considering the individual within the cultural context) (Stige 2002). Stige claims that the client, music therapist, and music create a core community around which the therapy evolves. More recently, Stige (2015) added his concept of "practice turn theories" into the milieu of theory-directed music therapy dialogue (p.6).

In 2005, Aigen published *Music-Centered Music Therapy*, in which he introduces the premise that the medium of music is central to all approaches and frameworks of music therapy. In a more recent publication, *The Study of Music Therapy* (2014), Aigen clearly delineates three stages in the development of music therapy theories: (1) the borrowing of theoretical ideas from other disciplines; (2) treatment models that developed from clinical practice; and (3) more indigenous and cross-disciplinary theories that are relevant to multiple models and forms of clinical practice. In summary, it seems that even though formal music therapy organizations were founded in the US and UK in the 1950s, it was not until more than a half century later that the profession was finally ready to claim its own theories of practice.

MODEL

Although the focus of this present book is not about theories of music therapy, theories are inevitably represented in models. Models act as mediators between theories and phenomena (Russo 1994). Simply put, a model represents an idea, such as a theory, in such a way as to make the idea more tangible. For that reason, models are essential to the development of theories (Haig 2010). Just like words function to represent concepts, models represent theories. Haig explains further that models spring from a creator's imagination to make clearer the subject matter of a given theory. Haig continues that a model successfully clarifies a theory; therefore, the model tends to be simpler and more accessible than the theory it represents.

French (1994a) perceives models from the bottom up. In his mind, a model represents a number of analogies between real-world phenomena and whatever is substituted for them in the model. To wit, based on French's interpretation, instead of representing abstract theories, models serve as metaphors for real-world phenomena. French claims that models are also different from theories because they incorporate certain simplifications that render the theories understandable and more accessible. Serving as the intermediary between theories and real-world phenomena, models more easily allow inferences to be drawn (French 1994b; Russo 1994).

Music therapy models

Music therapy publications have contained the term *model* so often that it has created what Wartofsky (1979) refers to as the "model muddle." In an earlier publication, Bruscia (1987) stated, for example, that improvisational models were primarily rooted in treatment theories (e.g., psychotherapy, communication, personality); this matches the definitions of model presented above. At the 1999 World Congress of Music Therapy held in Washington, DC, five internationally known *models* of music therapy and their founders were acknowledged: (1) Guided Imagery and Music (GIM) (Helen Bonny), (2) Analytical Music Therapy (Mary Priestley), (3) Creative Music Therapy (Paul Nordoff [deceased] and Clive Robbins), (4) Benenzon Music Therapy (Rolando Benenzon), and (5) Behavioral Music Therapy (Clifford Madsen). At this event, the term *model* reflected the name or creative ideas of a music therapy founder, and while all five models were based partially on theoretical orientations, they were also recognized according to their unique clinical techniques.

For music therapy models, the linguistic tide began to shift away from theory and more into specific clinical considerations. In 1998, Bruscia revised his definition of "model" as a "comprehensive approach to assessment, treatment and evaluation which includes theoretical principles, clinical indications and contraindications, goals, methodological guidelines and specifications, and the characteristic use of certain procedural sequences and techniques" (p.115). Bruscia also identified six major models of music therapy practice: Didactic, Medical, Healing, Psychotherapy, Recreation, and Ecological, with auxiliary, augmentative, intensive, and primary levels for each, and techniques to elucidate each level (1998, pp.172–173). Wigram *et al.* (2002), on the other hand, proposed that a music therapy *model* should contain the components of historical foundation, session format, clinical applications, documentation, and levels of clinical practice.

This brings us back to the dilemma of "model muddle" (Wartofsky 1979). It seems that the implied meaning of the term "model" has changed considerably from its inception, and now has multiple connotations. At this point in this chapter, it appears that the term "theory" is too abstract and "model" is too unstable in meaning to be useful for the basis of this book. While models are still necessary when discussing music therapy practice, they serve as the intermediary between theories and methods of music therapy.

METHOD

The term "method" comes from the Greek *meta* and *odos*, meaning *following after* (Stam 2010b, p.1345). According to De Leon (2000, p.92), a method includes "the activities, strategies, materials, procedures, and techniques that are employed to achieve a desired goal." De Leon used the example of *therapeutic community* to demonstrate how a method functions (2000). A therapeutic community (TC) is residential, long-term, and usually focuses on the treatment of persons with addictions. Its theoretical orientation is both holistic and psychoanalytic. The community involves the participation of therapists, family members, and patients, and serves as an alternative to inpatient psychiatric units. Its goal is to sustain each individual's full participation in order to achieve pre-established social and psychological goals of lifestyle and identity change, which is essential for recovery from addiction. The TC's membership establishes standards and means of participation to achieve these goals (i.e., activities, strategies, materials, procedures, and techniques). To wit, the community itself serves both as the *method* and the primary agent of treatment (Chen *et al.* 2012, p.1419).

Music therapy methods

Methods allow theoretical phenomena to become realized. When compared to "theory" and "model," the term *method* appears least often in music therapy publications, yet it is very prevalent in research literature. The *scientific method* is the "systematic way in which someone makes an observation, renders an hypothesis about that observation, goes about testing the phenomenon in question, and gathering and evaluating data to determine if the guess can be substantiated" (*Dictionary.com*, 2016). With the advent of reflexive and mixed methods research, the scientific method is no longer the cornerstone for conducting research. This has freed the term *method* to serve other functions, and even in current research contexts, methodology has become a more flexible and multi-dimensional means of exploring phenomena.

Earlier in this section, De Leon defined method as "the activities, strategies, materials, procedures, and techniques that are employed to achieve a desired goal" (2000, p.92). Similarly, Bruscia (2014, p.408) defined a music therapy method as "a particular type of music experience used for assessment, treatment, and/or evaluation." He differentiated between the terms *model* and *method* by stating that while a model was based on theoretical foundations, a method was not. In 2014, Bruscia identified four main methods of music therapy: improvisational, re-creative, composing, and receptive.

Advanced methods of music therapy practice
The problem with definitions

It has become apparent to me that no single definition belongs to any of the aforementioned terms. It is the nature of the English language to change. Each of the three terms first introduced in this chapter—theory, model, and method—have undergone massive semantic changes, not only in the field of music therapy, but also in the English language as a whole. Well-respected music therapy authors themselves have altered the function of these terms over time. And since the purpose of literature is to engage and hopefully change the reader's perspective, it seems that authors now have the freedom to choose terms that are the most congruent for them to express their ideas.

At this point, I feel compelled to point out a fascinating discovery I made regarding differences in semantics between the UK and US while traveling to conduct research for this book. In the US, the term *advanced* refers to the clinical Music Therapy training that is completed after a person completes a Master's degree. For example, at New York University, students must have a Master's degree in Music Therapy before pursuing advanced training in Nordoff-Robbins Music Therapy, Vocal Psychotherapy, Analytical Music Therapy, or the Bonny Method of Guided Imagery and Music. In the UK, *advanced* refers to the training that the students receive during their pursuit of a Master's degree in Music Therapy.

The word *training* also differs in semantics between the two countries. In the US, *training* usually refers to clinical environments, such as the internship site or field placements, and *education* takes place at university. In the UK, Music Therapy students receive *training* at university. Even within the UK, Music Therapy programs differ regarding when training, such as Nordoff-Robbins Music Therapy, should occur. One program in the UK offers a Master's degree curriculum that includes the entire Nordoff-Robbins training. In all other UK programs, the Master's degree is earned first, and then interested clinicians can opt to study an advanced method of music therapy practice.

Finally, the term *post-graduate* has multiple meanings. In the US, post-graduate refers to post-Master's degree Music Therapy education. In the UK, the same term refers to the post-Bachelor's degree level, which is where students begin their Music Therapy study. Because this text covers music therapy practices both in the US and the UK, music therapists in the two countries may misinterpret the terms used above, especially if they are not aware of the existence of the other definitions. Table 3.2 elucidates these semantic inconsistencies more clearly.

Table 3.2: Discrepancies in terms referring to music therapy

Country	Term	Meaning
US	Advanced	Post-Master's degree level of study
UK	Advanced	General level of music therapy study that takes place at Master's level
US	Training	Separate from music therapy education but taught in conjunction with educational content
UK	Training	What music therapy students receive at university
US	Post-graduate	After the student earns a Master's degree
UK	Post-graduate	After the student earns a Bachelor's degree

To standardize the language, I have chosen to use the US definition of *advanced* throughout the rest of this book. As much as possible,

I point out the equivalent content in the UK whenever I discuss something that is "advanced."

Defining "advanced"
An advanced method of music therapy practice results from the interaction of various components: (1) relationships between the music, music therapist, and multiple clients; (2) the music therapist's familiarity with current theories and models, both indigenous and related, when interacting with the music and the clients; (3) the music therapist's knowledge base, values, and interests; and, (4) various procedures, techniques, strategies, and artifacts employed within the clinical music therapy setting. The term

> ...*procedure* is defined as an organized sequence of operations and interactions that a therapist uses in taking the client through an entire music experience while a *technique* is a single operation or interaction that a therapist uses to elicit an immediate reaction from the client or to shape the ongoing, immediate experience of the client. Thus, a technique is a smaller, single operation within a procedure, while a procedure can be viewed as a series of techniques. (Bruscia 2014, p.410; emphasis added by author)

A *strategy* is defined as "a careful plan for achieving a goal" (Merriam-Webster 2015); this implies that a music therapist invents strategies to successfully combine techniques into a systematic therapeutic procedure. Finally, in the present context, an *artifact* is an object that is selected by the music therapist to enhance clinical techniques.

As demonstrated by the components and the many possible interactions during the formation of an advanced method, although theories and models influence the development of an emerging music therapy method, equally, so do the everyday musical and clinical practices used by music therapists as they experiment with emerging interventions for their clients. Figure 3.1 represents my schemata for advanced methods in music therapy practice. According to this model, an advanced method is not a product, but an ongoing, reflexive process (Bruscia 2014) that is living and changing. Bruscia defines *reflexive* as a therapist's "continuous efforts to bring into awareness, evaluate, and, when necessary, modify his work with a client—before, during, and after each session, as well as at various stages of the therapy process" (2014, p.160).

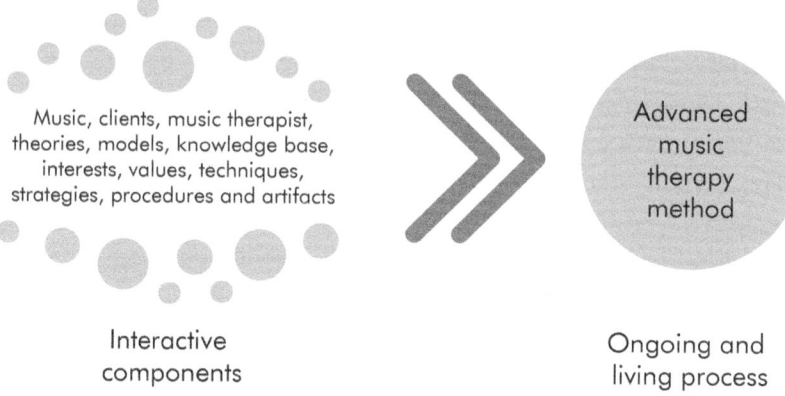

Figure 3.1: Formative process for advanced methods of music therapy practice

The music therapists who choose to pursue training in advanced methods of music therapy practice tend to make this decision after years as clinicians, akin to my own story in this book's Preface. To further define the qualities of such an advanced clinician, the AMTA *Levels of Practice* (LOP) (2006) document defines *"Advanced Level of Practice"* as the following:

> ...holds a Bachelor's degree or its equivalent in music therapy, a current professional designation or credential in music therapy, professional experience, and further education or training (e.g., continuing education, a master's degree, *a doctoral degree, or in-depth training in areas of specialization such as AMT, BMGIM, or NR-MT.* It is anticipated that in the future music therapists at the Advanced Level of Practice *will hold at least a Master's degree in music therapy* that includes advanced clinical education. The advanced music therapist demonstrates comprehensive understanding of foundations and principles of music, music therapy, treatment, and management in clinical, educational, research, and/or administrative settings. (2006, p.5; emphasis added by the author)

After careful consideration, I selected four advanced methods of music therapy practice as the basis of this book: Analytical Music Therapy (AMT), the Bonny Method of Guided Imagery and Music (GIM), Nordoff-Robbins Music Therapy (NR-MT), and Vocal Psychotherapy (VP). Three of the four areas of specialization are already listed in the above AMTA definition. This is not to say that other advanced music therapy methods do not exist, nor is this meant to slight other forms of advanced practice. My choice of the four selections are based not only on the fact that they were founded by music therapists, but because of the rigor of their training requirements: (1) Master's degree, or training occurring concurrently with Master's degree candidacy; (2) specified years of clinical experience prior to beginning the training; and (3) a time-intensive process that includes multiple workshops, clinical hours, supervised sessions, self-growth requirements, personal sessions, reading assignments, and final projects to complete the training and to receive the corresponding clinical designation.

QUESTIONS

To explore the four advanced music therapy methods, I employed techniques related to transcendental realism. Section II represents the inception, historical development, present training, current practice, and existing literature for each of the four methods. To standardize the language, I used the term *founder(s)* throughout the research questions to represent those individuals who created the method. The questions for Section II follow:

Questions about method founders

1. Approximately how long were the founders employed as music therapists (or were they music therapists?) before developing the method?

2. What are the basic concepts related to this method?

3. What are the techniques that are unique to this method?

4. What was the historical and political context under which this method developed?

5. Did the founders refer to this method as a form of music therapy, or did they use different words?

6. How many documents did the founder write about the method?

7. What kinds of documents did the founder write?

8. What were the salient themes established in the publications that were written by the founder?

9. How did the training for the method develop?

Questions about current practice and training

1. How many publications exist about this method that were not written by the founders? How many were published in non-music therapy sources?

2. Who were the authors of the publications about the method?

3. What were the salient themes established in the publications that were not written by the founders?

4. What are the current training standards and procedures for this method?

5. Do trainees earn a designation as a result of the training for this method?

Section II

Section II of this book contains Chapters Four through Seven, and presents answers to the first two sets of questions above, in narrative form. To answer the aforementioned questions, I examined all available publications about the method that were written in English by the founders or by music therapists who were trained in the method. In addition, I interviewed at least two expert music therapy practitioners/trainers per method who had trained with at least one of the founders to discern more specific information about the development of the method that may not have been published. The adult children of two of the founders served as experts regarding the early years of the development of the methods. I also used the results of a questionnaire sent to current trainers of the four methods along with training content websites to define current training practices.

Section III

The final section consists of Chapters Eight and Nine. Chapter Eight is based on qualitative inquiry regarding the data generated from five questions asked to experts of the four methods in the US and the UK. Chapter Nine covers the last two questions asked of the experts, and provides my speculations regarding the future of the advanced methods in relationship to the profession of music therapy. The material for this final section comes from presented case studies, both cross cases and within cases, and by using the *NVivo* software program, which analyzes the transcribed responses from the experts to the following seven questions:

1. What is it about this method that still resonates with you?

2. What has the advanced method taught you about music therapy?

3. Has your relationship with this advanced method changed over the years? If so, how?

4. Do you believe that the founders of this advanced method intended to create a new music therapy approach?

5. Do there seem to have been changes in the professional music therapy association's attitudes towards the method over time?

6. Do you consider this method to be a part of music therapy practice? Why or why not? Has your viewpoint on this changed over time?

7. Overall, what do you foresee for the future of this advanced method?

SECTION II

CHAPTER FOUR

MARY PRIESTLEY AND ANALYTICAL MUSIC THERAPY

Figure 4.1: A photograph of Mary Priestley

I visited with John Priestley, on March 21, 2015 at his home in Balham, UK, to speak with him about his mother, Mary Priestley. He showed me a slide show that he had assembled for Mary's 90th birthday party, which had just occurred a few days earlier. Although I had originally planned to visit with Mary, she was too ill to have visitors at that time. John began the slide show with an entry from Wikipedia about his mother, "that she was the premarital child of the English playwright, J. B. Priestley and mother Jane

Wyndham-Lewis, that she had a lifetime bipolar mood disorder, and that she had initiated a new model of music therapy known as Analytical Music Therapy" (John Priestley, personal communication, March 21, 2015). I asked John if he minded if I used his exact words in this book, and he said that he did not. It was at this point that I realized I was in the presence of the son of an extraordinary single mother who, although having struggled with financial and mental health issues for most of her life, had returned to university as an adult to study Music Therapy, and had later developed one of its most unique psychotherapeutic approaches.

MARY PRIESTLEY'S STORY

In this brief overview we look at Mary's early years into adulthood, her training in music therapy, and the role of psychoanalysis in her work.

The early years

Mary Priestley was born in 1925, the daughter of English playwright and author J. B. Priestley and Jane Wyndham-Lewis. Both were married to other people at the time of Mary's conception, and to save face, they put Jane's current husband's name down on the birth certificate as Mary's father (Hadley 2001). Jane and J. B. eventually divorced their first spouses and married each other while Mary was a very young child. During her childhood, Mary was never aware that she was conceived out of wedlock, and did not learn this truth until she was an adult (John Priestley, personal communication, March 21, 2015).

Mary's family moved quite often. She had little contact with her parents, who were often out socializing (John Priestley, personal communication, March 21, 2015). Her family also traveled a lot. John described a period in Mary's childhood when she got to spend two idyllic winters in Arizona, US, because her mother had a lung condition and needed to stay in a drier climate. John describes this as a simpler, happier time for Mary. She was homeschooled by her parents and got to spend more time with her family and to ride horses. In fact, John showed me a picture of Mary with her family, all on horseback, and Mary was dressed up in a western outfit, smiling.

In Mary's interview with Leslie Bunt (2004), she remembers one day in the UK when she and her father were in their drawing room having tea. Mary described her father as a gifted piano player who could play anything by ear and often improvised. He used to make up stories, and illustrated them on the piano. This seemed to be a very pleasant memory for her. When she was seven years old, Mary started taking piano lessons. To help her memorize the names of the keys, she took a piece of chalk and wrote "ABCDEFG" all the way up and down the piano keyboard. Her father was not pleased with this addition to his Bechstein piano, and her piano lessons were discontinued.

When she was 14 years old, Mary started playing violin and was awarded a full scholarship to the Royal College of Music in London, where she studied piano, violin, and composition for five years. She then went to the Conservatoire de Musique in Geneva. At an international competition in Geneva, she met a Danish violinist named Sigvald Michelsen, and they fell in love. When they returned from Geneva in 1949, Mary told her parents that she and Sigvald wanted to marry. In those days, it was customary for a couple to separate for six months before marrying to be sure of their decision. Mary's parents told them they had to wait for six months, and Sigvald responded that if they had to wait that long, Mary would have a breakdown (Bunt 2004). She did indeed have her first bipolar incident during that waiting period, and had to be hospitalized. Mary remembers receiving a "primitive form of electro-convulsive and deep insulin therapy, which was very horrible" (Bunt 2004, p.4). John also mentioned another possible cause of Mary's breakdown—during this time she found her birth certificate and learned the truth about her real father (John Priestly, personal communication, March 21, 2015).

Adulthood

Two years after her first breakdown, Mary and Sigvald got married on the Isle of Wight. For the next seven years, they lived in Denmark, and both performed for a living. Mary remained very healthy (Bunt 2004). Sigvald performed mostly in orchestras, such as the Danish Radio Orchestra, and Mary played in pit orchestras for American Musicals, such as *Annie Get Your Gun*. In 1951, when she was 26, Mary gave birth to male twins. In 1958, she gave birth to another son, David.

After seven years, however, the marriage broke up, and a divorce ensued. Sigvald had had an affair with the au pair, who consequently became pregnant. Mary returned to the UK taking her youngest son, David, with her. The twin boys were left in Denmark to live with their father and with the au pair, whom Sigvald eventually married. Mary suffered a tremendous breakdown and was hospitalized for a long time. When she was finally released, she was told that she would probably never play the violin again, and that she should look for another vocation.

In a short period of time, Mary had lost her husband, her home, her profession, and two of her children. But she persevered, retrained and became a shorthand typist, working in a typing pool where she could type 120 words per minute. She gradually worked her way into a job with the Thomas Cook Travel Agency and became a copywriter (Bunt 2004), writing travel brochures. It was with this agency that she wrote her first book, *Going Abroad* (Priestley 1965). John describes the book as, "about how you get to various European countries and what you expect to eat there and there's a very brief description of the national characteristics of the people" (John Priestley, personal communication, March 21, 2015).

Meanwhile, back in Denmark, Mary's twin boys were not faring well. Sigvald's second marriage had broken up, his house had been repossessed, and he was being treated for alcoholism. When the twins came to London to visit Mary in 1965, she asked them to stay. John describes this as "the first period of stability in his life." Mary became a caring and responsible single parent. She even used the revenue earned from her travel book to buy their first washing machine (Bunt 2004).

Music therapy training

Mary did not learn about music therapy until she was in her 40s. She heard about a lecture entitled, "Mutual Understanding Through Music" that was to be given by Juliette Alvin (Hadley 2001). She attended the lecture, during which Juliette discussed how she had used music with a French couple to help them communicate with each other. Mary was especially interested in this talk on marital therapy because many of the arguments with her ex-husband had been about music. During the lecture, Juliette announced that she was starting a course in Music Therapy (John Priestley, personal communication, March 21, 2015). Mary was intrigued, as Music Therapy seemed to incorporate two of her strongest interests, music and psychology. After Juliette's talk, Mary followed her into the women's restroom to inquire about the training (Bunt 2004). In 1967, at the age of 43, Mary began studying Music Therapy at the Guildhall School of Music and Drama in London (Hadley 2001).

Mary entered the second official Music Therapy class to be offered at Guildhall. She recalled that it was the first time in 12 years that she had "performed music properly." She described Juliette Alvin as a frightening teacher (Bunt 2004). Mary quickly realized that she could not do music therapy the way Juliette did, and that she needed to do it her own way. She took weekly violin and piano lessons along with improvisation classes with Alfred Nieman (Hadley 2001). John remembers that Mary commented that it was difficult because she had to learn to play in a different way; she had to learn to improvise on the piano (John Priestley personal communication, March 21, 2015). Straight from finishing her one-year training, Mary was hired as a music therapist at St. Bernard's Hospital along with her colleagues, Marjorie Wardle and Peter Wright.

The role of psychoanalysis

One of the most significant relationships in Mary's life was with Dr. Gerald Wooster (Bunt 2004), a Kleinian psychoanalyst and psychiatrist. She attended bi-weekly analysis sessions with him for ten years (John Priestley, personal communication, March 21, 2015), and they had a very close relationship. At one point, Mary sculpted two busts of Dr. Wooster, one that she gave to him and the other that she kept in her flat. In fact, Dr. Wooster and J. B. Priestley were the two major sources of feedback during the time that Mary wrote her two books. Every weekend she would write a chapter and send it to both. They, in turn, would make comments on the manuscript and quickly return them to Mary. Mary would then revise the chapter and prepare for the next, which would be reviewed the following weekend.

Mary also received ongoing supervision from Dr. Joe Redfearn at St. Bernard's Hospital and attended group work and family therapy courses at the Institute of Group Analysis (Bunt 2004). In addition, Mary, Marjorie Wardle, and Peter Wright met weekly on Tuesdays at her flat for *"Intertherap"* group improvisation sessions, where they practiced as each other's personal music therapist (Bunt 2004; Hadley 2001). At this stage of her life, Mary was integrating all of her experiences—her personal therapy, supervision, coursework, and the weekly improvisation sessions with her peers—into the development of her work with patients who had chronic mental ill health at St. Bernard's. Her personal struggles, victories, determination, and inclinations helped give birth to a method that she named "Analytical Music Therapy."

Mary Priestley passed away on 11 June 2017 at the age of 92.

THE METHOD

Analytical Music Therapy (AMT) is an analytically oriented, symbolic application of music that is improvised and then processed by the therapist and client (Abrams 2014). In AMT, music functions as a creative resource through which the client gains opportunities to explore their inner life, uncover and resolve conflicts, gain greater personal insight, and realize their greater potential. The aim of AMT is, through the active, lived experience of music, to build awareness and to remove obstacles that prevent individuals from realizing their full potential and from achieving personal goals (Abrams 2014).

During AMT treatment, the music is always improvised. Scheiby (2013, p.11) describes the functions of AMT improvisation as to:

- facilitate transparency of boundaries (e.g. my sound starts and ends here)
- serve as a medium for the transformation of emerged emotions
- provide support and enhance vitality and insight
- release symbols, images, thoughts, metaphors, emotions, and free associations
- facilitate new neuronal connections
- reinforce the internalization of emerged material
- stimulate the ability to endure being in silence and listening to one's personal inner music and to others' music and words at a deep level.

Brian Abrams, music therapist and AMT practitioner, discussed his personal experiences with receiving AMT:

> My experience of therapy was one I would characterize as a *relationship-centered, music-centered* space and time. The AMT therapy was *relationship-centered* because of the importance of mutual roles in each session, and because therapy was all about ways of being and working together. In many ways, I found that the therapy relationship itself was the core, transformative dimension of the work, independently of anything actually 'done' in therapy. For me, the element of *care* in this relationship was perhaps [its] most crucial facet. Personal AMT therapy sessions were

also *music-centered*. In the work, as therapy processes guided the improvisational music-making, the music likewise guided the overarching therapy processes. Whether improvisations were referential (titled) or non-referential (untitled), the process always felt very much 'about' the music to me, and I experienced numerous ways in which the dynamics of the therapeutic relationship were manifested within the music. The music-centeredness of the work has helped me to experience, on a direct, first-hand basis, a certain sense of consistency and alignment between the general nature of self-exploration and that of musical improvisation, the characteristic interplay of music and words in AMT. (2013, n.p.)

Psychodynamic foundations

John Priestley summarized his mother's impact on the therapeutic milieu of her times by stating that "for people who are interested in psychodynamic thinking and also music, [Mary Priestley] provided the bridge between these two different disciplines" (personal communication, March 21, 2015). He was referring to popular psychological theories such as psychoanalytic, humanistic, Gestalt, information systems, and cognitive-behavioral therapies. These were methods that were borrowed and enhanced through music therapy practice, but the music therapy never outshone the paradigm.

In this section, we will explore the psychodynamic foundations of AMT, the mentors behind Mary Priestley, and the issues of transference, countertransference and resistance.

Mary Priestley's mentors

Mary Priestley was not your typical music therapist, however. Unlike the psychological theories commonly paired with music therapy, AMT presumably emerged from Mary's relationship with the psychoanalytical concepts of Sigmund Freud, Carl Jung, and Melanie Klein (Hadley 2001). Due to her personal strength, commitment, intelligence, and experience with multiple therapeutic practices, Mary was a music therapist who chose to create theory from music therapy practice rather than relying on existing psychological theories (Scheiby 1999). Indeed, Mary was one of the first music therapists to try this. According to John, who himself became a Jungian analyst, Mary belonged to the Jungian school that was more intrigued with the theories of David Winnicott and Melanie Klein (personal communication, March 21, 2015).

From Sigmund Freud, Mary adopted the concepts of the super-ego, the ego, and the id. She believed that health results when these three components of the personality are balanced and that pathology occurs from an imbalance, and specifically, when one component overshadows the others (Hadley 2001). In addition, the human personality functions on three layers, the unconscious, the pre-conscious, and the conscious. One of the tenets of AMT is the role of musical improvisation to bring the unconscious into the conscious. Mary also incorporated her awareness of the many types of Freudian defense mechanisms into AMT practice (Priestley 1994).

From the works of Melanie Klein, Mary learned the term *projective identification* (Priestley 1994). This concept centers on the baby's fragile ego, inherent at birth, which is perpetually in fear of disintegration (Hadley 2001). This ongoing fear leads to the building of defense mechanisms as the child's ego splits between the good mother and the bad mother. Eventually, the individual projects the good or bad parts of the mother onto someone else, which results in projective identification (Hadley 2009; Priestley 1994). The music therapist's goal is to aid the individual in recognizing that this projection has occurred, and in integrating the good and bad parts back into themself.

From Carl Jung, Mary embraced the concept of the *shadow* (Hadley 2001; Priestley 1994). The shadow is that part of the self where lost memories, impulses, instincts, and thoughts that are not acceptable are repressed (Priestley 1994, p.231). Individuals may be unaware of their shadows or project them onto others. To be healthy one must acknowledge, explore, and fully accept the shadow. Mary wrote specifically about this phenomenon, and created a video with her colleagues at St. Bernard's entitled *Music and the Shadow* (1987).

Transference and countertransference

Mary Priestley was highly cognizant of the roles of *transference* and *countertransference* in AMT. *Transference* is the process by which the patient tries to experience, in current relationships, unfinished business from earlier relationships (Priestley 1975, p.238). In AMT, the client may project onto the music therapist, the music, or even a musical instrument (Hadley 2001). Transferences can be positive or negative, and can come from one's *conscious, pre-conscious,* or *unconscious. Countertransference* occurs when the therapist experiences the client in ways that reflect dynamics from the therapist's perspective or past (Abrams 2014; Priestley 1994). More simply put, it happens when the therapist emotionally reacts to the patient (Hadley 2001). For example, in AMT, the music therapist may create sounds to empathically resonate with the patient's feelings. According to Mary Priestley (1994), the music therapist may echo the client's projected feelings, called *complementary identification* or *e-countertransference*, or may identify with the patient's unconscious dynamics, called *concordant identification* or *c-countertransference*.

Resistance

Simply put, *resistance* occurs when the patient opposes the therapeutic process in a number of ways that counter positive change (Scheiby and Montello 1994). Resistance is sometimes verbal and sometimes musical. The role of the AMT therapist is to determine where the patient's psychic energy has been blocked, in what ways it has been blocked, and to musically mobilize the patient's inner energy so that it flows from the id to the ego to the super-ego, thus bringing their unconsciousness into the light of consciousness (Hadley 2001). Using her knowledge of psychoanalytic theories, Mary forged a link between music therapy practice and the theoretical constructs described above. She created improvisational techniques based on these theories to help access her patients' unconscious materials more effectively.

TECHNIQUES

In a typical AMT session, the music therapist does not set specific goals for the patient, but the patient creates personal goals throughout the therapy process—the analytical music therapist and patient define the goals together (Scheiby 1999). The patient does not need previous music skills or training.

Improvised music forms the basis of the AMT session. The music therapist must be able to play, vocalize, and communicate in any style needed depending upon the culture of the patient.

Scheiby (1999, p.268) defines the structure of an improvised session as follows: (1) identification of theme, metaphor, word, dream, etc.; (2) definition of roles for improvised music; (3) improvisation with music or movement; (4) processing of music verbally, if appropriate; and (5) musical or verbal closure.

The improvisations can be instrumental, vocal, or both. Clients mainly choose percussion instruments—both pitched and unpitched—to play, while music therapists primarily use the piano to evoke, guide, and contain all that is expressed (Wright and Priestley 1972). Scheiby (2010) recommends instruments from a variety of cultures such as singing bowls, rain sticks, bells, Native American flutes, and gongs. AMT can be done with an individual, a dyad, or a group (although a group functions best with 6–8 clients). AMT sessions tend to last for 60–90 minutes (Wright and Priestley 1972).

Mary often audio-recorded her sessions so that she and the patient could listen together afterwards. Sometimes the patient was invited by the music therapist to move creatively to the recorded improvisation. If appropriate, the music therapist and patient discussed the music improvisation and how it related to the patient's life. Also common during improvisations were spontaneous images experienced by the patient (Eyre 2007). These often became the title of the improvisation, and the music therapist and patient often explored the images together, either musically or verbally.

Concomitant with its strong theoretical foundations are the indigenous AMT techniques so skillfully developed by Mary and her colleagues. These can be organized into three categories: (1) consciousness probing; (2) accessing the unconscious (Cooper 2012); and (3) ego strengthening (Kowski 2007).

Consciousness probing techniques

Examples of consciousness probing techniques include the following:

- *Holding:* Allowing the patient to experience emotion all the way through to the climax through sound expression while the music therapist acts as a container for all of the patient's musical expression, also called "containing" (Priestley 1994, p.38).

- *Splitting:* When the patient has projected themselves onto another and has lost the emotion invested in this person. The patient is encouraged to musically role-play conflicts and projections to explore feelings that have been lost or repressed (Priestley 1994, p.40).

- *Investigation of emotional investment:* When the patient's emotions are explored musically instead of verbally. The music therapist serves as accompanist and as a quiet listener (Priestley 1994, p.43).

- *Entering into somatic communication:* When the patient experiences physical symptoms and lets the music therapist musically role-play the patient while the patient role-plays the symptoms (Priestley 1994, p.45).

Accessing the unconscious techniques

Examples of accessing the unconscious techniques include:

- *Guided imagery:* When the music therapist works musically to ground or concretize the patient's imagery. This is often followed by verbal processing or artwork (Priestley 1994, p.48).

- *Myths:* When the patient feels threatened by personal imagery or emotions. The music therapist will read a simplified version of a myth or fairy tale. Using the holding technique, the therapist and patient then improvise the myth together (Priestley 1994, p.53).

- *Dream intracommunication:* When the music therapist acknowledges the patient's dream and splits the dream into fragments. The patient enters each fragment and explores verbally. The music therapist and patient improvise on parts of the dream, and then process how the dream applies to real-life situations (Priestley 1994, p.54).

- *Dream resolution:* When the patient reviews a nightmare or disturbed dream and musically improvises a different ending to the dream (Priestley 1994, p.55).

Ego strengthening techniques

Examples of ego strengthening techniques include:

- *Reality rehearsal:* When the patient is battling with overcoming inner fears and negative patterns of responding. The patient musically practices changes and responses that have been identified in therapy for implementation into daily life (Priestley 1994, p.57).

- *Wholeness:* When the patient chooses an instrument and plays alone while the music therapist listens. The patient is told to play as if without pathology or illness (Priestley 1994, p.58).

- *Exploring relationships:* When the patient takes on the role of another with whom there are problems and role-plays, with the music therapist acting as the patient (Priestley 1994, p.59).

- *Affirmations/celebrations:* When life, joy, and peace are celebrated musically by the patient and music therapist (Priestley 1994, p.60).

- *Sub-verbal communication:* When improvised music is created by the patient and music therapist without a dedicated title or a focus (Priestley 1994, p.60).

- *Patterns of significance:* When musical improvisations create ways to experience feelings about significant events in the patient's life (e.g., death, birth) (Priestley 1994, p.61).

- *Suicide:* When the patient expresses suicidal tendencies. The patient musically experiences what this event would be like (Priestley 1994, p.63).

- *Programmed regression:* When the patient musically returns to a desired, younger age, and experiences what it is like to be there (Priestley 1994, p.65).

Observing an AMT session

On March 5, 2015, I observed an individual AMT session with a client whom I will call "Janet." The session opened with verbal processing. Janet verbally recounted a negative experience that had happened to her earlier that week, and the music therapist suggested that Janet choose an instrument to represent her feelings about the incident. Janet chose a guitar. The music therapist then asked if there was any instrument that Janet wanted her to play. Janet did not respond. The music therapist brought over an Indian cedar flute and asked Janet to incorporate her voice into the improvisation.

Janet started the improvisation, which was based on an E minor scale, and primarily played the two lowest guitar strings (E and A). Only at one point did the music change, and that was when it dropped to a lower octave. While the improvisation was continuing, the music therapist put away the flute and moved to the gong and keyboard. She played the gong once and then supported the improvisation on the keyboard primarily by playing an E minor chord. At one point the music therapist began to vocalize, but Janet did not join her. Then Janet stopped the improvisation abruptly. The music therapist asked her if she wanted to play another instrument or keep playing the guitar, and Janet said that she didn't want to do either.

Janet immediately began talking about how the negative incident from last week related to the rest of her life and her lack of control. I was impressed with how much the seemingly simple, short improvisation had opened Janet up. The music therapist mentioned that they needed to move back to the music for more clarification. She again directed Janet to use her voice in the improvisation, and asked how she would prefer doing that. Janet did not answer. She seemed resistant towards using her voice in a musical, non-verbal manner.

The music therapist moved her chair closer to Janet and demonstrated some breathing exercises that resulted in downward vocal swoops. Janet joined her. The music therapist then took Janet's hands, and they began toning. The client stayed primarily in the range of 2–3 tones, while the music therapist either sang in unison or a fifth below her. The vowel remained an *[a]*. Halfway through this improvisation, I saw the client "let go" and rest her feet underneath the music therapist's chair. They continued with this vocalization for five additional minutes.

Following the improvisation, Janet again disclosed what realizations came from the musical experience. For example, Janet was able to identify how the incident last week had triggered the same dynamics as many of her personal challenges. The music therapist asked Janet what seemed to work the best from the session, and Janet said the toning. The music therapist mentioned how much Janet had let go of physically during the breathing and vocalizing.

The session lasted approximately one hour. Based on the AMT techniques provided above, it seemed that the music therapist had used two types of *consciousness holding* techniques (Priestley 1994): (1) the *holding* technique that allowed Janet to experience emotion through sound expression while the music therapist acted as a container; and (2) the *investigation of emotional investment* technique, which is when Janet's emotions were explored musically instead of verbally. In this case, the music therapist served as accompanist and as a quiet listener. I was very impressed with how the music therapist handled this client's resistances and used the music in a powerful way to help the client identify her stumbling blocks. The music she supplied was very supportive in nature. Never was the music therapist's music self-conscious, nor did it move the client too far away from her emotional home base.

TRAINING

I was able to find one active training program that focused entirely on AMT in the US and none in the UK. Benedikte Barth Scheiby coordinates the US program. Scheiby studied personally with Mary from 1978–1980. She made it one of her life goals to train others in AMT (Benedikte Scheiby, personal communication, March 9, 2015). Mary worked in New York City, where she had a private practice. She also provided individual and group music therapy supervision as an adjunct faculty member at New York University, Molloy College, and Montclair State University and directed the Institute Analytical Music Therapy, an AMT training program for post-graduate level music therapists who wish to become AMT practitioners (Benedikte Scheiby, personal communication, September 6, 2016).

Students entering the Institute for Analytic Music Therapy must have the minimum of a Master's degree in Music Therapy and prior experience in music psychotherapy, either individually or in groups. It takes AMT students an average of four years to complete training, which consists of the following requirements:

- 48 personal music therapy sessions with an AMT-trained music therapist

- 15 Intertherap group sessions and corresponding documentation (i.e., case assessment, application paper)

- 48 individual supervision sessions and corresponding documentation, including video/audio documentation

- completion of an ongoing reading list.

Students in AMT training have to demonstrate the following skills:

- be skilled musicians in piano and voice, and skilled in other instruments such as guitar and percussion

- accompany a client on at least one major instrument, on the piano, and with the voice

- improvise in most idioms

- be good sight-readers so they can learn new repertoires

- use their bodies as communication tools and as instruments, and to express themselves musically as well as bodily.

Benedikte Scheiby, personal communication
(March 9, 2015)

Upon completion of the training program, the music therapist earns a certificate and receives the designation of *"AMT therapist."* The Institute also offers additional workshops for AMT therapists who wish to become trainers.

WRITINGS

This section of the chapter summarizes both the writings of Mary Priestley and other authors who have published about AMT. First, I searched for any piece of writing, published or unpublished, which had been written by Mary. Using electronic retrieval and the Music Therapy Archives at Temple University in Philadelphia, Pennsylvania (PA), I found 24 documents that had been written by Mary between 1969 and 1995. In all but two documents, Mary was the sole author. Twelve of the 24 articles (50%) were published in the *Journal of British Music Therapy*. The types of documents and names of periodicals can be found Appendix 4-A.

The best word to describe the selected topics of Mary's writings is "eclectic." As I read through the essays that Mary had written during the last ten years before her retirement, it seemed that she openly shared her revelations about music therapy as they occurred to her, and so her articles were about music therapy and community, love, the shadow, listeners, the cycle of life, fantasy, and linking sound and symbol. Her writings during the first ten years, in contrast, were more anecdotal and focused on how Analytical Music Therapy related to Freudian theory and psychoanalytic practice. During the following ten years, it seemed to me as though she let go of the stronghold that Freudian theory had held in her life and work, allowing her to explore new ideas about the conceptual nature of music and symbols. (See Appendix 4-A at the back of this book for the bibliography.)

Mary wrote two books about music therapy. *Music Therapy in Action* (1975), her first book, was published early in her career by St. Martin's Press in London and centered on her clinical experiences and techniques as a music therapist in psychiatric hospitals. Her second book, *Essays on Analytical Music Therapy* (1994), was published by Barcelona Publishers the year before Mary retired, and contains a collection of all of her writings and lectures, including portions of her first book and the *Herdecke Lectures on Analytical Music Therapy*, which she wrote in German while teaching at the Herdecke Community Hospital in Germany. These were later translated into English.

Works by other authors

I searched for any literature about AMT that had been published in refereed journals or books through 2014. Appendix 4-B (p.190) contains a bibliography of all the publications about AMT that were written by persons other than Mary Priestley. It contains the year of publication, author's name, type of publication, and abridged publication title. In summary, 35 documents written specifically about AMT (but not by Mary Priestly) were published in English between 1987 and 2014. Twelve different authors contributed to the writings. Benedikte Scheiby has written the most literature on the topic of AMT (14, 40%).

When I looked to identify themes for the publications not written by Mary, I discovered that 23 percent focused on clinical populations and 23 percent were written about the psychoanalytic components of AMT. Other publications provided overviews of AMT or AMT education and supervision. In the early years of publication (i.e., 1987–2001), many of the writings were psychoanalytic in nature. The articles seem to have become more clinical, as evidenced by the last article about AMT (2014), which focused on group AMT with refugee women. A list of themes of the writings of persons other than Mary Priestley can be found in Appendix 4-C (p.194).

Only one book about AMT was written by someone other than Mary. Johannes Eschen, who edited the book *Analytical Music Therapy* (2002), was Professor of Music Therapy and Founding Director of the Institut für Musicktherapie der Hochschule für Musik und Theater in Hamburg, Germany. The book featured 12 chapters written by different experts on AMT in the UK and the US. The chapters were based on lectures about AMT that had been presented at the 1999 Ninth World Congress of Music Therapy. It was at this conference that AMT was acknowledged as one of *Five International Models of Music Therapy*.

SUMMARY

Due to the current lack of available trainers, I am concerned about AMT's future as a discrete therapeutic approach. The primary trainer of the method in the US is Benedikte Scheiby, and she is very determined to continue AMT practice and the training of AMT practitioners. Indeed, new AMT training programs in the US are in the development stage (Benedikte Scheiby, personal communication, April 1, 2017). Although Mary taught at Herdecke University in Germany, the Guildhall School of Music and Drama in London, England, and then privately from her London residence, few AMT academicians remain. One reason may be that this method is deeply rooted in psychoanalytic theory, which is now out of vogue. The practice of music therapy, both in the US and in the UK, where most of the students trained with Mary, is limited by national, state, or regulatory restrictions. For that reason, a therapeutic approach as time-intensive as AMT may well struggle to survive in its traditional form.

I contacted Inge Nedergaard Pedersen, a music therapy academician who resides in Denmark. Pedersen was hired to teach music therapy at Aalborg University. When I asked her how she incorporated AMT into her teaching, she responded:

> "I am not a trainer in this advanced method as an isolated method called Analytical Music Therapy. I am a practitioner and trainer of important ideas and elements from this advanced method, which in my working situation now is applied as 'the roots' of a broader and integrated training course in music therapy." (personal communication, June 10, 2015)

Regarding the training of AMT in Europe, Helen Bonny (1997) stated that AMT had gained greater acceptance in Europe in the 1970s than in the US, where music therapy relied too much on a behavioral psychology base (p.67). Bonny also purported that many forms of music therapy improvisation in Europe are based on AMT.

Elements of AMT have been incorporated not only into training at Aalborg University (Denmark), but also at the University of the Arts (Berlin), Institut für Musiktherapie der Hochschule für Musik und Theater (Hamburg), Seitoku University (Japan), Westfalische Wilhelms-universitat (Munster), New York University, Molloy College, and Michigan State University. In addition, AMT-trained music therapists are now working with client groups who were not treated in the past, when Mary Priestley was developing the method (i.e., patients in medical hospitals; patients in rehabilitation facilities; individuals with learning disabilities or emotional problems; those on the autism spectrum; persons with acculturative stress and cultural adjustment issues; and individuals in forensic settings) (Benedikte Scheiby, personal communication, November 16, 2016). I therefore assert that Mary's ideas and techniques will not be lost, but will continue to be assimilated into current improvisational, psychodynamic, music-centered music therapy training and practice in the future.

CHAPTER FIVE

THE BONNY METHOD OF GUIDED IMAGERY AND MUSIC

Figure 5.1: A photograph of Helen Bonny

The aim of this chapter is to expose the reader to the life, spirit, and vision of Helen Lindquist Bonny. Writing this chapter has been a labor of love for me. Helen was my teacher, mentor, and friend from the moment I began my Bonny Method training until her passing in 2010. I still feel her strong presence in my life. My friendship with Helen included her wonderful family—her three children, their spouses, and her grandchildren.

Our friendship first began when Helen was living in Salina, Kansas (KS) and teaching for the Bonny Foundation, her training program, in Wichita, KS. Her modest house was the center of the Bonny Foundation. All of the training materials were stored in her basement, which is also where she led individual and group sessions.

Presiding over her living room was a mammoth grand piano that belonged to a local community orchestra with which she played. It was in the Salina house that I conducted a three-day interview with Helen about her choice of music for the original 18 core Guided Imagery and Music (GIM) programs. I always felt at home in her house. I remember one particular evening when I went over to her house, and I lay under the piano while she played Schubert. I still recall how the vibrations from the piano filled me, as though I were melting up into the music.

HELEN BONNY'S STORY

In this brief overview, we look at Helen Bonny's life, from childhood to becoming a mother, the role of the violin throughout her life, and the events that led her to create Guided Imagery and Music.

The early years

Helen Lindquist Bonny was born in Rockford, Illinois (IL) in 1921. One of her pivotal childhood memories occurred when the family moved from Illinois to Kansas in 1923. According to Helen, they traveled in an old Ford to Lawrence, KS, where her father was hired as the religious work director for the Haskell Indian Institute. Helen's father was a Congregational minister who dedicated his life to working with Native Americans (Cohen 2004).

Helen came from a home with a strong musical maternal lineage. Her mother and grandmother were both musicians. Helen's mother received a degree in piano and organ in 1915 from Oberlin Conservatory at a time when most women did not pursue college degrees. Helen remembered being fascinated with the piano as a child and wanting to play it. She remembered reaching up over her head to touch the piano keys as a toddler; later her mother would stand her and hold her on the piano stool so she could more fully explore the keyboard. Her mother played often; Helen especially remembered falling asleep to the soothing sounds of her mother performing Chopin nocturnes. Helen credited these early childhood memories to her first experiences with music in an altered state of consciousness.

Helen's mother also loved Caruso songs, and Beethoven, Brahms, and Mozart symphonies. They would listen together to the Texaco Opera Theater on the radio every Saturday morning. Helen stated that, "If she could pick a mother, she could not have picked a better one, because she taught me mothering" (Cohen 2004, p.11). She described her mother as a strong-willed woman who instilled the love of music in her.

Helen's father was gone a lot. He was on the road for about two-thirds of the year, visiting Indian missions. Helen credited her father for her Swedish heritage, looks, and innovative tendencies. When her father was home, Helen remembered the family standing around the piano making music while her father listened. She also had a clear memory of her mother playing Schubert songs while her father sang. Although Helen's family lived through the Depression, her father worked for a well-known non-profit organization in Boston, Massachusetts (MA), and they did not struggle financially.

It was clearly Helen's mother who instilled the love of music in Helen. Helen began her formal music study at a very early age, around five years old. She remembered studying piano with a woman in Yonkers, New York, with deliciously smelling perfume, and giving a recital when she was only six-and-a-half years old. Even as a child, Helen's senses played a large role in her relationship to music. After her family moved to Lawrence, KS, Helen continued her piano studies briefly with an "unimaginative, pedantic, and tired" piano teacher, which caused her to stop taking lessons. As Helen simply explained, "She did not love the piano" (Bonny 2002, p.3).

In third grade, Helen heard a classmate play the violin. She was enthralled by the instrument and asked her mother to buy her a violin. Her first violin was quarter-sized and not of good quality; neither was her first violin teacher. At Helen's urging, her mother bought her a full-sized instrument and asked Karl Kuersteiner at the University of Kansas (KU) to accept Helen as a student (Cohen 2004). He remained Helen's faithful teacher and mentor for nine years. Helen claimed that he was a gentle man, whom she just "adored" (Cohen 2004, p.11). After three years of study, Helen performed in her first student program, where she played the slow movement of the *Wieniawski Violin Concerto.*

Helen and her family faithfully attended Plymouth Congregational Church in Lawrence, KS. When Helen turned 12, she was finally allowed to participate in a Christmas pageant and to walk down the aisle dressed as an angel while holding a candle. Helen had looked forward to this event for years. When it occurred, she had this wonderful out-of-body experience. Helen said it was like "I was an angel" (Cohen 2004, p.12).

The violin suited Helen well. She described herself as a "fairly shy person, but at home performing" (Cohen 2004, p.11). Helen loved being on stage (Bonny 2002). She grew to her substantial adult height when she was only 13–14, and the violin remained her emotional release during her awkward teenage years in the 1930s. Music became Helen's safe passage. She won many contests at state and national level during high school, and spent an exhilarating summer at Interlochen Music Camp in Michigan.

Following high school, Helen attended the Oberlin Conservatory of Music in the footsteps of her mother. There, in her early 20s, she studied violin performance with Reber Johnson. Although she had many years of performance experience prior to her collegiate study, it was with Reber Johnson that she encountered one of the most useful lessons about music. She learned that it was not enough for the performer to produce the correct tones. To make music, according to Helen, one needed both the skill of the player and the *intention* behind the playing (Bonny 2002). This emphasis on intention became a foundation for how Helen later selected the music for her GIM programs.

Helen always remembered having a strong faith, albeit one that transformed over the years. Not only was her father an ordained minister, but so too was her future husband, Oscar Bonny. They met at a wedding where Helen was a guest violinist and Oscar was the preacher, and they married in 1943. Oscar was pursuing a theological degree from Oberlin, and eventually became a Congregationalist minister. His first pastorate was in Cleveland,

Ohio (OH). Helen thus became a minister's wife and the mother of three children.

Helen as Mother

Helen and Oscar's first daughter and oldest child, Beatrice (Bea), was born in 1945. Bea describes her parents' relationship as one that was conceived in music. The family moved to Kansas City between the years of 1952–1962. Helen hosted weekly prayer meetings for the churchwomen in their home, created a liturgical dance group, and conducted children and adults' choirs. Despite fulfilling the tasks of being a minister's wife and mother, she still found time to continue her music career. Bea recalls being proud of her mother for continuing her own work "at a time when many women did not have their own careers, especially ministers' wives who were expected to be at home co-ministering with their spouses and taking care of the needs of the congregation" (Beatrice Stoner, personal communication, August 23, 2010). Beatrice has a fond memory of listening to her mother play *"Ave Maria"* on her violin while Beatrice was laying her head on Helen's pregnant belly. She clearly remembers the music moving through Helen's body to her own. Bea recalls how hymns were a given part of their lives as they sat on the front pew each Sunday to listen to Oscar's sermons and Helen's choir anthems. Even now when she sings a hymn, Bea can hear Helen and Oscar's voices singing next to her.

Helen and Oscar's first son, Erich, was born in 1947 in Cleveland, OH. They moved the family six weeks after Erich was born, to Anthony, KS, where Oscar began a new church position. Like his older sister, Erich remembers Helen catering to the needs of the congregation while also maintaining her violin performing; however, he always recognized Helen's drive to move beyond just being a minister's wife. He describes their home as constantly filled with music, especially hymns, classical music, and Helen's violin playing. Erich remembers the "earlier experiences as a minister's family in church settings as ones that reflect the most transformative moments in his life" (personal communication, August 23, 2010).

Their youngest child, Francis Albert, was born in 1950 in Lawrence, KS. The family lived in a rectory a half block from the Congregational church. Francis was born while his father was attending Heidelberg University in Germany. He remembers hearing music while still in Helen's womb, which he found comforting and entertaining (Francis Bonny, personal communication, August 23, 2010). He felt that the music shaped his body and mind, and did not want to leave the womb when it was time. Thus, he was three weeks late for delivery. As a child, Francis recalls the house being filled with Helen's female friends and classical music. Francis credits his father for grounding the children in an appreciation of the outdoors and for encouraging intellectual pursuits. He describes how his father would say the prayer at the dinner table in German, and how spiritual an experience that was for him.

All three children remember the annual vacations the family took during the summer to Palm Beach, Florida, to visit Helen's parents. They would stop and camp along the way. Bea remembers watching Helen swim in the ocean, and recalls that Helen seemed most happy and carefree during those days at the beach. Helen's cooking was another noteworthy part of the annual beach trips. Francis remembers that she was a wonderful cook who used unusual spices and flavors. The house was usually filled with delicious smells. He credits Helen for his love of cooking today.

Although Helen and Oscar attempted to establish a supportive, spiritual environment for their children, their marriage was troubled. Bea claims that Helen found the most meaning in her professional and spiritual endeavors, but was absent frequently from home to avoid marital tensions.

As adults, the three children seem to have been influenced by different parental virtues when choosing their careers. Bea chose a career that emulated the deep faith in her home environment, and was appointed a national staff position in her church's denomination. Helen and Oscar were strong catalysts in Bea's spiritual life cultivation and calling in lay ministry. She states about Helen:

> "I was proud of her abilities and the ways in which people acknowledged her giftedness...her ability to listen, her unconditional love, her humility, her deep faith-rootedness, her openness, and her acceptance of all people." (Beatrice Stoner, personal communication, August 23, 2010)

Erich chose a career as a therapist. Some of his fondest moments are when Helen moved in with him after leaving her troubled marriage, and he and Helen traveled together to the Catholic University of America in Washington, DC. He remembers their conversations about emerging psychological concepts. During that time, Helen was Director of Music Therapy and Erich was completing a degree in Developmental Psychology. He later completed a Master's degree in Clinical Social Work and established a private practice. Erich was the only child who studied GIM and became a Fellow. He was involved in the Leadership Circle of the Association for Music and Imagery (AMI), and assisted Helen with GIM training.

Francis began playing the trumpet when he was ten years old, and was already playing professionally by the time that he was 15. His musical calling seemed to come to him from beyond the womb. Francis remembers sitting next to Helen in church when he was a young boy:

> "I recall sitting next to Mom in the church pew when she wasn't singing, dancing, or playing in church in my early youth. I would methodically touch and look at each of her fingers over some time during the service. I now know it was the energy emanating from and the shape of her fingers that spoke to me. The last day I spent with Mom in May, she did the same, holding my hands. Since her passing, I now feel we were in many ways one another." (Francis Bonny, personal communication, August 23, 2010)

Helen in transition: The violin experience

Helen had always been extremely sensitive to the energies emanating from music and from the universe. Her out-of-body experience as a 12-year-old angel was the first of such events in her life.

Looking back, she discussed *omens* of what was to occur in her life. In August 1948, three weeks before the violin experience, Helen was asked to play the violin at her brother's wedding. Having some free time before the wedding, she was reading in a dormitory room where she had been housed. Suddenly she felt a presence in the room and offered herself to it. Helen predicted that this experience was like a prelude to other mystical experiences and was a way of getting her attention (Cohen 2004).

On September 21, 1948, Helen decided to attend a church-women's meeting in Manhattan, KS to hear Dr. Frank Laubach speak about his literacy technique called *Each One Teach One* (Bonny 2002, p.5). Helen was inspired by his commitment to world literacy and his books on prayer. She decided to bring along her violin on the trip since she was preparing for a performance, and her accompanist was also traveling with her. The day began with a spectacular sunrise, which was enhanced by the open skies and prairies of Kansas (Bonny 2002, p.5). Later, Helen would refer to the sunrise as another indicator for what was to come.

Dr. Laubach overheard Helen and her accompanist practicing together during an afternoon break, and asked them to perform for the service that evening. His exact words to Helen were, "You play as if God speaks through your violin" (Bonny 2002, p.5). That night at the service, Helen thought of his inspiring words as she played "The Swan" from Saint Saens' *Carnival of the Animals*. During the repetition of the first theme, everything changed. Helen described this as, "it was as if the violin was not my own; bow arm and fingers were held in abeyance to a light and wonderful infusion that created an unbelievable sound I know I had not produced before" (Bonny 2002, p.5). This music was exquisitely graceful, and no technical adjustment by Helen caused any changes to the sound. The music continued like this all the way through the piece. Helen was trembling upon finishing the song, and shook even more violently when she sat down. Dr. Laubach spoke, "The violin was so beautiful, I cannot speak. Let us meditate for a while" (Bonny 2002, p.6). He spoke briefly and then asked Helen to play again.

By this point, Helen was shaking uncontrollably and knew that technical control would be impossible. Nevertheless, she agreed to play "Ave Maria" by Bach/Gounod. Again, the exquisite music played through her violin.

That evening Helen could not sleep, and finally realized that what she had experienced was a conversion though music. It felt like an epiphany to Helen and lasted for weeks. To Helen it was "an indescribable event" (Bonny 2002, p.6). Dr. Laubach communicated with Helen that he, too, had experienced an epiphany that evening, and recommended to Helen that she practice daily meditation and form a prayer group to reach out to others. The violin experience not only revealed to Helen the beautiful aspects of her life, but also spotlighted the painful remainders of unfinished business. It was under Dr. Ken Godfrey's psychotherapeutic care that Helen was finally able to heal from the death of her brother, which happened when she was a young child.

Helen Bonny and music therapy

As can be expected, the violin experience transformed Helen's life. Most relevant to this would be Helen's decision, in 1960, to pursue training in music therapy exactly 12 years following her musical conversion. She studied at the University of Kansas (KU) in Lawrence, KS with Dr. E. Thayer Gaston, who had founded the first graduate music therapy degree program in the US (Davis and Gfeller 2002). Helen told Dr. Gaston about her violin experience and how she believed that magic through music could happen to others as it had happened to her. To her surprise, he shook his finger at her, stated that KU taught "behavioral psychology," and warned her never to mention mysticism again while she was a student there (Davis and Gfeller 2002, p.7). Helen remained at KU for six years and graduated with a second Bachelor's degree and a Master's degree in Music Education with a specialization in Music Therapy. During that period of development in the US, few academic programs conferred actual Music Therapy degrees, and most music therapists actually earned Music Education degrees with specializations in Music Therapy and the subsequent music therapy registration.

Dr. Gaston's warnings did not thwart Helen's exploration into music and consciousness, but did indeed represent the mindset of most of the membership of the National Association for Music Therapy (NAMT) at that time. Helen remained in Lawrence, KS from 1966–1968, where she served as the office coordinator for NAMT. In 1969, she was invited to join the research staff of the Maryland Psychiatric Research Center (MPRC) in Baltimore, Maryland (MD). Helen was hired to explore the clinical effects of mind-altering drugs, such as lysergic acid diethylamide, or LSD (Meadows 2010). This groundbreaking approach to exploring the psyche in a laboratory setting via mind-altering drugs was also labeled psychedelic psychotherapy. Helen's role at the center was to choose and produce music programs for the experimental drug sessions, which could last as long as 8–12 hours (Bonny 2002; Meadows 2010).

THE METHOD

The MPRC served a variety of patients (e.g., those with neurotic tendencies, substance abuse issues, and terminal cancer). As Helen focused on the listening experiences of the patients, she discovered that music had many benefits, such as:

- helping the patient relinquish the usual controls to enter an inner world of experience
- facilitating the release of intense emotionality
- contributing toward peak experiences
- providing continuity in the experience of timelessness
- directing and structuring the therapeutic experience.

(Bonny 2002, p.22)

Helen concentrated on how music listening could be used to mine both the conscious and unconscious realms and to retrieve the materials evoked in the form of imagery. She discovered that the most effective music to use for guiding during these sessions was classical music (Bonny 2002). It seemed able to bring the patients to the extremes they needed and then to bring them back. Helen worked not only on choosing music, but also on the guiding techniques necessary when a patient was in a deep state of consciousness.

It was only a matter of time before these mind-opening drugs found their way to the streets. As they began to be produced incorrectly, this resulted in overuse and toxic experiences for the users and their eventual restriction in 1972, even in clinical settings such as the MPRC. When they were no longer accessible, Helen began creating music programs to emulate the effects of the drugs and the length of the drug profile, but without the contraindications. She researched the effects of these music programs on a group of patients diagnosed with alcoholism, and found that the results from listening to these longer music sessions were not promising. Through her collaborations at the MPRC with many famous therapists in the 1970s (i.e., Stanislav Grof, Walter Pahnke, Jean Houston, Ram Dass, Charles Tart, Huston Smith, Joseph Campbell, and Hanscarl Leuner), Helen began to birth a new form of music psychotherapy (Bonny 2002). She realized that without LSD, she needed much shorter music programs, a way to facilitate relaxation responses (which the drugs had previously done), and a focus at the beginning of the music to prime the patient's imagery. She started creating shorter music programs that still simulated the stages of the drug effects (i.e., pre-onset, onset, building to peak, peak, re-entry, return to normal consciousness), and practiced these both with groups and individual patients (Meadows 2010). She found that the deeper parts of the psyche, when it was ready, could still be reached via this non-drug approach, and it resulted in less abrupt or traumatizing effects (Bonny 2002).

The 1970s were an extremely busy time for Helen. As mentioned earlier, she had a troubled marriage. In 1973, she co-wrote *Music and Your Mind* with Dr. Louis Savary. She separated from Oscar in 1974, and they later divorced. She returned to school and completed her PhD at Union Graduate College. With Sr. Trinitas Bochini, Helen founded the Institute for Consciousness and Music (ICM). This became the means through which to publish and disseminate materials about GIM and to train new practitioners. It produced Helen's music programs on cassette tapes and made them available for the GIM trainees; these were called the *original GIM programs*. Along with the tapes, the Institute published three monographs from 1978 through 1980 based on sections of Helen's dissertation (Ventre and McKinney 2015), and later published another small monograph by Linda H. Keiser entitled, *Conscious Listening: An Annotated Guide to the ICM Taped Music Programs* (1986). During the same decade, Helen took a full-time job as Director of Music Therapy at The Catholic University in Washington, DC. She remained there until 1980, when she suffered a serious cardiac episode and had to receive emergency surgery. This event forced Helen to retire temporarily from all activities.

Following her surgery, Helen moved to Port Townsend, Washington (WA), to live with her sister during her recuperation. She stayed in Port Townsend until moving to Salina, KS, to be with her daughter, Bea, in 1987 (Beatrice Stoner, personal communication, August 23, 2016). While in Salina, Helen created the Bonny Foundation. Through the Foundation she published the *Music Rx Manual* (1983), which consisted of six cassette tapes with healing music and instructions to be used in hospital settings that was based on her own experiences as a patient. Helen taught with the Bonny Foundation until she fully retired in the late 1990s. After retirement, she moved to Vero Beach, Florida (FL) in 2002, to again live near Bea, who had moved there years before. She remained in Vero Beach until her death in 2010.

Theoretical foundations

In one of her earliest publications (the article, "Music and consciousness," 1975), Helen presented an egg-shaped diagram of *psychosynthesis*, as introduced by Dr. Roberto Assagioli (1965).

The diagram represented the self and consisted of various layers of consciousness (i.e., unconscious, ego, pre-conscious, and super conscious); these were based solely on Freudian theory. She next presented her original *cut-log diagram of consciousness* in the same article. This represented the multiple levels of an altered state of consciousness that are accessible through methods of relaxation, concentration, and classical music. The growth rings in the cut log are a metaphor for continuing growth (Goldberg and Dimiceli-Mitran 2010). The cut-log diagram was an essential foundation for the development of GIM, as it represented not only psychotherapeutic levels but also spiritual levels. From the theories of Carl Jung, Helen borrowed concepts such as guided scripts, archetypes, myths, collective unconscious, and meeting the shadow, and incorporated them into GIM practice (Abrams 2002).

Helen primarily based GIM on two psychological constructs that were popular in the 1970s: humanistic and transpersonal psychology (Bonny 2002). Prior to these, psychoanalytical and behavioral theories provided the basis for most music therapy practice. Earlier in this chapter, E. Thayer Gaston had warned Helen not to mention words like "magic" or "mystical" while studying Music Therapy in university because he was strongly associated with behavioral psychology and its reign over music therapy.

From humanistic psychology, Helen gleaned the concepts taught by Abraham Maslow and Carl Rogers. From Maslow she incorporated the concept of peak experience as a source of healing into her work (Goldberg and Dimiceli-Mitran 2010), and even created a music program that contained elements that could trigger a peak experience. She believed, like Rogers, that humans were endowed with self-wisdom and could explore the depths and heights of their potentialities (Goldberg and Dimiceli-Mitran 2010, p.12). Humans could give and share thoughts, experiences, and actions (Trondalen 2009). Helen embraced the transpersonal theories proposed by Stanislav Grof, Charles Tart, and Ken Wilber. From their perspectives, she explored the limits of space and time. Helen believed that GIM could help humans transcend the limits of their individual personalities and egos to encompass larger aspects of life, such as the psyche and the cosmos (Abrams 2002). And she believed that classical music was the ideal vehicle for such transpersonal experiences. Helen credited other writers for helping her shape GIM practice through the elements of music and psychological theories of art. They include Viktor Zuckerkandl, Leonard B. Meyer, Pinchas Noy, and Susanne Langer (Bonny 2002).

Defining GIM

As I was looking for the most salient definition of GIM for this book, I realized that I had already read numerous definitions and was no closer to choosing the right one. Most of the definitions came from the inner experience of the authors, and so each was viable in its own way. It was at this point that I decided to select the definition that I believe Helen would have preferred the most in her later years. Although the entire definition can be attributed to Fran Smith Goldberg and Louis Dimiceli-Mitran (2010), Goldberg published this earlier, condensed version of it in 1995:

> [GIM is] depth experience in which specifically programmed classical music is used to generate a dynamic unfolding of inner experience. [It] is holistic, humanistic and transpersonal, allowing for the emergence of all aspects of the human experience: psychological, emotional, physical, social, spiritual, and the collective unconscious. (Goldberg 1995, p.114)

I liked this definition immediately because it was simple, yet inclusive. It combines Helen's emphasis on the spiritual nature of the human experience and her acknowledgement of humanistic, Jungian, and transpersonal theories. It uses the term *depth experience* to represent the ineffable nature of the GIM session instead of citing psychoanalytical terms. It describes GIM as a holistic, or *synergistic*, process where the entire experience creates much more than the sum of its parts (Stokes 1992).

In addition, other authors have enhanced the understanding of GIM as follows:

- GIM is a music-centered transformational therapy (Cadrin 2005).

- GIM harnesses the refined energy of classical masterworks to evoke imagery in travelers' inner journeys (Clarkson 2005).

- Music then becomes a servant stretching the imagination and leading us beyond our current mode of presence to people, events, and things (Beck 2005).

- The focus is on the client's unfolding and spontaneous imagery process (Kirkland 2009).

- Symbolic images [that] have aesthetic, autobiographical, archetypal, and transpersonal dimensions (Körlin 2009).

- GIM is based on the reflexive mode in music therapy (Bonny 1997).

I would like to pause and address this last entry. Helen decided to be a music therapist when she was 40, and always proudly considered herself a music therapist. In the 1970s, at the inception of Helen's relationship with the National Association for Music Therapy (NAMT), a number of its members were highly critical of her work or any mention of spirituality or mysticism in music therapy in general. For that reason, GIM training and practice developed in relative isolation from NAMT for many years (Summer 1997). Helen attempted to heal this rift through her ongoing research, publications, and conference presentations that showcased the clinical value of GIM, and intentionally did not focus on concepts that might be misconstrued by music therapists who were operating from a behavioral paradigm. Once the unification between NAMT and the American Association for Music Therapy (AAMT) occurred in 1998, the new association members of the American Music Therapy Association (AMTA) seemed more open to the potential of music therapy as a form of psychotherapy. In 1999 the AMTA finally honored Helen Bonny and GIM for founding one of five prestigious international music therapy models. Helen even proposed that a spiritual track be added to Bonny Foundation training in the late 1990s for trainees who wanted to focus more on spiritual and transpersonal work, but this never came into being.

TECHNIQUES

The techniques used now by Bonny Method practitioners were carefully honed over the years that Helen was creating the music programs in MPRC. Helen learned very early on that music by itself could not engage a person. It had to be a specific kind of music, and people had to be opened up so that the music could enter them at a deeper level. To do that, Helen experimented with relaxation techniques, such as modified progressive relaxation (Jacobson 1938), Hanscarl Leuner's guided precursors (1984), and verbal guiding skills to accompany the music. The Institute for Consciousness and Music was the first association to oversee the standardized training of Bonny Method practitioners. From this early training evolved the techniques that are now used by Bonny Method therapists around the world.

The Bonny Method music therapist's goals for the first session would be to develop rapport with the client, to assess the client's needs and functioning levels, and to determine whether the Bonny Method was appropriate for the client. Usually the music therapist begins to determine the primary issues that brought the client to pursue the Bonny Method, which include the client's level of happiness, social skills, self-knowledge, and blocks in creativity. If the music therapist deems the client appropriate for Bonny Method work, a contract is usually signed between the music therapist and the client that stipulates a certain number of sessions, the cost of each session, and other pertinent information that may need to be included depending on the nationality and mental health certification of the music therapist. The first few sessions involve a more extended verbal exchange at the beginning so that the music therapist can gather extra information about the client (e.g., childhood, family of origin, therapeutic experiences, other non-ordinary state of consciousness experiences, relationships with music).

To teach trainees how to guide a Bonny Method session, Helen divided the session into four essential sections: the prelude, induction, music, and postlude. The Bonny Method session usually lasts 90 minutes. Although the section names may have changed over the years, their functions have not.

Prelude

The prelude, preliminary conversation, or pre-session makes up the first part of a Bonny Method session. This is when the music therapist and client meet to develop rapport, to focus on the here-and-now feeling state of the client, to review what the client has been experiencing since the last session, and to discuss possible goals, foci, or intentions for the music session. The prelude usually lasts 15–30 minutes (Bonny 2002).

Induction

The induction is the shortest portion of the Bonny Method session and usually lasts for 5–10 minutes. Prior to the induction, the client usually sits in a lounge chair or lies on a mat on the floor facing up with a pillow under the head and a blanket covering the body. The music therapist sits to one side of the client's head so that the face and body of the client can be observed, and a music speaker is normally placed behind the client's head. The induction usually contains two basic elements, physical relaxation and psychological concentration (Bonny 2002). The function of the physical relaxation is to help the client feel more comfortable, to relax, and to access a deeper level of consciousness. The music therapist guides the client through the relaxation without any music playing. Modified progressive relaxation (Jacobson 1938), which is typified by the contraction and release of different muscle groups in the body, is one common relaxation technique used in Bonny Method sessions. Once the client is noticeably relaxed, the music therapist will verbally suggest some form of psychological concentration, such as a visual image, emotion, or a sensation in the body. The function of this is to allow the client to become more aware of the deeper self but not to bring the client back into the cognitive realm. Helen called this moment of psychological concentration the *focus* of the session. More recently, some training programs teach that the second part of the induction involves the formulation of a therapeutic intention for the session that is mentioned by the music therapist right before the music is played.

The music

The aforementioned parts of the Bonny Method session are conducted to prepare the client for the moment when the recorded music is turned on with verbal guidance (e.g., "let the music take you where you need to go," "let the music join you in your feelings of peace," or "let the music join you on your path"). The music program is chosen by the music therapist based upon the here-and-now state of the client, the client's intention for the music, and the specific relaxation and induction used. Once the music begins playing, the client is verbally encouraged by the music therapist to relay impressions, scenes, and feelings. The music therapist is there to hold the space of the client, to intervene as needed, and to help guide the client's experience through the use of verbal reflecting and matching. The healing occurs through the music and the supportive nature of the dialogue between the client and music therapist.

The music may run from 25 to 45 minutes, depending on the specific program. Once the music has ended, the music therapist will slowly guide the client back to the here-and-now. The client will be encouraged to sit up, but only when ready. Often at this point the music therapist gives the client some mandala paper—drawing paper with a circle drawn in the middle—and drawing media, such as oil pastels, and directs the client to draw. The sensory connection between the client, the pastels, and the paper helps to transition the client more fully back to consciousness.

Postlude

Otherwise known as the post-session or post-session integration, the postlude also helps to transition the client back to full consciousness. Often the client will feel more vulnerable during the postlude and will experience a heightened state of sensory awareness. After the drawing of the mandala, a circular representation of the Self, the music therapist will slowly begin to discuss the session with the client, and will focus primarily on the mandala, the initial focus of the session and how the session related to that, any pivotal or charged moments or images that may have occurred in the session, and finally, ways to process this elements from the session until the next session. The session should end only when the music therapist observes that the client is physically grounded enough and back in a full state of consciousness. The postlude usually lasts for 15–20 minutes.

Bonny Method music programs

One of the salient features of Bonny Method practice is that the practitioners use recorded music as the primary source of therapy. Most of the time, these programs are based on classical Western music, although as new music programs are introduced, they sometimes contain contemporary, jazz, or ethnic selections instead. Early in the development of GIM, Helen pieced together cassette tapes of music programs to support the differing parts of the LSD experience, literally using vinyl recordings, cassette tape, scissors, and scotch tape. She sometimes chose not to use an entire movement of music but to create excerpts of that movement that maintained the same quality throughout (e.g., Richard Strauss' *Ein Heldenleben*). She often labeled her programs based on their therapeutic intentions (e.g., *Comforting/Anaclitic, Peak Experience*).

Seven early music programs were identified in Helen Bonny's dissertation and Monograph #2 (Bonny 1978): *Positive Affect, Death/Rebirth, Peak Experience, the Comforting/Anaclitic, Affect/Release, Imagery, and Group Experience*. Eighteen core programs are recommended for training purposes and practice across all Association for Music and Imagery (AMI) training programs (*Education Standards and Procedures for the Bonny Method of GIM*, 2015), and include these additional programs: *Creativity I, Expanded Awareness, Explorations, Emotional Expression I, Grieving, Inner Odyssey, Mostly Bach, Nurturing, Quiet Music, Relationships, Serenity,* and *Transitions*. Helen created the core programs over a period from 1973 to 1989. In 1994, Helen and Linda Keiser-Mardis revised *Comforting/Anaclitic and Nurturing* tapes, creating two new programs, *Caring* and *Recollections* (Grocke 2002).

One of the changes in copyright law in the early 1990s was that duplication of recorded music for personal or professional use was forbidden. Therefore, Bonny Method practitioners could no longer buy the ICM cassette tapes, but had to purchase the music recordings that they needed individually. Ken Bruscia (1996), in collaboration with Naxos Recording Label, created a set of ten compact discs entitled *Music for the Imagination,* from which Bonny Method trainees and practitioners could piece together and create the programs. Although some of the original pieces used by Helen were not available from Naxos, Ken painstakingly found other pieces of Western art music recorded by Naxos that would work in substitution. As a trainee during that time, I am very grateful to Ken for creating this collection. This made my task of creating the programs much easier, especially since I did not know much about the music. However, some of the Naxos programs did not seem to be as effective as the original music chosen by Helen. In addition, some of the selections from the Naxos recordings, even if they were the same pieces that were chosen by Helen, were not as musically evocative as the ones that Helen had used. Regardless, the *Music for the Imagination* series was extremely helpful for those Bonny Method practitioners and trainees making the shift from already-produced cassette tapes to self-created programs made from compact discs. As a researcher at heart, I discovered that some of the recordings from the core 18 programs were no longer in print, and I spent hours and literally thousands of dollars locating the individual pieces that were missing from the Naxos collection or that did not match the quality of the pieces that Helen had originally chosen.

TRAINING

> "That's why the [GIM] training is so important. You have to know how to get the person to accept you as a person, to accept the music, and for you to use music that is easy to open to at the beginning and then more difficult later on." (Helen Bonny, personal communication, May 16, 2002)

The AMI holds a number of functions, including the ongoing approval of Bonny Method practitioners, trainers, and training programs. Students enrolled in Bonny Method training programs are called "trainees." When trainees finish all of their training requirements, they receive the designation of "Fellow of the Association for Music and Imagery" from AMI. AMI began in 1986 and has published a professional periodical entitled the *Journal of the Association for Music and Imagery* since 1992. In 2009, the AMI Leadership Circle officially decided to change *Guided Imagery and Music* to *The Bonny Method of Guided Imagery and Music*, to distinguish it from other guided imagery trainings with fewer requirements and lower standards of practice. To standardize the language, I use the term *Bonny Method* in this section to represent the Bonny Method of Guided Imagery and Music (GIM).

The AMI has currently endorsed seven Bonny Method training programs in the US and 13 outside of the US; two of these are in the UK. This means that 35 percent of the training programs are in the US, 10 percent are in the UK, and the remaining 55 percent are located elsewhere throughout the world. In 2015, AMI maintained a roster of 45 approved primary trainers; these are individuals who have met the AMI requirements to teach all levels of the Bonny Method training. In a similar pattern to the training programs, 19 (42%) of the trainers are located in the US, two (4%) are in the UK, and the remaining 24 (53%) are located throughout Western and Eastern Europe, Australia, New Zealand,

Singapore, South Korea, Japan, Mexico, Canada, and South Africa (AMI 2015a). Simply put, more than half of the Bonny Method training programs and trainers are located outside of the US and the UK.

All the details involved in the approval and endorsement of Bonny Method training are included in the *AMI Education Standards and Procedures for the Bonny Method of GIM* (rev. 2015). This document contains a detailed explanation of the content and specific requirements for all three levels of training. Table 5.1 represents the prerequisites for entry into each training level and the minimum instructional hours per level. In most cases, these instructional hours take place in a workshop format with a group of trainees at the same level.

Table 5.1: Prerequisites for each Bonny Method training level and minimum hours per level

Level	Prerequisites	Minimum instructional hours/level
I	Bachelor's degree or equivalent	35
II	Bachelor's degree or equivalent Required training to practice as credentialed mental health practitioner in own country Two years' clinical experience in clinical mental health field	50
III	Bachelor's degree or equivalent Required training to practice as credentialed mental health practitioner in own country Three years' clinical experience in clinical mental health field	100 (3–4 modules)

AMI has specifically worded the pre-requisites to address whatever educational level is required in each country to practice as a credentialed mental health practitioner. In most countries, that equals the equivalent of a post-graduate level of training, either at a post-Master's or post-doctoral level. Years of clinical experience are also required for those trainees applying for the second or third level of Bonny Method study. Table 5.2 represents the minimum prerequisites established by AMI for a trainee to enter each level of Bonny Method or to complete the entire training. Because of the immense growth in the number of Fellows and training programs outside of the US, and after years of planning, the European Fellows officially established the European Association for Music and Imagery (EAMI) on September 11, 2016. I send my heartfelt congratulations to all of my European Bonny Method colleagues who will now help shape the new generation of Bonny Method practitioners to meet the specific needs of the European countries and peoples.

Table 5.2: AMI Bonny Method clinical prerequisites to reach next level and Fellow status*

Level	Client sessions	Supervisions	Personal GIM sessions	Admission to level
Prerequisites for Level I			1	
Prerequisites for Level II	6		2	Trainer approval
Prerequisites for Level III	10		4	Trainer approval
To reach Fellow status	75	15	15	Trainer approval

Note: * Different AMI training programs may require more than the above numbers.

In addition to the clinical prerequisites listed in Table 5.2, written assignments are required by AMI during Level III training in order for trainees to reach Fellow status. These written assignments include, but are not limited to:

- two separate case studies based on ten sessions with two different clients
- 15 book reports

- learning and using at least 12 different core music programs in client sessions

- conducting at least two thorough analyses of GIM music programs

- a culminating project (research, musical awareness, or case study).

These requirements are the *minimum* that must be completed to reach Fellow status (AMI 2015a). Each training program has the freedom to add its own assignments to this list, including additional required personal sessions, client sessions, personal growth training, consultations, or other tasks. Some training programs require a research study for the final task, while others require more of a clinically based project.

It is difficult to estimate how long it takes a Bonny Method trainee to reach Fellow status. Most Bonny Method training programs currently organize their training seminars so that they can be completed in three years if the students take all of the classes in succession. Unlike Analytical Music Therapy or Vocal Psychotherapy training, which are usually completed in two years, the complete Bonny Method training often takes longer to complete. Most of the work is done individually once the trainee reaches Level III, save for group participation in 3–4 modules. Trainees may have to travel long distances, even internationally, to attend trainings or to receive personal GIM sessions.

In 2016, AMI had 287 members, 253 of whom were Fellows (Maryann Napavar, personal communication, July 9, 2016). AMI Fellows are currently practicing in over half of the US and in 25 countries worldwide. According to the AMI website, 92 Fellows (38%) come from the US, 4 (2%) from the UK, and the remaining 149 (61%) from the rest of the world (AMI 2015b). To demonstrate the healthy state of growth in AMI, in 2015 alone, 14 new Fellows completed their training and one new training program was added (Maryann Napavar, personal communication, July 10, 2016).

WRITINGS

I searched for any piece of writing, published or unpublished, which had been written by Helen. Using electronic searches through my university library system, my home GIM library, and hand searches through the Music Therapy Archives at Temple University in Philadelphia, Pennsylvania (PA), I found 36 documents that had been written by Helen between 1965 and 2002. The entire bibliography can be found in Appendix 5-A, which represents the year each document appeared and the source of the document.

The documents are categorized into the following types: journal articles, books, chapters, conference presentations, conference proceedings, monographs/manuals, miscellaneous, and a dissertation. Between 1965 and 2002, Helen wrote 36 documents. She produced a steady stream of publications from 1965 to 2002. In the earlier years, between 1965 and 1973, she tended to share authorship with others and to publish in music therapy journals. After the publication in 1973 of Helen's first book, *Music and Your Mind*, which she co-wrote with Louis Savary, she tended to maintain solo authorship of her writings. Helen's three monographs were taken from her doctoral dissertation, *"Music and Psychotherapy."* Table 5.3 represents the types of documents Helen Bonny wrote in descending order of frequency.

Table 5.3: Writings of Helen Bonny by type (*N*=36)

Type	Number	Percentage
Journal articles	16	44
Conference presentations	8	22
Monographs/manuals	3	12
Books	2	5
Chapters	2	5
Conference proceedings	2	5
Miscellaneous	2	5
Dissertation	1	3

Helen primarily wrote articles for refereed professional journals (44%), followed by papers for conference presentations (22%). When I was looking through her unpublished writings at the Temple University Archives, I noticed how fastidiously she had prepared her conference presentations. She began with an outline, typed out the first draft of the presentation, then revised and retyped the presentation. I saw many pages with Helen's comments on small pieces of paper taped to the pages of the draft version in preparation for her next revision. She used the same procedure for her journal articles. Each publication had at least two rough draft versions before she typed her final document, and she saved all of her rough drafts. It was for this reason that I chose to include her conference presentations as written documents based on extensive research.

Two of the documents never found their way to the public and are listed under the category of "*Miscellaneous.*" Joseph Moreno, a music therapy colleague, invited Helen to write a chapter for a book he was planning, entitled, *Music Therapists of Our Time: Profiles in Creativity.* Helen wrote the chapter in 1997, but the book was never published. Another book about GIM that never materialized was one of Helen's own planning. She wrote out an outline with the titles of all the planned chapters and their authors organized into sections. My speculation is that Helen's decline in health caused her to postpone her plans for this book. Both unpublished documents can be found in the Bonny Foundation Archives at Temple University Library.

In a manner similar to Mary Priestley, Helen published her books either at the beginning or end of her career. Her first book, *Music and Your Mind: Listening with a New Consciousness* (1973) was co-authored by Helen Bonny and Louis Savary, her colleague at the Institute for Consciousness and Music. In 1976, Helen completed her dissertation, entitled, "*Music and Psychotherapy: A Handbook and Guide*" from the Union Graduate School. From 1978 to 1980, the Institute for Consciousness and Music published three monographs: *Facilitating GIM Sessions, The Role of Taped Music in the GIM Process,* and *GIM Therapy: Past, Present, and Future Implications.*

Finally, Barcelona Publishers invited Helen to publish her collected writings in *Music and Consciousness: The Evolution of Guided Imagery and Music* (2002). All of the writings in this collection were written by Helen and had been previously published. This anthology was Helen's last publication. She passed away in 2010.

Table 5.4 represents the themes of the documents written by Helen. The largest percentage of documents (42%) was written about music therapy. They include conference presentations that Helen gave as well as speculative pieces about the future of music therapy. The next largest percentage of writings focused on GIM in the form of overviews and updates.

Table 5.4: Themes of the writings by Helen Bonny ($N=36$)

Theme	Number	Percentage of writings
Clinical	1	3
Emotionally disturbed clients	1	3
GIM and art therapy	1	3
GIM overview	5	13
LSD music research	1	3
Mandala	1	3
GIM in medical setting	3	8
Music programs	3	8
Music therapy	15	42
New techniques	1	3
Psychiatric	1	3
Theoretical	3	8

Works by other authors

I searched for any literature about the Bonny Method that had been published in refereed journals or books through 2014. The purpose of the second literature review was to represent how each advanced method of music therapy practice had developed by analyzing the writings of practitioners of the method. All writings in this content analysis had to be written or translated into English. Some dissertations are included. Appendix 5-B, which can be found at the back of this book, contains 181 publications written about the Bonny Method between 1981 and 2014 by persons other than Helen Bonny.

According to Table 5.5, 25 different publication sources exist. Out of these, 100 articles (55%) appeared in the *Journal of the Association for Music and Imagery*. The book, *Guided Imagery and Music: The Bonny Method and Beyond*, published by Barcelona Publishers, contained 26 chapters (14%). *Inside Music Therapy: Client Experiences* was a related text that contained eight chapters (4%) specifically dedicated to GIM. The *Nordic Journal of Music Therapy* published six articles about GIM (3%), and seven dissertations/Master's theses were based specifically on GIM research (4%). Out of the 181 publications found, 96 percent (175) were music therapy resources, and 4 percent (6) were not.

Table 5.5: Sources of publications about the Bonny Method (N=181)

Source	MT or non-MT	Number	Percentage
Journal of the Association for Music and Imagery (JAMI)	MT	100 articles	55
Guided Imagery and Music: The Bonny Method and Beyond (Book)	MT	26 chapters	14
Inside Music Therapy: Client Experiences (Book)	MT	8 chapters	4
Dissertations/theses	MT	7 works	4
Nordic Journal of Music Therapy	MT	6 articles	3
Music Therapy (MT)	MT	4 articles	2
Journal of Music Therapy (JMT)	MT	3 articles	2

Music Therapy Perspectives (MTP)	MT	3 articles	2
Qualitative Inquiries in Music Therapy (Book)	MT	3 chapters	2
Voices (Journal)	MT	3 articles	2
Music and Medicine: Integrative Models in the Treatment of Pain (Book)	MT	2 chapters	1
Mind, Music and Imagery (Book)	Non-MT	1 book	0.76
Music Therapy at the End of Life (Book)	MT	1 chapter	0.76
Case Studies in Music Therapy (Book)	MT	1 chapter	0.76
Clinical Applications of Music in Therapy (Book)	MT	1 chapter	0.76
Conscious Listening (Book)	Non-MT	ICM monograph	0.76
GIM in the Industrial Setting (Book)	MT	ICM monograph	0.76
Healing Imagery and Music: Pathways to the Inner Self (Book)	Non-MT	1 book	0.76
Health Psychology	Non-MT	1 article	0.76
Introduction to Approaches in Music Therapy (Book)	MT	1 chapter	0.76
Journal of Clinical Nursing	Non-MT	1 article	0.76
Journal of Mental Imagery	Non-MT	1 article	0.76
Listening, Playing, Creating Essays on the Power of Sound (Book)	MT	1 chapter	0.76
The Arts in Psychotherapy (Journal)	MT	1 article	0.76
Literature Review of GIM (not published)	MT	1 article	0.76

Source	MT or non-MT	Number	Percentage
Variations in GIM: Taking a Closer Look (Book)	MT	1 chapter	0.76
Unlocking the Treasures of Your Mind (Book)	MT	1 chapter	0.76

Note: MT = music therapy.

A total of 99 authors contributed to the 181 pieces of literature written between 1981 and 2014 about the Bonny Method. The authors who were the most prolific were Ken Bruscia (9%), Lisa Summer (9%), Virginia Clarkson (8%), Denise Grocke (7%), Fran Goldberg (6%), and Cathy McKinney (6%). Table 5.6 contains the names of the authors who wrote at least two pieces, in descending order of publication, and the number of authors who published 1–2 pieces. According to Table 5.6, 20 authors published more than two pieces of literature, 18 authors published two pieces, and 62 authors published one piece.

Table 5.6: Authors of Bonny Method literature: 1981–2014 ($N=100$)

Author	Number of publications	Percentage
Bruscia	9	9
Summer	9	9
Clarkson	8	8
Grocke (Erdonmez)	7	7
Goldberg	6	6
McKinney	6	6
Meadows	5	5
Pickett	5	5
Abrams	4	4
Beck	4	4

Moe	4	4
Ventre	4	4
Borling	3	3
Burns	3	3
Kasayka	3	3
Körlin	3	3
Merritt	3	3
Scott	3	3
Short	3	3
Skaggs	3	3
Others2	2 (18 authors)	2% each
Others1	1 (62 authors)	1% each

Books written specifically about the Bonny Method, from the earliest to the most recent, were *GIM in the Institutional Setting* (Summer 1997); *Music, Mind, and Imagery* (Merritt 1990); *Healing Imagery and Music: Paths to the Inner Self* (Bush 1999); *Guided Imagery and Music: The Bonny Method and Beyond* (Bruscia and Grocke 2002); and *Variations in Guided Imagery and Music: Taking a Closer Look* (Muller 2014).

I discovered 20 salient themes out of the 181 publications written about the Bonny Method between 1981 and 2014 by persons other than Helen Bonny. The following themes appeared the most often: Clinical Practice, Procedures, and Techniques; Theoretical; Music; Myth; Archetype; Imagery, Culture, and Psychotherapy; and Combined Therapies with GIM. Many of the publications could have fallen into more than one category, so I chose what seemed to be the most representative category for each. Table 5.7 displays the number and percentage of documents belonging to each thematic category.

Table 5.7: Themes of publications not written by Helen Bonny (N=23)

Theme	Number	Percentage
Clinical Practice, Procedures, and Techniques	20	11
Theoretical	15	9
Music/Music Programs/Music and Imagery	**14**	**7**
Archetype/Metaphor/Myth/Culture	12	7
Related Therapies/Psychotherapy	12	7
Abuse/Domestic Violence, PTSD, Incest	11	6
Medical	10	6
Psychiatric	10	6
Research (not case studies)	9	5
Informational/General	8	4
Case Studies	7	4
Grief and Death	6	3
Transpersonal	5	3
Adaptations/Modifications	4	2
Miscellaneous*	4	2
Review of Literature	4	2
Spirituality	4	2
Lifespan: Children/Adolescents/Elderly	3	2
Shamanism	3	2
Autism	2	1
Holocaust	2	1
Mandala	2	1
Pivotal Moments	2	1

Note: * Helen Bonny Interview, Breath, Music Therapy, Performance Anxiety, Gender, Inner Family.

SUMMARY

According to the above information about Helen Bonny' writings, almost half (42%) of her 36 scholarly publications focused on music therapy practice. Out of the 181 publications written about the Bonny Method between 1981 and 2014 by persons other than Helen, 99 percent of the authors were music therapists; however, no salient theme emerged as most representative of the literature. The highest number of publications by other persons was based on Bonny Method Clinical Practice, Procedures, and Techniques. In fact, my overwhelming observation about the literature published in English between 1981 and 2014 by persons other than Helen is that no salient themes actually evolved. Instead, the topics shifted rapidly to reflect popular themes, emerging techniques, or the individual tastes of each author. Perhaps one reason for a lack of standardized themes in this literature is that the trainees in many of the programs were required to conduct a research study as part of the training, and so many of the publications resulted from these research requirements. In addition, although Helen was a music therapist and self-identified as one over the course of her adult lifetime, not all Bonny Method practitioners or trainers are music therapists. Bonny Method training is not limited to music therapists, but is studied by many mental health practitioners, such as psychotherapists, pastoral counselors, licensed psychologists, psychiatrists, licensed professional counselors, and other medical practitioners.

CHAPTER SIX

NORDOFF-ROBBINS MUSIC THERAPY

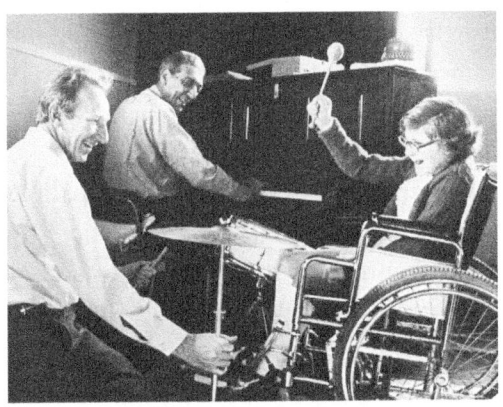

Figure 6.1: A photograph of Paul Nordoff and Clive Robbins (Paul Nordoff at the Piano, Clive Robbins assisting with the cymbal)

I was part of the third generation of music therapists in the US. During my college years in the 1970s, very few universities offered Music Therapy degrees. I was fortunate to receive my undergraduate training at Duquesne University in Pittsburgh, Pennsylvania (PA). A private parochial school, it was just large enough to be culturally infused by the many social movements that were sweeping the US and small enough that I did not ever feel like a number in any of my classes. My music therapy professor was Richard Gray, a kind and humble man who had been one of the first internship directors in the US and who had written a chapter in E. Thayer Gaston's landmark text, *Music in Therapy* (1968). Out of all of my experiences at Duquesne, the most salient was in 1976 when we watched the film, *The Music Child* (Parry 1976), which had been filmed at the Benhaven School for Autistic Children in Connecticut and the Charles V. Hogan Regional Center in Massachusetts. The three music therapists featured in the film were Vera Moretti, Beverley Wilson, and Donna Chadwick. All three were trained in the approach created by Paul Nordoff and Clive Robbins. Vera and Donna came to the university for the showing of this film.

I was young and very impressionable, granted, but something in me changed the day I watched this film. The musical cries and deep moans coming from the "psychotic-autistic" children, as they were called in those days, shot right to my core. I felt as though I was witnessing music therapy so powerful that I could not fathom how to do it. I became star-struck and dreamed of someday reaching a crossroads where I could finally comprehend how to be a music therapist like those three women.

As the years went by, I took a different path, and practiced behavioral music therapy at the state school where I was hired. But I never forgot the impression that this film made on me. During my attendance at professional conferences during the 1980s and 1990s, I often had the pleasure of attending presentations given by Clive and Carol Robbins. It was then that I realized that the approach the three music therapists in the film had been practicing was Nordoff-Robbins Music Therapy. I always left the Robbins' presentations teary-eyed, altered, and emotionally moved by the beautiful work that they did. Clive always showed videotapes of them working with clients who were autistic. The children in the videos were alive with music. Carol was an excellent musician and therapist, and Clive was a captivating speaker and co-therapist.

Roll ahead 20 years. In 2015, I had the privilege of interviewing Dr. Alan Turry and Dr. Kenneth Aigen from the US and Dr. Gary Ansdell from the UK about Nordoff-Robbins Music Therapy (NR-MT) for this book. Today I am older and wiser, and through the process of writing this chapter, I am determined to begin to comprehend the full potential of NR-MT.

PAUL NORDOFF AND CLIVE ROBBINS' STORIES

The early years

The following section will contain an exploration of the lives of Paul Nordoff and Clive Robbins, the founders of this exceptional method.

NR-MT developed through the partnership of Paul Nordoff, an American pianist-composer, and Clive Robbins, an English special educator. Both founders preferred to call what they created an "approach." The seeds for Nordoff-Robbins Music Therapy were sown in 1959, when Paul took a leave of absence from his professorship at Bard College of Music in Connecticut to visit the UK. According to Dr. Alan Turry, although Paul had a lucrative career as a composer, pianist, and music professor, he felt something was missing in his life in regard to his relationship with music. He craved to explore music in a therapeutic capacity instead of just performing for select audiences (Alan Turry, personal communication, November 12, 2016).

Paul Nordoff was born in Philadelphia in 1909. He studied music at the Philadelphia Conservatory of Music and The Juilliard School. Although he began as a piano performance major under the tutelage of Olga Samaroff, he switched his major to composition and studied with Rubin Goldmark (Robbins 2005). He received many honors for his compositions, including two Guggenheim Memorial Fellowships and a Pulitzer Travelling Fellowship (Aigen 2005a). He was Head of Composition at the Philadelphia Conservatory in 1938, appointed Assistant Professor of Composition at Michigan State University in 1945, and then hired as Professor of Music at Bard College from 1949–1959 (Aigen 2005a; Simpson 2009). Paul was awarded an honorary doctorate from Combs College of Music in Philadelphia in 1958 (Simpson 2009). His compositions were very tonal and written in more traditional forms, as opposed to the avant-garde music that was popular in the mid-20th century. He believed that music should mirror society at large, and not just the elite intellectuals of the day.

Paul was involved in the study of *anthroposophy*—an "influential European movement of social, cultural, and spiritual renewal" (Simpson 2007, p.27). It is based on the writings of Rudolf Steiner, an Austrian philosopher and teacher. Anthroposophy literally means "wisdom of man" (Simpson 2007, p.27), and emerged as a study of the spiritual nature of humanity and the cosmos in the middle of the 20th century. Steiner's writings addressed a multitude of topics, including education, special education, medical health, the arts, and ethics (Simpson 2007, p.27). Most salient to anthroposophical work is its emphasis on creativity, healing, freedom, and responsibility. Paul was deeply involved in the study of anthroposophy, which led him to join Threefold Farm in Spring Valley, New York, an anthroposophical community, in 1946. It was there that he met his wife Sabina, who had been a dancer on Broadway. After they married, Sabina became a practitioner and teacher of *eurhythmy*, a practice of art in movement (Simpson 2009). Paul and Sabina had three children and lived together at Threefold Farm.

Clive Robbins was born in 1927 in Handsworth, Birmingham, UK, and was raised in a baker's family marred by illegitimacy. Clive only discovered when he was 17 that the woman he had believed to be his older sister was actually his mother. Clive remembers feeling incomplete and confused during his childhood, and was always looking for something to bring him a sense of meaning (Simpson 2009, p.18). When recorded music became available, Clive remembers that listening to it together brought the experience of having a relationship to his family members (Robbins 2005). What he most remembers about his childhood was his strong reaction to hearing songs. He felt the "vulnerability to music's emotional impact, and how unquestioningly the open, unschooled mind of a child would accept the messages conveyed in the form of a song" (Robbins 2005, p.3). Songs brought a sense of grandeur and dignity to Clive's childhood life.

In 1944, during World War II, Clive joined the Royal Air Force and suffered an injury that resulted in a partial paralysis of his left arm and hand. After his rehabilitation and release, he worked at various jobs and finally returned to his family home and bakery in Smethwick in the West Midlands. While working at the bakery, he met and later married Mildred. They lived in a small trailer, and Mildred worked as a nurse at Sunfield Children's Home, an anthroposophical residential facility for intellectually and emotionally disabled children and adolescents (Aigen 1998). At Mildred's request, Clive visited Sunfield on Christmas Eve, 1953, where he experienced a sense of "spiritual values being lived practically" (Robbins 2005, p.7). Although neither were familiar with anthroposophical values or communities, Clive and Mildred decided to join the Sunfield community, towed their trailer there, and Clive took on the position of a student teacher in curative education (Simpson 2009), and later became a curative educator and house parent.

While living at Sunfield, Clive and Mildred had two children, Tobias (b. 1954) and Jennifer (b. 1956). Although Clive resonated with the anthroposophical belief that human beings are reborn from a spiritual essence where they draw their own learning and development (Simpson 2009, p.19), he found that he was not able to apply what he believed to the immense needs of children in his classroom, especially when they became adolescents (Aigen 1998). Clive grew frustrated with the children's lack of progress (Robbins 2005).

Paul Nordoff and Clive Robbins meet

Back in the US, Paul was living in New York at Threefold Farm with his wife and three children and teaching at Bard College. In 1958, Paul received a sabbatical to tour Europe and find venues for performing his compositions. While visiting England, he toured the Sunfield Children's Home due to its reputation for promoting music in curative education. On the evening of his tour, he gave a concert of his compositions in Sunfield's auditorium. Clive remembered sitting on a small balcony immediately above Paul, who was seated at a grand piano (Robbins 2005). During the performance, Paul read poems and then played his settings of the poems on the piano. Later in the concert, he accompanied a movement of one of his classical pieces for violin and piano, and concluded with a setting of *The Frog Prince*, which was written for storyteller and orchestra. Clive clearly remembered thinking about Paul, "This is a sun among men. This is a man who radiates warmth and a certain strong regard for human life. He is a radiant person" (Robbins 2005, p.11).

Paul was 49 years old when he first visited Sunfield. He continued his tour of Europe and then returned to Philadelphia, where he asked for an extension to his sabbatical from Bard in order to investigate music therapy further. His request was refused. After deciding to leave his job, Paul sought out information about music therapy from the National Association for Music Therapy (NAMT), from music therapy literature, and from observing music therapy practitioners in the US (Aigen 1998). Even then, he found that NAMT academicians tended to favor behavioral psychology techniques over all others, and to value rigor and scholarship above clinical practice and exploration (Robbins 2005). This didn't match his perceptions about music therapy.

In 1959, Paul received a 15-month grant to tour various anthroposophical institutions in Europe. It was at this point in his life that he made the decision to discontinue his composing and teaching to work with children with disabilities. Between 1959 and 1960 Paul returned to Sunfield for 10 months. At first, he worked alone to develop formats for his work with individual children, groups, and the integration of music with movement (Aigen 1998). Clive remained very aware of Paul's impact on the children. Paul had the intuitive, musical, and compositional skills. Clive, however, had the insight and vision that Paul lacked (Aigen 1998). When they finally began working together, it was with individual children. At first Paul would ask Clive to play an instrument next to the child while he played the piano, and only later did Paul begin to let the child play instruments while Clive assisted as co-therapist.

During the last five months of his tour, Paul and Clive toured other curative homes in Europe and gave lecture demonstrations wherever they went. They visited 26 homes during this period, although their reception by the anthroposophist communities was lukewarm

(Simpson 2009). At the end of the tour, Paul invited Clive to return with him to the US to create curative homes there. Clive agreed to join him, and with that decision, chose to leave his wife and family to work with Paul (Simpson 2009). In 1960, traveling in a Ford Consul filled with musical and clinical equipment and tapes, they boarded a freighter with passenger accommodations that was heading to the US (Aigen 1998; Simpson 2009).

In the United States

Paul and Clive intended to begin their curative home project at Threefold Farm, where Paul had lived. However, word of their work together had traveled among the anthroposophist communities from Europe to the US, and the Threefold Farm community was not receptive to Paul's plans for an anthroposophical music degree or his background in curative education (Aigen 1998). Paul and Clive found work at Devereux, a residential school in Philadelphia. With the assistance of Nellie Lee Bok, a friend of Paul's, they found financial support through the American Foundation Pilot Project to work with psychotic-autistic children at Devereux. The University of Pennsylvania clinic at Mercy Douglass Hospital brokered a five-year grant for them from the National Institute of Mental Health (NIMH) to work with psychotic children under the age of seven. They remained in Philadelphia for six years. During that time, they began to teach their approach to college students at the Crane School of Music and the State University of New York at Potsdam.

While they were in Philadelphia, Clive joined NAMT in 1961 and became a member of the Mid-Atlantic region. Paul applied twice for NAMT registration and was twice denied (Robbins 2005). In 1966, Paul and Clive were invited to present at an NAMT conference. E. Thayer Gaston, also known as the "Father of Music Therapy," happened to be in the audience, and invited them to contribute a chapter ("Improvised Music as Therapy for Autistic Children") in his 1968 landmark book, *Music in Therapy* (Robbins 2005). This helped to improve their relationship with

NAMT. However, Paul was never recognized by NAMT as a music therapist in his lifetime. In 1971, the American Association for Music Therapy (AAMT) was founded at New York University (NYU), and both men were invited to become members.

On the road in Europe

The year 1967 was magical for music therapy in the UK. At the Guildhall School of Music and Drama, the British Society for Music Therapy began the first music therapy training program, with Juliette Alvin as Director. Although Paul and Clive were often in London, there seemed to be conflict between Juliette and the two men. Speculation about their uncomfortable relationship was that Juliette was established within a well-known academy, whereas Paul and Clive were "floating around" (Gary Ansdell, personal communication, March 19, 2015.) Also in 1967, the American Scandinavian Foundation and Van Ameringen Foundation sponsored Paul and Clive in a lecture demonstration tour of all five Scandinavian countries. Until 1974, they continued their international traveling, teaching, and demonstrating while co-writing three books: *Therapy in Music for Handicapped Children*, *Music Therapy in Special Education*, and *Creative Music Therapy*.

In 1974, Sybil Beresford-Peirse, a music lecturer who was interested in music therapy, arranged for the Music Therapy Charity of Great Britain to coordinate funds that she raised to support a six-month training course taught by Paul and Clive at Goldie Leigh Hospital in London, UK (Aigen 2005a). In many ways, the time at Goldie Leigh was the culmination of their work. The entire six-month course was audio-recorded for future preservation. Paul functioned primarily as composer, musician, and ethnographer of music. He had brought these strengths naturally into his clinical work with children for years, and now they were becoming integrated into his training of music therapists (Aigen 2005a). Clive functioned as an archivist, collecting documentation via audiotapes to ensure that Paul's legacy was preserved. As he so articulately stated, their team had been the "intermeshing of the abilities of two individuals" and a "fusion of identities that produced a greater whole than either single individual could have produced on his own" (Aigen 2005a, p.11). Nevertheless, Clive's role had grown beyond archivist and co-facilitator.

The Goldie Leigh course was the last time that Paul and Clive would teach collaboratively. Paul was not in good health. After 17 years as a team (Aigen 2005a), each began to crave different experiences. Clive began to teach more on his own, as if the apprentice had become the teacher. He also became romantically involved with one of his students, Carol, who had studied NR-MT since 1966. Clive and Carol married in 1975, and the couple began to work together at the New York State School for the Deaf in Rome, NY. They received a three-year federal grant, and the culmination of their work was the publication, *Music for the Hearing Impaired and Other Special Groups* (1981). The couple continued working and teaching, and were hired as adjunct faculty at NYU to teach and direct the Nordoff-Robbins Music Therapy Center, an autonomous facility housed at NYU that trains music therapists with Master's degrees who are seeking the NR-MT designation. New York was not the only place where NR-MT training was offered. In the late 1970s, the first NR-MT Centre was established in London, UK. In the 1980s, in Germany, the Institute for Music Therapy taught NR-MT techniques at the Community Hospital in Herdecke. In 1984, Carol and Clive founded the NR-MT Centre in Australia.

Paul Nordoff passed away from cancer in Herdecke, North Rhine-Westphalia, West Germany, in 1977, at the age of 67. I could not find out if he had remained married to Sabina for all those years or whether they had gotten divorced at some point. Carol Robbins passed away in New York City in 1996 at the age of 54 from cancer. Clive Robbins married Kaoru Mochizuki in 1998, and he passed away in 2011 at the age of 84 in New York City.

What's in a name?

In early March 2015 I had the pleasure of interviewing Dr. Alan Turry, Managing Director of the Nordoff-Robbins Center for Music

Therapy on the NYU campus. One of the first questions I asked him was, "What is the difference between Creative Music Therapy and Nordoff-Robbins Music Therapy (NR-MT)? Was it called Creative Music Therapy first and then did the name change to NR-MT?" Reinforcing my premise was the title of the last of the three landmark texts by Paul and Clive, *Creative Music Therapy* (1977). Kenneth Bruscia labeled the approach *Creative Music Therapy* in his book *Improvisational Models of Music Therapy* (1987), and Alan speculated that this reference probably reinforced the original name of the practice for others. Gary Ansdell published a book in 1995 entitled, *Music for Life: Aspects of Creative Music Therapy with Adult Clients*. In 1996, Clive chose the name *A Journey into Creative Music Therapy* for his autobiographical narrative. This is not surprising, however, as Clive was writing an historical account. So why and when did the name of the practice change to Nordoff-Robbins Music Therapy? Alan remembers Clive's remark that "they did not own creativity, nor were they suggesting that no other music therapists are creative" (Alan Turry, personal communication, March 6, 2015). It seems, nevertheless, that at some time Clive favored changing the name of the approach.

From 1998 to 2003, Alan published many articles. In all this literature, he referred to the approach as Nordoff-Robbins Music Therapy. When Clive was honored in 1999 as founder of one of the five international models of music therapy at the World Congress of Music Therapy, the model was called Nordoff-Robbins Music Therapy (Wheeler 2012). It therefore appears that sometime in the late 1990s, the name began to change officially in publications and perhaps in the US, followed by the UK. Nowadays, Alan explains that those people who are trained in NR-MT are called "Nordoff-Robbins music therapists," and those who embrace the approach refer to it as "Creative Music Therapy" (personal communication, March 6, 2015).

TECHNIQUES

This was the most challenging section to write in this chapter. The reason is that, unlike the other advanced music therapy methods with their more tangible foundations, I believe that NR-MT can only be conceived in its totality by its two founders, who are no longer on this spiritual plane. Even then, what they called Creative Music Therapy has transformed into a clinical practice that matches the needs of modern-day healthcare, the music therapy profession, and the clients.

Group clinical improvisation

One way that NR-MT is practiced is as group clinical improvisation. When this occurs, the clients in the group choose instruments and play together without any external musical plan. The music is created spontaneously with a resultant group sound and with the group members getting to explore their own musical contribution. It is the role of the primary music therapist at the piano to give structure to the different instrumental voices. The co-therapist may play instruments to model musically, direct others to play, recognize each player's contributions, or attempt to create a meaningful interaction between group members. However, it is the clients who have the ultimate say in determining the onset, sound, and duration of the music.

The benefits of group clinical improvisation include: (1) internal awareness, (2) realization of one's creative impulses, (3) courage and self-esteem, (4) awareness of others' activities, (5) direct interaction, (6) a real-life experience rather than an artificially imposed musical re-creation, and (7) a momentary erasure of all differences that separate one from another.

Indigenous techniques

Certain techniques are commonly identified with NR-MT practice, and include the following:

- *Non-directivity:* Using techniques to facilitate, express, support, and encourage participation, rather than issuing directives, within the clinical context of improvisation.

- *Engagement:* The music therapist's process of getting the client to participate musically by using musical interventions, gestures, or cues. Engagement alternates with non-directivity.

- *Supportive music coactivity:* The music therapist's offering of supportive musical responses. This occurs when the therapist musically acknowledges the sounds created spontaneously by the clients in order for the clients to recognize their own music. This technique is meant to affirm the value of the clients' music.

- *Aesthetic shaping:* Shaping the clients' music into a larger context. In aesthetic shaping, the music therapist not only matches but also enhances the clients' music. In this manner, the aesthetic qualities of the music will intensify the experience for the clients. This creates the likelihood that the clients may engage in more music-making.

- *Awareness and response:* When clients are directed by the music therapist to the participation of others, this facilitates awareness among the clients of their indigenous creative potential. This, in turn, facilitates a flexible and evolving musical structure.

The video: *Irvin Can Beat the Drum*

I find it always best to describe a session rather than just identifying a method's techniques in a dry manner. I would therefore like to recount my responses to the opening segment of the video, *Irvin Can Beat the Drum*. Through this narration, I believe that the reader may feel the musical impulses come alive. The first few minutes of this video are saturated with aesthetic meaning, expression, and group energy. Here I relate the narrative to the NR-MT indigenous techniques introduced above.

In 1972, Paul and Clive produced a video meant for publicity purposes, entitled *Irvin Can Beat the Drum*. As the video begins, Paul is seated at the piano, and Clive is sitting behind Paul, next to a standing drum, drumstick, and cymbal. Clive moves the drum in place and then sits incredibly still, poised with attention and presence. A girl stands before the drum and begins to play sturdily, and often the wooden drumstick creates a bouncing effect on the drum head. It seems as though her right-hand motor function is impaired. Paul matches her by playing with light, staccato musical support in the middle range of the piano (*aesthetic shaping*). He creates an open texture with an upper, dotted melody in the right hand enhanced by intervals of perfect fourths and fifths below. The camera zooms out, and a circle of children who have a developmental disability, many of them with Down syndrome, are seated around the girl and the drum. They watch her play and seem to listen intently, despite the cameras revolving around them. It is as though the music eclipses anything else that is happening (*awareness and response*).

Paul is playing a snippet of the "Hello Song," one of the most popular and best known of the *Children's Play Songs* (1962), with words written by Clive and music composed by Paul. Paul proceeds to follow the unsteady beat of the child at the drum, and begins accompanying in two different meters alternated between his left and right hand (*supportive music coactivity*). Rather than complicating and confusing the girl, this musical technique creates a music container for her so that anything she plays becomes reinforced (*non-directivity*). She seems to gain confidence, and Paul leads her into a percussive climax, followed by a release into a faster tempo (*engagement*). At this point, she has completely become the music, and yet she is still in the lead (*non-directivity*). She plays freely and with expression. The other children respond to her music by moving their bodies to the tempo and by watching intently (*awareness and response*).

I can only try to express my full appreciation for the creative and spiritual energy created by the work of the many Nordoff-Robbins music therapists who now work with a variety of clients (e.g., adults with neurological impairments, older adults in memory care settings). However, due to my personal experiences with NR-MT, this approach will be related to children in my mind, first and foremost.

I cannot help but return to Clive Robbins when he was a young father and student teacher of curative education, before he met Paul. At that time, he stood outside his small trailer, frustrated that his work and his beliefs did not coincide. The children he worked with were challenging, and he could not seem to reach them. Contrast that with the Clive Robbins I watched in the video and had the privilege of hearing many times, a person who was always full of contagious energy for those around him, especially the children, and for the musical techniques that he so lovingly created with Paul Nordoff.

TRAINING

A transformation in NR-MT training has occurred since the first course at the Goldie Leigh Hospital in 1974. Most of my information regarding current training in the US was shared with me by Dr. Allen Turry, Managing Director of the Nordoff-Robbins Center for Music Therapy on the NYU campus (Alan Turry, personal communication, March 3, 2015). I was also fortunate to visit with Ken Aigen in his office at NYU, and to observe an NR-MT training session while visiting the Center. Finally, I met with Dr. Gary Ansdell, Director of Education at the Nordoff Robbins Centre, London, who spoke about NR-MT training in the UK (Gary Ansdell, personal communication, March 19, 2015). In addition, I reviewed the websites for both training centers (http://steinhardt.nyu.edu/music/nordoff/training, www.molloy.edu/academics/graduate-programs/graduate-music-therapy/nordoff-robbins-training and www.nordoff-robbins.org.uk/training), which remains the best way to find out the locations of current training centers.

In the US, board certification in the country of origin is required to begin training. Students who complete the first level of the training at the Steinhart School at New York University or the Rebecca Center for Music Therapy at Molloy College are required to have a Master's degree in Music Therapy and to be a board-certified music therapist. In the UK, training in NR-MT and Master's-level Music Therapy occur concurrently. Trainees cannot practice NR-MT in either country until after they achieve their Master's degree.

Although training is offered at three levels, entry level to practice is Level One. Level One training at NYU takes ten months. It is competency-based, but some candidates remain longer to receive additional supervised clinical work. During the training, the candidate is required to take the following courses/workshops: four clinical improvisations, practice and theory of group music therapy, and a certification seminar. Recommended but optional is the *Introduction to Nordoff-Robbins Music Therapy* course, which is open for all Music Therapy Master's-level students at NYU. Additional requirements for Level One training include:

- completion of interview and audition
- clinical practice on-site
- client/group sessions: minimum of two sessions as primary music therapist, two as co-therapist, two groups (usually 6–9 sessions by the second semester)
- session review and processing, individually or with a co-therapist, including "indexing"
- personal sessions in the method—suggested, but not mandatory
- other personal growth requirements—personal therapy is recommended but not mandatory
- supervisions/consultations—one hour of supervision each week
- final research study, written, and a 60-minute presentation.

At the end of Level One training, the music therapist receives the designation "Nordoff-Robbins music therapist." Level Two focuses on the supervision of trainees and advanced clinical work, and Level Three prepares the trainee to teach NR-MT courses and/or to begin a training program.

In the UK, the training program as described by Gary Ansdell takes two years and is divided into three sections (Nordoff Robbins Centre, London 2011):

- Section One (September to December): Nordoff-Robbins foundational training

- Section Two (January to December, three terms): (1) gaining and consolidating basic skills in communicative and social musicianship; (2) learning to make productive use of supervision; (3) becoming familiar with key literature, resources and concepts relating to the Nordoff-Robbins approach

- Section Three (January to June, three terms): The student is responsible for setting up the third placement in an environment where no music therapist is employed.

At the end of training in the UK, the student receives both entry-level Nordoff-Robbins designation and becomes a creative arts therapist who is regulated by the UK Health and Care Professions Council (HCPC).

WRITINGS

Now that the historical development and current training requirements for NR-MT have been covered, I would like to review the writings of the founders, Paul Nordoff and Clive Robbins. I will then discuss the writings of Clive Robbins and Carol Robbins, and finally, other authors who wrote about NR-MT.

Appendix 6-A contains 27 pieces of literature written by Paul and/or Clive from 1961 to 2005. This includes unpublished documents that were used in teaching or for conference presentations. I intentionally decided to delimit these materials to those in print: articles, chapters, books, conference proceedings, grant-funded materials, and teaching materials. Not included in this analysis are training videotapes, videotaped interviews, or brief newsletter articles written by Clive for the newsletter of the *International Association for Nordoff and Robbins*. My main reason for delimiting video or audio materials is that these materials are located wherever Paul or Clive taught, and it would be difficult to locate and identify the entirety of them. For example, when I visited NYU in March 2015, I observed many shelves of videotapes, as videotaping is an inherent part of the NR-MT approach.

Paul and Clive collaborated in their writing primarily between 1961 and 1971. From 1971 to 1974, Paul wrote individual pieces, and Clive did not publish. In 1974, Paul and Clive published their third and final book, *Creative Music Therapy: Individualized Treatment for the Handicapped Child*.

From 1980 to 1991, Clive and Carol Robbins collaborated in their writing. After Carol's death in 1996, Clive wrote individually until the publication of his final book in 2005, *A Journey into Creative Music Therapy*. Of note during this period was the case study, "*Edward*," which had actually been conducted much earlier by Paul and Clive, but was finally published in 1998 in the *Nordic Journal of Music Therapy*. It appears to me that Clive preferred to collaborate with others when he wrote. This reflects his warm, outgoing, and engaging nature. For example, out of his 21 documents, he wrote only four by himself, and the rest were the result of collaborations with others. Clive and Carol published one book together in 1981 about music for persons who were hearing impaired. Clive later wrote two books; one was an homage to Carol (1997) and the second was an homage to Creative Music Therapy (2005).

The list in Appendix 6-A is not designated by author, but represents the total number of articles, books, chapters, conference proceedings, and teaching materials written by these exceptional authors. It contains all 21 pieces of literature published by Paul and Clive in chronological order, from 1961 to 2005.

What did these eminent authors write about? Their topics are clearly presented and strongly related to the specific clinical populations with whom they were working, or to specific elements of music. The themes follow a chronology that begins in 1961 at Devereux, where Paul and Clive first worked. Their first publication was an introduction to the music work being created at this school. From 1964 to 1971, their literature focused specifically on the clinical populations or environments in which they were working (i.e. children with autism, handicapped children, and in special education). In 1974, Paul produced two sets of teaching materials about musical techniques for music therapy students.

In the 1980s the literature was primarily written by Carol and Clive Robbins and focused on music therapy with children who were hearing impaired. In 1988, Paul created his final teaching manual, entitled, *The Whole Tone Series*. In the early 1990s, Clive and Carol explored more esoteric topics in their literature, including time as a phenomenon in music therapy and self-communication in Creative Music Therapy. From 1993 until 2005, Clive wrote alone about topics such as creativity, a tribute to Carol that was published the year after she passed away, and a final monograph, *A Journey into Creative Music Therapy*.

Works by other authors

Although Paul and Clive toiled to disseminate information about their approach via their writings and presentations, it is their trainees who have kept NR-MT alive and thriving in both the US and the UK, in part through the sheer number of publications about NR-MT in professional texts and journals. I searched for any publications about NR-MT in refereed journals or books.

Appendix 6-B contains 42 publications by authors other than Paul, Clive, or Carol about NR-MT. The publication dates span from 1987 through 2014. Since Paul and Clive began publishing in the 1960s, it appears that it took almost two decades for the first group of trainees to begin to publish their own research and scholarship about the approach. The first book written by a non-founder was not published until 1995.

In the period between 1987 and 2015, only 21 articles were published about NR-MT, with most journals averaging only one article within the 28-year period. Authors published more articles (29%) about NR-MT in *Music Therapy Perspectives* than in any other periodical. Only two publications (5%) were located in non-music therapy journals, and only one of the 13 chapters was published in a non-music therapy related book.

SUMMARY

My sojourn into Nordoff-Robbins Music Therapy has left me wiser and more appreciative of the immense skills and presence that an NR-MT therapist must have. Out of the four advanced practices in this book, NR-MT clearly requires the highest levels of musical ability and spontaneity. I also believe that this method is grounded in musical foundations, whereas the others also share related psychological or philosophical theories.

CHAPTER SEVEN

DIANE AUSTIN AND VOCAL PSYCHOTHERAPY

Figure 7.1: Diane Austin

In March 2015 I met with Dr. Diane Austin in my hotel room near Washington Square, New York City, to conduct an interview. This was the first time I had talked with her. Now as I recall the evening with her, I can better understand why I chose Vocal Psychotherapy (VP) as one of the advanced music therapy approaches for this book. It is younger, whereas the other three methods started in the 1970s. Diane is still very vital and very involved in the development of VP.

VP techniques were created over time and are aligned with different theoretical constructs that Diane studied in the 1980s and 1990s. From my examination of the three older methods, I have observed that it takes a good 20–30 years before other authors begin to publish about the approach. The youth of the method of Vocal Psychotherapy will allow the readers of this book to witness the blossoming and maturation of a new form of music psychotherapy. This chapter begins with Diane's childhood, and follows the natural path that is the story of Vocal Psychotherapy.

DIANE AUSTIN'S STORY
The early years

Vocal Psychotherapy involves the use of the voice, breath, natural sounds, improvisation, toning, singing, and the speaking voice within an analytic orientation to promote intra-psychic and interpersonal change (Austin 2007, Preston-Roberts 2011). It is the brainchild of Dr. Diane Austin. Born in New York City, one of Diane's earliest childhood memories was sleeping beneath a piano (Austin 2008). It happened one evening when her father was performing with his jazz trio, and her mother couldn't find a babysitter. According to Diane, she woke up on the stage under the piano in a "cocoon of rhythm, melody and harmony" (Austin 2008, p.11). She remembers feeling held by the music. Since then, whenever she has felt lonely or unsafe, she has turned to music.

Diane made her vocal debut at a jam session when she was about ten. She sang the song, "Where is Your Heart?" while her father accompanied her at the piano. After that, he accompanied her often when she performed. Diane remembers how much she loved to sing and how vital an experience it was for her as a child. Her childhood was not always happy. When she sang, she could block out anything unpleasant. Singing provided a safe container in which she could express emotions and the darker aspects of herself (2004, p.5). Along with singing, the young Diane liked to make many kinds of vocal utterances, such as screams or animal sounds. She thrilled at the feel of her voice echoing back to her. Diane refers to these vocal sounds as *primal* or *pre-vocal*, and they allowed her to express the inexpressible (Preston-Roberts 2011).

Adulthood

Music has always been the center of Diane's life. She studied Theater Arts at Emerson College in Boston (Austin 2008, p.12). Through acting, Diane thoroughly enjoyed becoming the different characters she portrayed through voice, movement, and song. Although she did not come to this realization until much later on, these expressive experiences were very therapeutic for her. In fact, she claims that, "music and the arts changed her life" (Austin 2004, p.4). Following college, Diane moved back to New York City and performed professionally in musicals. She became disillusioned with acting. As Diane described it, "I was tired of playing roles" (Austin 2008, p.12). One aspect of musicals that tired her was the redundancy inherent in the text and music. Also, she wished to do more self-exploration. Diane began to work with a Jungian analyst and found that it was a "good fit" (Austin 2004, p.6).

After quitting her acting jobs, Diane became a performing vocalist and songwriter. Her songwriting process was empowering and helped her to gain a clearer perspective on the issues she was discussing with her analyst. To augment her income, Diane also taught voice lessons. She sensed that singing gave her students permission to feel, and discovered a strong emotional connection between singing and people's inner dialogues. It was at this juncture that Diane pursued a Master's degree in Music Therapy at New York University (NYU). She continued to teach voice lessons and also worked with many clients, including women in prison and battered women and children, while completing her internship (Diane Austin, personal communication, March 8, 2015). Diane most clearly remembers how the music therapy theories of Florence Tyson and Mary Priestley influenced her during her education. She completed her Master's degree in Music Therapy in 1986 (Austin 2008).

Although Diane could have been hired by different psychiatric hospitals in New York City following her internship, she felt uncertain about the aesthetic limitations of the environments in which she would work. As she studied more and more music therapy, her voice lessons had begun to convert into therapeutic singing lessons (Preston-Roberts 2011). She summarized this conversion as, "I had clients who were students, and then they turned into clients" (personal communication, March 8, 2015). She began to identify her practice as music psychotherapy. Diane continued her own analysis and training in Jungian psychology. Her work started to attract music therapists and creative arts therapists, who came to her for therapy sessions.

Although Diane established a music psychotherapy practice, she still felt inadequately prepared to function as a primary therapist for clients who needed longer-term and more in-depth treatment. At that point, Diane began studying object relations theory, trauma theory, psychodrama, addiction theories, and depth psychology (Austin 1999, 2004; Diane Austin, Personal Communication, March 8, 2015). Although Diane was conscious of newly emerging constructs upon which to practice psychotherapy, she also found that her therapeutic approach was becoming primarily verbal. As Diane describes it, "the distance from the couch to the piano increased. I was losing the music" (Austin 2011, p.14). What she wanted was to musically and vocally "facilitate an ongoing dialogue between the conscious and unconscious elements of the client's psyche." She called this approach "analytically oriented music therapy "(2011, pp.14–15). To find her way back to the voice, Diane pursued further Jungian training and completed a doctorate in Music Therapy at NYU in 2004. In collaboration with Director Barbara Hesser, she established Vocal Psychotherapy training at NYU as part of the Music Therapy and post-graduate curriculum.

TECHNIQUES

The analytically oriented music therapist, like most music therapists, will conduct an assessment on a new client. Diane emphasizes the observation of certain vocal behaviors. For example, she will listen to the client's voice to determine whether there are prosodic (melodic) elements, whether the speech is monotonic, or if the voice changes when the client talks about certain topics. She listens to determine a flow to the music of the voice, whether the client listens to the music therapist as well as the music therapist listening to the client, and whether there is a natural give-and-take in the conversation. The assessment also incorporates non-verbal mannerisms, such as holding the breath, restricted body movements, and facial expressions (Austin 2011). Once the assessment is completed, the music therapist chooses to utilize one of the following vocal interventions: client's speaking voice, natural sounds, breath, toning, or vocal improvisation skills.

The *speaking voice* is defined as the tone of the voice. It is normally made up of a small range of natural phonated frequencies that are produced when conversational verbalization occurs. It is demonstrated as flexible (e.g., clients speed up and talk quickly, slow down and fade out at the end of sentences, or speak lethargically). Certain musical elements, such as tempo, pitch, loudness, rhythm, and prosody, are present in the speaking voice.

Natural sounds occur spontaneously and are pre-verbal in nature. They represent whatever we are experiencing at a given moment. Natural sounds include, but are not limited to, gasping, sighing, yawning, sneezing, groaning, sighing, screaming, and laughing. When natural sounds begin to emerge in a VP session, they often represent primal sounds of emotions long repressed (Austin 2008, p.27). Clients may be naturally uncomfortable with these sounds at first, and a major intention of VP is to guide clients to access, acknowledge, accept, and integrate those sounds into their voices.

The *breath* represents how well clients can inhabit their bodies. The way we breathe impacts how we feel at any given moment. The first step in connecting to the voice is to learn to breathe deeply. Singing, naturally, helps to facilitate deep breathing. When people hold their breath or experience tension in their throats, chests, or abdomens while breathing, they become cut off not only from their deep breathing but also from their deeper emotions. This restriction manifests itself as an impaired quality in both the speaking and singing voice.

Toning is a vocal technique first introduced by Keyes (1973). It involves the humming or chanting of vowel sounds over a succession of pitches to increase awareness of the breath, to release tight articulators, to energize the chakras, and to encourage a vital flow in the voice.

Vocal improvisation comes from a natural impulse which, when not blocked, releases free vocal expression and spontaneity (Austin 2007). When a voice is spontaneous, a natural stream of musical and textual impulses can emerge from the client's authentic self. Vocal improvisation can be combined with instrumental accompaniment or be sung a cappella.

Once the vocal behaviors above have been assessed, the music therapist will determine the most appropriate VP technique: vocal holding, vocal mirroring, vocal grounding, and free associative singing. All of these techniques can use an accompanying instrument or be sung a cappella.

Vocal holding is the use of two chords and the music therapist's voice to create a stable and consistently safe musical container (Preston-Roberts 2011). It is the simplest technique and is used to form a bond between the music therapist and client or to encourage a reparative experience. During vocal holding, both the client and the music therapist sing in unison. There is a regressive, *symbiotic* quality created by this technique. The music therapist plays and sings a rocking rhythm, like a lullaby, and the repetition creates a safe, non-ordinary state of consciousness. This stage emulates the feel of the mother and child in unison. It is especially useful when working through early developmental injuries caused by a break in the mother–child relationship (Austin 2008, p.147), and reinforces Winnicott's (1971) concept of the *good enough mother*, a situation in which the developing infant creates what it needs.

Vocal grounding simulates the first stages of separation between a baby and mother. It occurs when the music therapist plays and sings the tonic of the chord while the client vocally explores, comes back home to the tonic, explores again, etc. Diane considers this stage like to be Mahler's *rapprochement* in object-relations theory

(Bond 2008). For example, musically, a little girl may want her mother to share every new skill and experience. She moves away from the tonic and then comes back, which is akin to saying, "See, Mommy!" The mother reiterates the tonic, thus saying, "Yes, you did it. Great." In a healthy relationship, the mother stays in contact with the child and supports her efforts to individuate.

Vocal mirroring occurs when the client sings a melodic phrase and then the music therapist echoes it back. Mirroring helps to find, strengthen and ground the client in their authentic voice (Austin 2008). Mirroring also helps the client become aware of new parts of the personality as they emerge as sounds. Vocal mirroring promotes encouragement and reinforcement.

Free associative singing occurs when words enter the vocal holding process (Austin 2008, p.158). Similar to Freud's technique of *free association* (1938), the client sings any words that comes into their head, but the music therapist is also contributing to the musical stream of consciousness by singing or speaking verbal interventions and through playing the musical accompaniment. The musical accompaniment is kept simple, such as a two-chord holding pattern or repetitive motive. Due to the more complicated involvement of the music therapist, transference and countertransference become more complex than with the simpler techniques (see Analytical Music Therapy, p.183).

Free associative singing often begins with deep breathing or with the music therapist mirroring or repeating the words or melody back to the client. All of the techniques introduced above can be used within the free associative context.

In addition, specialized free associative techniques include the *double*, which represents the inner voice of the client. The music therapist uses the first person "I" when singing as the double (Austin 2008, p.160). Another technique is called *essence statements*, which occurs when the music therapist reflects the content of the client's text by singing "I feel" or "I need" or "I want". These essence statements help to deepen the therapeutic process and to increase the client's self-awareness (Austin 2008, p.160).

Observing a free associative singing session

I discovered a video of a VP session on the internet. This video, *Vocal Psychotherapy—Free Associative Singing*, came out almost a year after my interview with Diane, and I was very eager to watch it. It was a powerful demonstration of all of the VP techniques: vocal holding, vocal mirroring, vocal grounding, and free associative singing.

Diane was the music therapist in this video, and I refer to her as "the therapist" here, and I shall call her client "Joan." I am very grateful to this client for sharing her inner struggles. It seems that this woman was a perfect match for VP, as she expressed that she loved to sing, and quickly went into a regressive state once the singing began.

The video began with a verbal introduction to VP by the therapist. She claimed that the voice is a primary instrument. When we sing, she says, our voices and bodies become the instruments through which the music is sounded. When people sing, they are immediately connected to the source of the sound and its vibration. Singing results in both internal and external connections. Internally, our physiological rates (e.g., respiratory, cardiac) decrease and our voices resonate inwardly. Externally, our voices express our emotions and connect with other voices. Singing also allows us to give voice to that which is inexpressible, to all the parts of us that long to be heard and to integrate them.

Then the therapist discussed how singing impacts persons who have been traumatized. Singing connects to feelings. People who are traumatized may cry incessantly, but not be able to find the words to express their emotions. It is up to the vocal psychotherapist and client to get to the source of that feeling and then to re-source it, like a diver finding a beautiful pearl and resurfacing to share it with the world.

In the video, Joan sat to the right of the therapist, with both facing the piano keyboard. They seemed to be in a small room with an upright piano. The therapist instructed Joan to sit up straight and to make an audible sigh, which they did together. The therapist demonstrated deep breathing by matching Joan's respiratory rate for a few breaths. Then the therapist asked Joan to make a soft whisper, which created a descending sigh-like sound. When she asked Joan what kind of chords she wanted, Joan was unable to specify and said she liked them all. That question made me wonder if Joan might be a music therapist, since not many clients have the musical know-how to identify chordal sequences. The therapist played a sequence that Joan had used previously in another session, which was a IV–I progression with a 3–2 melodic suspension. Joan said that the music was too sad. The therapist then played the same chordal progression, but played the tonic chord in inverted form with a 3–4 melodic suspension. Joan immediately started singing sounds.

The therapist told Joan that she could start without words, but when a word popped into her head…the client immediately said "a word" and sat up straight as though she had gone back to a cognitive place. The therapist reminded Joan to start singing without words. The client began to sing the 3–4 melodic phrase, and the therapist sang it with her three times. Then the therapist dropped down to the tonic pitch, which was still close to where Joan was singing. Joan seemed to relax and close her eyes while singing. The therapist dropped down to the fifth below the tonic pitch, and that seemed to cause a strong response in Joan. She said "I want to sing help" and the therapist reflected "help" in a singsong manner. Joan began singing "Help me heal" on a 3–4–3 melodic pattern while the therapist sang in unison with her. The therapist again dropped down to the tonic, and this time the musical support felt downright palpable. She began to sing "It's been long enough," and Joan's voice began to break up. At that moment, the therapist went back to the tonic pitch and sang "It's been scary." The client tearfully joined her and they sang that in unison. Joan initiated singing "I felt so alone" on a 1–2–3–1–1 melodic pattern. She sang raspily, "I was alone in that room not knowing if I would live or die." Joan sang "scared" and the therapist responded "terrifying," with a strong emotional inflection. By this point, Joan was visibly crying. The therapist continued singing, "So awful, so scary, so lonely" and sang down to the fifth below the tonic on the word "lonely."

Later in the video, the therapist led the singing and the client mirrored back. They sang, "Nobody to be with" and "Nobody to hold my hand." The therapist looked right at Joan as she sang, with clear support radiating from her face and voice. She sang how she was going to stay with Joan, "I won't leave you." The next part of the improvisation was a narrative of the Joan's time in a medical isolation unit when everyone had to be masked and gloved to enter. Joan sang, "I don't like to feel helpless" and the word "helpless" bounced back and forth between the two voices. Joan sang out, "I had to depend on people I didn't know," and her voice took on a new quality of awareness and wisdom. After that, the two women brought the vocal improvisation to an end by slowing down the tempo and singing more softly. Joan sang that she liked being an "enigma." The therapist sang back, "What's an enigma feel like?" and the client answered, "A puzzle" followed by "As long as I can put in the last piece and make me whole. That's what I will be. I will be whole." The improvisation concluded with Joan singing by herself while the therapist accompanied her on the piano.

Following the improvisation, the two women verbally processed the session. Joan admitted that the singing helped her access her emotions. She was very surprised when she sang "help" and then "help me heal." The therapist explained that Joan had accessed her unconscious. She asked Joan how it was when she was singing with her. Joan answered that although she had been feeling so alone in her whole process, suddenly she was harmonizing without even being conscious of it. Joan concluded, "It felt like teamwork." Joan's final statement was that the process had gotten to her heart and her soul, those places that are so hard to reach.

TRAINING

The majority of the information about VP training came directly from Diane, founder of this method. I also found helpful information on the website http://dianeaustin.com/music.

VP trainees must have a Master's degree in Music Therapy to apply for training. In addition, applicants need to have "singing ability, improvisational singing skills, and basic piano skills" (Diane Austin, personal communication, March 8, 2015). Diane mandates an essential requirement for anyone interested in the training: "[He or She] is or has been in psychotherapy or is willing to begin psychotherapy and takes part in the psychotherapy section of the sessions" (personal communication, March 8, 2015). Each prospective trainee receives an interview as part of the application process. Below is a description of the training:

> Participants will be trained in Vocal Psychotherapy, a model that utilizes breathwork, natural sounds, vocal improvisation, songs and chants. Students will have opportunities to observe, participate in and conduct voice-centered therapeutic experiences and interventions. The course format includes participation in individual and group vocal exercises and experiences, lectures, discussions and demonstrations. A certificate is awarded upon the completion of the program. (Diane Austin, personal communication, March 8, 2015)

Each training group is limited to eight students per year. It takes a student a minimum of two years to complete VP training. The trainee must attend weekly sessions lasting two-and-a-half hours from September through the end of May. Diane describes the training as a combination of experiential and didactic learning. Other requirements include:

- 64 client/group sessions
- 6 personal sessions in the method
- 40 observations of group members working
- 4 personal supervisions
- weekly group supervisions
- conducting vocal warm-ups and song leading
- required reading (except for her book, none of the other assigned readings are about music therapy; this suggests that

Diane's work is so new and cutting edge that she is really the only music therapy source on this approach to date)

- a paper on countertransference with the trainee's primary clinical population
- singing a personal song and discussing it with the group
- conducting a final project/research study on the experience of being a therapist working with a client using vocal holding and free associative singing.

Diane Austin, personal communication (March 8, 2015)

Full VP training usually takes place at the Music Psychotherapy Center in New York City, which was founded in 2003 (dianeaustin.com). Following completion of all the requirements, the trainee receives a certificate of completion and is qualified to use the acronym "AVPT" (Austin Vocal Psychotherapist). Two distance-training courses are now offered: one in Vancouver, British Columbia and one in Seoul, South Korea. These programs help to reach and recruit interested students in locations other than New York City, which is where Diane practices and teaches. Just recently, Diane also began a training program for those AVPT practitioners who wish to offer VP classes to others.

WRITINGS

Diane has written 17 documents about VP from 1991–2014 (see Table 7.1). She co-wrote one of her early articles with Dr. Janice Dvorkin, but was sole author for the rest of the writings about VP. She has primarily written book chapters, save for a few articles. Her landmark work, *The Theory and Practice of Vocal Psychotherapy: Songs of the Self*, was published in 2008 by Jessica Kingsley Publishers. This is the best resource on VP to date. Table 7.1 depicts the types of documents written by Diane in descending order of frequency.

Table 7.1: Types of documents written by Diane Austin (N=17)

Type of publication	Number	Percentage
Book chapter	11	65
Article	3	17
Dissertation	1	6
Book	1	6
Foreword	1	6

Table 7.2 represents the different themes addressed in Diane's writings. Since some of the themes overlap, I chose what I considered to be the salient theme in each publication. When VP was first introduced to the Music Therapy profession, Diane wrote two book chapters that primarily gave an overview of the salient points and techniques featured in VP. Diane's primary therapeutic focus clearly concerns persons who have experienced trauma, including children, adolescents, and adults. Her strong affinity with psychodynamic theory, singing, and their interrelated function in the treatment of trauma is also clearly represented in her writings.

Table 7.2: Thematic material in documents written by Diane Austin (N=17 references)

Type of publication	Number	Percentage
Trauma	5	29
Psychodynamic Music Therapy	4	24
Miscellaneous*	3	18
Overview	2	12
Case Histories	2	12
Pre-Vocal Psychotherapy	1	5

Note: * Grief, Psychiatric Music Therapy Setting, Foreword.

Works by other authors

I searched for any publications about VP that had been published in refereed journals or books by someone other than Diane. All writings in this chapter were written or translated into English. Table 7.3 contains a bibliography of all the publications about VP that were written by authors other than Diane, and contains the year of publication, the authors' names, titles, and publication sources. Simply, three publications about VP exist that have not been written by Diane. One of the documents was published in a non-music therapy journal (*Canadian Music Educator*), and one resource addressed both music therapy and special music education. Two of the documents were general introductions to the practice of VP and one publication was an interview with Diane.

Table 7.3: Documents written by writers other than Diane Austin (*N*=3)

Date	Author	Title	Publication
2010	Evangelia Papanikolaou	From out of our voices	Approaches: Music Therapy and Special Music Education
2011	Patricia Preston-Roberts	An interview with Dr. Diane Austin	Voices
2013	Amy Clements-Cortès	Vocal psychotherapy: Connecting to the self via the voice	Canadian Music Educator

SUMMARY

I began this chapter with the knowledge that Vocal Psychotherapy is the newest music therapy method discussed in this text and in its infancy, really. The first VP distance learning courses have just been offered, and a VP teacher training program has just started. In fact, one of the reasons I chose VP, along with the fact that I so strongly believe in its power to heal, is to compare a younger method with the other methods that are more seasoned.

My overriding question guiding this comparison was, "What can the Vocal Psychotherapy specialists learn from what has already been experienced by practitioners and teachers of Analytical Music Therapy (AMT), the Bonny Method, and Nordoff-Robbins Music Therapy (NR-MT)?" I returned to the earlier years of publications about AMT, and discovered that although Mary Priestley had publications since 1969, her landmark book on AMT did not appear until 1975. Even more interesting was that it took until the early 1990s for other music therapists to begin to publish about AMT. This means that Mary alone was writing about AMT for *almost 20 years* before others joined her.

I then reviewed the bibliography of Helen Bonny's writings, which were first published in 1965. Helen's landmark book (co-written with Louis Savary) was published in 1973. Again, I found that it was not until the early 1980s that other authors began to write about the Bonny Method. That means that Helen alone was writing about Guided Imagery and Music (GIM) *for 15 years* before other authors began to join her.

If it takes this long for information about advanced methods to be shared by more than just the founders, my prediction is that music therapists will begin publishing about VP much more within the next few years. Diane has been writing about VP since 1991. And just like the other two methods, it took *almost 20 years* (2010) for the first article about VP to be published that was not written by Diane.

It seems that founding an advanced music therapy method is akin to birthing a baby. At first, the mother (founder) stays very close to the infant. It is not until a generation later that the child learns to speak for herself, move into the world, individuate, be noticed, and transform.

SECTION III

CHAPTER EIGHT

QUESTIONS

The Advanced Methods in Context

Now that the four methods of advanced music therapy practice have been presented in Section II, I would like to share the responses to a set of seven questions that I asked representatives of each method, both from the US and the UK, during the Spring of 2015. With the exception of Diane Austin, who is a founder, the 11 people I interviewed had all known the founders of the advanced methods, were reputable trainers of the methods, and were also academicians in some capacity in institutions of higher learning. It was my intention to consider their responses as general representation of persons highly knowledgeable about at least one of the four methods. In case the reader is wondering, I did not interview the founders except for Diane because one was in very poor health and the rest had already passed away. Following the interviews, each expert was sent a transcript with my request to member-check the document and send me back a corrected version. Along with the corrected interview transcripts, I kept field notes of my travel experiences and of the music therapy sessions that I observed. Upon my return to Texas, I transcribed each interview using F5 software (version 3.2.2; Doerner 2017) and then used *NVivo* software (QSR International 1999) to analyze the collected data.

The idea for this discourse came from a book by William Elliott, *Tying Rocks to Clouds: Meetings and Conversations with Wise and Spiritual People* (1996). In it, he asked identical questions to a number of spiritual leaders. While the responses were wholly unique to the persons being interviewed, they simultaneously reflected their shared values. Using Elliott's method, I plan to pinpoint similarities and differences between the four methods based on the responses from the experts and from my own notes. The first five questions form the basis of this chapter, and the last two questions are discussed in the final chapter.

QUESTION ONE: WHAT IS IT ABOUT THIS METHOD THAT STILL RESONATES WITH YOU?

This generated the largest variety of responses, which I then organized into themes. According to the respondents, the methods still resonated with them because of: (1) receiving the method, (2) music, (3) the imagery, (4) self-discovery, (5) the challenge, and (6) the relationships.

Receiving the method

All the respondents had known the founders of the methods, with the exception of Diane Austin, who is currently a founder. Often the trainers were required to receive personal sessions in the method before being able to practice on others. One respondent described her experience with Analytical Music Therapy (AMT): "One of the most powerful things was that you have to be in your own AMT [sessions] first in order to be training other people in it and in order to understand it." This expert described what it was like to work specifically with Mary Priestley: "Why did I resonate so much with the method? [Because of] the way she was. Very powerful. Very powerful trainer. And very deep. And very exciting and interesting in each and every way."

Although highly charismatic, the founders did not expect their students to simply parrot their ideas or imitate their techniques. One expert said about Mary, "She didn't expect students to imitate her as a teacher." Likewise, Helen Bonny encouraged, "Take from me what you can use and make it your own method."

The music, period

The presence of the music as core to the therapy is what drew the respondents to all four methods. As one woman concluded, "But the primary is the music." A salient principle behind music therapy is that all persons are capable of engaging with music. As one respondent summed up, "Music is for everyone, no matter how impaired." The interviewees were drawn to the music for personal reasons. For some, music was the vehicle for an expression far beyond what is verbally possible. For others, music drew you into the deeper self, the unconscious, around which the music interacts in the forms of imagery, musical improvisation, vocalizing, composing, or art-making. In fact, in three of the four methods, the music is improvised. In the Bonny Method, the music used has been recorded from high quality classical performances, and the elements of the audible music evoke the imagery.

The elements of the music are essential to all four advanced music therapy methods. In Vocal Psychotherapy (VP), the primary instrument is the timbre of the human voice in all of its manifestations. While some methods connect the elements of music to psychodynamic ends and follow it with analysis, others rely solely on the power of creative musicking. In Nordoff-Robbins Music Therapy (NR-MT), the purity of the music as it unfolds is what resonates with the music therapists and clients. Ironically, both in NR-MT and AMT, the founders religiously recorded the sessions. In Mary Priestley's case, she recorded the sessions to recognize the psychodynamic indicators in the improvised music. In Paul Nordoff and Clive Robbins' case, the sessions were recorded to analyze the elements of the music, as they evolved, in relation to the client and the music therapists' musicking.

The aesthetic qualities of music also bring healing experiences that go beyond the capacity of the very best music therapist. In all four methods, art and artistic expression are also part of the process.

The artistic aspects of music bring the music therapist and client in touch with a beauty that may not otherwise be experienced. In this state, music may transport a client to a place of unconditional love and other-worldliness.

The imagery

Since all four music therapy methods are psychodynamic in nature, they rely on the power of music-evoked imagery to provide a creative access to the psyche. Some of the respondents mentioned that the imagery resonated with them. Certain methods identify imagery as a salient part of the therapeutic approach. In the Bonny Method, for example, the musical elements are what awaken emotions, which, in turn, evoke imagery that unfolds from the continuing music and emotions (Goldberg 1992). As one expert explained, "[music] therapists are discovering that the skilled use of musically induced imagery allows the conscious mind to grasp insights more profound than words can communicate."

Self-discovery

The flexible and resilient qualities of music provide pathways for self-discovery. When asked how a method first resonated with him, one man explained that it was "the essence of engaging through your own relationship to music and challenging yourself to expand and grow as a sensitive, musical, humanistic person." He continued that this relationship to oneself was "a kind of life approach…a way of feeling you're going to learn and grow and develop and stay engaged in something that's life affirming."

Many practitioners feel a spiritual awakening via the musical methods they practice. In other words, working with music allows music therapists to bring their spirit and whole self into the work. As one female respondent claimed, "Analytical music therapy resonated with me because it seemed to be based on subjective, creative expressions of symbols, sensations, and feelings through music."

To this person, the internal expression seemed more resonant than aesthetic trappings of musical expression.

The challenge

Most of the individuals I interviewed are academicians or are associated with an institute of higher learning. Inherent in that world are expectations of continued scholarship in the form of research, publications, and presentations. Most of these experts are serious scholars. Identifying as trainers or clinicians of these four methods is not an inherent component of the "publish or perish" mentality. In fact, in many cases, these methods were not accepted by the early music therapy associations and were not taken seriously. Therefore, accepting the call to follow one of these methods involved taking a risk. As one respondent commented, "This was an interesting choice. It both resonated and was a risk, I suppose, to make that move."

Not only the music therapists, but also the clients are challenged through music therapy. According to Paul Nordoff and Clive Robbins, no matter how disabled someone is, that person wants to be challenged. Challenging a client isn't cruel or mean. As one NR-MT respondent explained, "it shows an ultimate level of respect which implies that music is for everyone, no matter how impaired." Also, music therapy is challenging because the opportunity to work at something is what makes us feel human and gratified.

Another challenge for practitioners of these methods is the need to be aware of our own shadows, as well of our clients'. I recommend continued personal therapy for all practitioners of these methods and am grateful that most of the trainings require a certain number of personal sessions to be completed. Due to the psychodynamic nature of these methods, it is crucial as a music therapist to decipher whether it's the therapist's material that's being activated or the client's material that's activating the therapist. This adds another layer to the levels of awareness that are ongoing in the practice of these methods.

The relationships

"Relationships" is the final theme that resulted from the question. Akin to the concept that practicing these methods leads to self-discovery, it also leads to intrapersonal relationships that reflect the imprints of one's previous life traumas. Many music therapists come to their profession because they have experienced a previous trauma, and music emerged as a lifeboat to take them to safety. Diane refers to the *wounded healer* in her book, *The Theory and Practice of Vocal Psychotherapy: Songs of the Self* (2008). Diane studied Jungian psychology and the terms used in her VP mirror the Jungian vocabulary. Carl Jung (1951) introduced the wounded healer in his text, *Fundamental Questions of Psychotherapy*, where he describes how only a physician who had been wounded can treat effectively. This archetype emerges when a person struggles with physical or emotional challenges and, after returning to health, is called to bring healing to others. It is akin to the shamanic conversion, when a person experiences a monumental trauma and then returns to health, but now with the knowledge of being called to heal. When asked how her method resonated with her, Diane responded, "Oh, my God. It's so intimate. It's like the most intimate kind of music therapy you can do." She continued, "When I developed free associative singing, that's so creative, it remains challenging because you don't know what's going to happen…where the client is going to take you. And you have to be able to go where they need to go" (Diane Austin, personal communication, March 8, 2015). One of her students, now a vocal psychotherapist herself, recalls what she learned in her first class with Diane and how it still resonates with her. She describes her therapy with clients and "really tapping into the countertransference that's going on in the moment with the client and trusting in your own experience as a therapist."

One reason that relationships form the basis of these methods is that it is easier to achieve a playful and creative contact with a client when you are making music, art, or movement than when you are processing verbally. The reason, according to an NR-MT expert, is that people want to make music and are motivated to make music. As a musician, the music therapist can then respond to the desire that comes from the client. How the music therapist meets that desire and works creatively with someone in music is the heart of NR-MT principles, beliefs, and practices. This expert concluded, "that's as true today, it's as true this afternoon...as it was during the first work I experienced in 1986." Another expert described the relationship between music therapist and client as, "It's amazing and magical to witness what happens in the therapy process because the client oftentimes feels safer to go into the feeling that I picked up on or that I'm checking out with them, whatever the sensation is." The element of respect from the music therapist in these relationships seems to be a crucial facet.

Finally, the experts describe their relationships to the founders, with whom they studied or practiced. In many cases, the founders related to these experts as mentors and were described by the respondents as "highly charismatic." Along with the internal relationships within themselves and external relationships with their clients, the vision and courage of the founders motivated these experts to continue with the methods. It is as if the founders passed their calling to the next generation of students. As one respondent summarized, "All of those things made me really want to commit my career to it, because I think it is so worthy of survival as music therapy develops into the future."

QUESTION TWO: WHAT HAS THE ADVANCED METHOD TAUGHT YOU ABOUT MUSIC THERAPY?

One of the experts mentioned *music-centeredness* in his response to this question:

> "...the music-centeredness of the work has helped me to experience, on a direct, first-hand basis, a certain sense of consistency and alignment between the general nature of self-exploration and that of musical improvisation."

Music-centeredness relates to the text, *Music-Centered Music Therapy* (Aigen 2005b), which was introduced during the first decade of the 21st century. It is considered one of the landmark indigenous music therapy theories, and it places music and musical experiences in a central role. The text also includes chapters about NR-MT, the Bonny Method of GIM, and AMT as forms of music-centered music therapy. To wit, this respondent emphasized both the constructs of self-exploration and the resultant manifestations of improvisation.

The respondents identified how the advanced methods had taught them about depth. One expert discussed depth in terms of the power of the music. In this manner, it is the music produced through vocal psychotherapeutic improvisation that mirrors both the power experienced within and the music that is evoked. This respondent stated:

> "The obvious thing is that a song goes much deeper than a word spoken. And that's probably obvious, but with two chords and my voice supporting and I use the double, it's so powerful. It's so incredibly powerful. And the combination for me of music and words, music and lyrics, that's so powerful."

Another expert replied that the entire music therapy process is considerably deeper for her now since she is using an advanced method. The reason is twofold: the music therapist must learn the specific techniques, which require highly developed clinical and musical skills, and must also comprehend related theoretical constructs which drive the process. As one expert explained:

> "It's taught me how much deeper music therapy can go with a client, through studying not only the techniques, but also the vast theoretical foundational knowledge. It's taught me that I can help a client really go below the surface. I think my work prior to that didn't go as deeply as it could have gone."

QUESTION THREE: HAS YOUR RELATIONSHIP WITH THIS ADVANCED METHOD CHANGED OVER THE YEARS? IF SO, HOW?

The experts seemed eager to answer this question, as many relationships with the methods had changed to reflect self-growth or to match the changes in the surrounding culture since they had been taught by the founders. Some of the major themes I discerned were personal reconstruction, relationships with music, amendments, roots, and new populations.

Personal reconstruction

Personal reconstruction is defined as changes made in the advanced method as the practitioner learns personal self-growth techniques or seeks new skills and knowledge. For example, one respondent sought training in bioenergetic techniques. Bioenergetics was first introduced by Alexander Lowen in 1994 and focused on body–mind integration via physical exercises and breathing techniques. This music therapist began to practice yoga and to meditate 20 minutes a day. Not only did the bioenergetics enhance her quality of life, but she also integrated the exercises, combined with musical expression, into her AMT sessions with clients. According to this expert, Mary Priestley had also used some of Lowen's techniques, yoga, and tension-release work in her sessions.

A different expert studied mindfulness-based stress reduction (MBSR), invented by Professor Jon Kabat-Zinn from the University of Massachusetts in the 1970s. MBSR is a form of therapy that encourages mindfulness through meditation, body awareness, and yoga techniques. This music therapist began to combine some of the MBSR meditations that she had learned with music, and then she incorporated them into her sessions with clients. In both cases, these new techniques were not part of what was considered the classical method (Martin Lawes, personal communication, February

10, 2017), but they definitely enhanced the work and moved it in a new direction.

Relationships with music

Relationships with music naturally grew as the practitioners became more skilled in their therapy work. Although students of these advanced methods must have highly developed musical skills as criteria for study (with the exception of the Bonny Method), the longer one practices the method, the more attuned one becomes to the music. This attunement occurs in multiple ways: the relationship of the music therapist to the music, the relationship of the music to the client, and the relationship of the client to the music therapist within the container of music. As one music therapist stated, the advanced method "has taught me that it is of vital importance for the music therapist to emphasize equally an understanding of the relational dynamic forces inside and between the client, the music and the music therapist."

As a music professor, I entered my Level One Bonny Method study highly confident about my musical knowledge. I soon discovered, however, that my knowledge was only cognitive, and did not interact with my inner relationships with music. It was only when I experienced my first GIM session in a non-ordinary state of consciousness that I experienced music in its pure emotional directness. Part of my training was to write up quarterly summaries about how my relationship with music had changed. My relationship continues to change to this day. More specifically, music now creates a spiritual pathway for me to a world beyond consciousness. Although at first it was primarily the GIM recordings that moved me so extensively, now I respond to any music that is live and performed with integrity. For example, I weep with joy when I hear my voice students sing.

Amendments

Amendments represents the small changes that individual practitioners and trainers have made to the advanced methods over the years. One respondent shared a perfect example of an amendment with me. I will call this expert "AMT" due to the advanced method she teaches:

> AMT: "He improvised and saw an image of himself flying, being very ungrounded, so he made that image on the Buddha Board, and then we just watched it disappear. Slowly. And that was very therapeutic…to help the person to let go of being anxious. I use that sometimes."
>
> NC: "And you added some of yourself to that."
>
> AMT: "Yes, I added some ideas of what I like."

Roots

Roots represent those practitioners who have incorporated the principles or techniques of a specific advanced method but have moved beyond the method. Often this occurs if the method reflects a time period where therapy occurred differently to how it does today. For example, one expert teaches Music Therapy at university level. She has incorporated many of the principles of AMT, but no longer labels what she teaches by that name:

> "Analytical Music Therapy (as created by Mary Priestley) seems to me to be really meaningful as the roots for an integrated music therapy program. In the eighties, and partly the nineties, we used the term Analytical Music Therapy. This was followed by Analytical Oriented Music Therapy in the first decade of the 21st century at the university program. These terms did not resonate with many of the working situations of our candidates. Many of them were working with clients without verbalization possibilities, and/or working in social and educational cultures where the term analytic did not really resonate with the existing culture."

New populations

The final theme, *new populations*, depicts the new areas of clinical emphasis that music therapists are expected to follow. When most of the advanced methods first appeared in the 1960s–1970s, some therapeutic practices were clearly psychoanalytical, such as AMT. Mary Priestley borrowed techniques and vocabulary that mirrored the psychoanalytic paradigm, but added the power of music. Her patients lived in psychiatric facilities and were treated for long periods of time. When Paul Nordoff and Clive Robbins began their method, they sought to create a new approach that focused primarily on children who were "psychotic-autistic" due to the funding they received. In the early years, Paul was not impressed with the types of techniques that most music therapists in the US demonstrated, which were often behavioral in nature. Music therapy had not really even started in the UK at that time. In another example, Helen Bonny worked in a research program for persons with psychiatric diagnoses who volunteered to take LSD to explore its potential as a healing agent. Only Diane Austin focused primarily on traditionally able persons who were seeking a different form of therapy for their depression, anxiety, etc.

The profession of Music Therapy has changed considerably since the 1970s. Music therapists are treating new kinds of clients, such as hospice patients, hospitalized children, infants in neonatal units, patients in rehabilitation facilities, children in foster homes, and patients in oncology units. For this reason, music therapists must stretch to apply the techniques they have been taught to new client populations. This also applies to music therapists who have been taught the advanced methods that are the basis of this book. It behooves trainers to change the content of their training to meet the needs of these new clinical challenges.

Practitioners are now conducting research using NR-MT with individuals with traumatic brain injuries. Many Bonny Method practitioners have studied the impact of GIM on physiological responses in patients with cancer. Bonny Method practitioners are also experimenting with adaptive techniques, such as shorter sessions or lighter music, for clients who may not be able to benefit from a full GIM session. Practitioners of AMT have studied its effects on persons who are medically and psychologically compromised, with promising results.

QUESTION FOUR: DO YOU BELIEVE THAT THE FOUNDERS OF THIS ADVANCED METHOD INTENDED TO CREATE A NEW MUSIC THERAPY APPROACH?

This was the question that generated the most controversy. Interestingly, some of the experts started out by stating "yes" or "no," but by the time they had finished talking about it, they had switched to the opposite answer. As this question represents one of the main reasons I wrote this book, I was fascinated by the number and variety of reactions. Even different experts representing the same method gave varying answers to this question, and sometimes contradicted their own answers.

Mary Priestley

During the time that Mary Priestley developed AMT, Music Therapy was in its infancy in the UK. She was in the second class of Music Therapy students at Guildhall under the tutelage of Juliette Alvin. The first AMT respondent chose to explain what had impacted Mary's decision to call her method "Analytical Music Therapy:"

> "After receiving intensive psycho-analysis herself, she chose to call her approach 'analytical.' This decision represents her theoretical and self-experiential training in psychoanalysis (i.e., Freud, Jung, Klein, Adler, Lowen). Her general philosophy behind the method is based upon analytical and psychoanalytical principles and phenomena such as transference, countertransference, resistance, and projection."

She then reconsidered the question and answered:

"She did intend to create a new MT approach. She bridges psychodynamic concepts, psychodrama concepts, and different ways of looking at and working with trauma by creating this method. It's very unique in the music therapy world."

A second AMT expert contributed a very thorough response to this question:

"I never heard Mary Priestley talk of herself and her work as something that should be an approach in itself. She started her model for students training at the Guildhall School of Music and Drama in London—after she herself terminated this study. She had undergone psychoanalytical therapy in addition to the music therapy training and she thought the Guildhall program strongly needed the element of students learning from being in the client's position. She also thought music therapists needed self-experience or experiential training in music therapy during their training, and not only self-experience as an additional verbal therapy. I think she was really foresighted there."

Here it appears that Mary did not condone the type of training that students were receiving at Guildhall, and was attempting to offer them an alternative form of Music Therapy study. This explanation doesn't mean that she intended to create a new form of music therapy, however, but rather that she intended to create a new kind of Music Therapy training.

The second respondent continued:

"When Mary Priestley first offered this training for students at Guildhall School of Music and Drama, it was illegal for the students to attend Mary Priestley's training at the same time as being a student at Guildhall. Later it became legal, but always non-mandatory. Johannes Eschen, one of the first followers of Mary Priestley, combined her analytical training elements into a full-time program in the Mentorenkurs Herdecke, Germany. This program in some ways was the first integrated music therapy program in the world—using both Nordoff–Robbins and Analytical Music Therapy, but also presenting other models for us as students."

During Music Therapy's infancy in the UK, it seems that two of the strongest Music Therapy personalities in London were Juliette Alvin and Mary Priestley, and that the two women did not agree regarding basic training principles for Music Therapy. To complicate matters, Mary had been a student of Juliette's, but had not accepted all of what Juliette had taught her. This second expert finally discusses Mary's choice of the name, "Analytical Music Therapy:"

> "Mary Priestley herself doubted the name Analytical Music Therapy, and wrote in her first book, that she also thought of 'Heuristic Music Therapy' as a possible title for the approach [Priestley 1975]. Later history in the world of music therapy would show that Mary Priestley's ideas, together with the way they were further developed by Johannes Eschen, certainly had a vital influence on the number of training courses which now include experiential training elements in the form of self-experience, and how these elements are highly valued as an important platform for developing the identity of music therapists."

What was compelling to me was that none of the AMT respondents clearly answered the question. A third respondent chose to answer the question by discussing Mary's impact on Music Therapy training. He answered simply, "But still, they were psychotherapists, and music therapists were considered activity therapists." In other words, even if Mary self-identified as a music therapist and perceived that what she was creating was music therapy, the hierarchical structure created by psychoanalytic practice would have labeled her work as activity or adjunct therapy at best. Although Mary was courageous and a pioneer, she was also very familiar with psychoanalytic theories and practices. After re-reading and considering these responses, my impression is that although Mary did not originally intend to create a new music therapy approach, she did wish to present Music Therapy students with an alternative method of study. After her method was accepted and taught at Herdecke, AMT grew into an advanced method, with Mary Priestley at the helm as its founder.

Helen Bonny

Since 1960, Helen had always considered herself a music therapist. She studied Music Therapy at the University of Kansas (KU) with E. Thayer Gaston, who warned her never to mention her violin experience or mysticism while she studied there. She worked diligently at the National Association for Music Therapy (NAMT) from 1966–1968, when it was located in Lawrence, KS. Ironically, one of the reasons that GIM was not considered music therapy is because her work at the Maryland Psychiatric Research Center (MPRC) was rejected by many NAMT members, and she was not made to feel welcome. In fact, according to one expert, "Helen had more psychiatrists and social workers training with her than she had music therapists. But I don't think it's because she didn't think it was music therapy. It's because the field didn't think it was music therapy."

Helen never stopped trying to reconnect with the Music Therapy profession. In fact, she changed the language of her publications and presentations at Music Therapy conferences to fit in better with clinical perspectives and the vernacular. However, the field was just not ready for Helen's work, even in its modified form. In fact, it wasn't until after the unification of NAMT and the American Association for Music Therapy (AAMT) in late 1999, at the World Conference for Music Therapy, that Helen's work was finally recognized as one of five international models of music therapy. I was present at that conference and witnessed how graciously she accepted the honor bestowed upon her. But I am also certain that was not what compelled Helen to create GIM. She was called by a force much stronger than notoriety. Her true talent lay in her vision of music and consciousness. I believe she would have created GIM regardless of the profession of music therapy.

Paul Nordoff and Clive Robbins

When Paul Nordoff first became interested in music therapy and observed music therapists in the US, he did not like what he saw.

In fact, as one respondent recounted, "Clive used to say, in the early days when they first started the work, that they were ambivalent about calling it music therapy because they didn't want to associate their work with what they'd seen in the US in the 50s." In fact, although both men were aware of the profession of music therapy, they were not satisfied with it, and wanted to create an alternative. In this way, they were akin to Mary Priestley, who did not approve of the only Music Therapy education in the UK, and so decided to create a different training approach.

Why were Paul Nordoff and Clive Robbins disenchanted with the practice of music therapy, both in the US and the UK? Perhaps they thought that the potentials of music were not being fully realized. As one respondent explained, "I know that they wanted to create something new." The anthroposophical facilities they visited did not use music effectively for children with disabilities. The two men seemed disappointed that people were not working with music creatively. In other words, their vision far surpassed their perception of the existing profession of music therapy. In fact, Clive believed that he had a moral obligation to bring the highest level of clinical musicianship possible to music therapists. According to another expert:

> "I remember Clive saying they didn't call it music therapy. They said, 'making music with the children.' I think they got very serious about studying music therapy...and they certainly thought they had something to contribute to the field of music therapy and later they began to call it music therapy. But in the very beginning they called it, making music."

Diane Austin

As the youngest founder, Diane Austin did not originally intend for VP to become a form of music therapy practice. She was disillusioned with the selection of clinical techniques available in music therapy, however, and created an entirely new method, although I do not believe that she intended to do so. She was very gifted and creative, and forged ahead with her voice work. Nothing could stop her.

Diane also did not believe that her work was accepted by the NAMT. She did not identify what she was doing as music therapy practice: "Honestly, I was so humble about it, I didn't know if it was anything. And meanwhile these amazing things were happening. I was shy...it's hard to own your own thing" (Diane Austin, personal communication, March 8, 2015). Diane credits Paul Nolan, Director of Music Therapy at Drexel University, Philadelphia, Pennsylvania (PA), with giving her the first chance to be noticed by the music therapy profession. He invited her to contribute an article and recording to a volume of *Music Therapy Perspectives* (*In Search of Self*, Austin 2001) that he was editing. This was the first time that Diane's work was widely shared with the music therapy profession.

Diane wrestles with the lack of support she receives as a clinician while she feels compelled to present and disseminate information. She does not receive travel assistance or remuneration for presentations. Diane is torn between the need to present on VP in order for more music therapists to know about it and the tremendous cost for her. She explains, "So I went and did a conference. Nobody paid me. I went and presented. I'm not on sabbatical. I don't get a full professor's fee. I just have to do this." Diane recalled one conference that she did attend: "But I did go to one after, it was when Clive died, and they finally gave me a Professional Achievement Award."

Although most of the founders, save for Paul and Clive in their early years, self-identified as music therapists, none seemed to envision that what they were developing was a new music therapy method. These founders had different reasons for creating their methods, such as improving practice or training or using techniques that they believed were more effective. For this reason, present-day music therapists may not realize what a wealth of music therapy clinical opportunities they now have available to them.

QUESTION FIVE: DID THERE SEEM TO BE CHANGES IN THE PROFESSIONAL MUSIC THERAPY ASSOCIATION'S ATTITUDES TOWARDS THE METHOD OVER TIME?

The answer to this question from all respondents was an unequivocal "yes." All agreed that the professional associations' attitudes towards the advanced methods had improved over the years. Yet, also present in the majority of the experts' answers, was unresolved resentment at how the founders were originally treated by members of the music therapy profession.

Although Mary Priestley spent most of her time developing AMT, acceptance towards that method did not come quickly from the various Music Therapy institutions in Europe. Two students who taught at Aalborg University in Denmark after training with Mary recount how they were first met with skepticism and misunderstanding regarding their practice of AMT. Later, they felt a positive shift, as witnessed by the sheer number of music therapists who began to integrate AMT practice into their music therapy work in medical and psychiatric hospitals.

Helen Bonny's rejection by some of the members of NAMT wounded her. Even though she traveled and gave GIM demonstrations and training, her students tended not to be music therapists, but other mental health professionals. For example, one respondent explained:

> "[She was] rejected totally and utterly. Helen, who gave her lifeblood and was the secretary/director for two years... I just re-read her biography over the weekend. She loved Gaston, but NAMT rejected her utterly...and thought she was a witch."

Ironically, most music therapists who were NAMT members knew about the advanced methods. According to one person, "Everybody at least knew about the methods, whether they liked them or not. Helen traveled all over the world demonstrating her method." In Helen's case, it was not until late in the 20th century that an increasing number of music therapists began to explore GIM.

Aware that the mindsets of this new generation of music therapists were changing, Helen definitely felt better about the music therapy association by the time she died. As she explained, "It was as though I had been reunited with an old friend."

Likewise, Clive Robbins and Paul Nordoff were never brought into the fold with NAMT. While they were in Philadelphia, Clive joined NAMT in 1961 and became a member of the Mid-Atlantic region. Even though he was admitted as a member, he had to struggle endlessly by attending music therapy workshops and by presenting at conferences to try to convince music therapists about the value of NR-MT. Paul applied twice for NAMT registration and was denied twice (Robbins 2005). One expert commented on how Clive and Paul were treatment by NAMT, "It just was really horrible, how they were treated. That's what I will tell you, rejected." Another respondent explained that after AAMT was formed in early 1971, she helped make sure that they both received certification.

Clive repeatedly stated that although Music Therapy students accepted NR-MT, music therapy academicians had a harder time with it. He believed that the Music Therapy faculty might have been threatened by the high level of musicianship required for NR-MT practice. According to one respondent, Clive would walk into a room of music therapists and "he'd have to be careful not to get tripped up."

Diane Austin responded that she believes a change in the music therapy profession occurred. She explains, "I was on the first panel they did on new methods or new innovators in the field. So that was, I thought, nice, that they did that."

As the two US music therapy organizations transitioned towards unification, the barriers between them began to erode. After unification, music therapists began to realize that there was more than one way to define music therapy. Most importantly, they began to move away from behaviorism as the basic construct behind clinical practice and to explore related or indigenous paradigms.

As part of this shift, they became aware of new potentialities in music therapy practice, such as the methods covered in this book. Other options also exist and are not to be overlooked: pursuing a

Master's degree in Music Therapy, pursuing a Master's degree in a different field, or signing up for shorter clinical training sessions such as Neurological Music Therapy or NICU Music Therapy training. To some music therapists, their current jobs bring them all the joy and satisfaction they desire, and they have no need to move beyond their current level of practice. Neither choice, one being the desire to study advanced methods and the other to remain at a current level of practice, are better than the other. Neither are they in competition with each other. The point I wish to elucidate at the end of this penultimate chapter is that music therapists have a choice regarding their level of clinical practice. And this has made all the difference.

Chapter Nine

THE TWO TREES

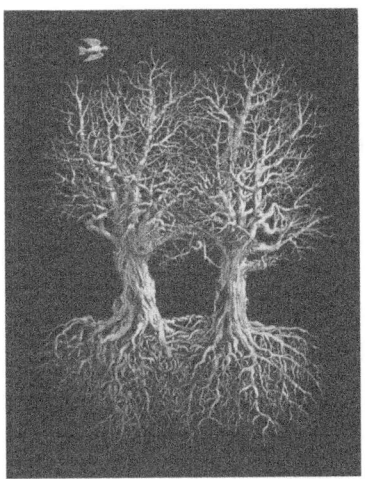

Figure 9.1: Two Trees II by Thomas Wood

When I was studying Music Therapy during the 1970s, behaviorism was the dominant paradigm. In the US, Public Law 94-142, or the *Sunshine Act* (1975), provided the right to free education for all children, regardless of disability. Behaviorism supplied the perfect vehicle to meet the needs for curricular management and classroom control. The public schools and state hospitals began to use a specific clinical vernacular (e.g., learning objective, short-term goal, long-term goal, condition, criteria, indicator behavior, reinforcement, extinction, punishment) that became standardized across the US. Since many music therapists were working in educational venues, they experienced success by focusing primarily on teaching pre-academic or academic skills.

Just as the founders of the four advanced methods in this book experienced great resistance from the music therapy associations, the experts who answered Question Six unanimously agreed that professional attitudes towards the methods have improved. It is my personal assertion that when behaviorism started loosening its grasp on music therapy practice, it led to new concepts of learning and therapeutic paradigms by music therapists. The unification between NAMT and AAMT was, in part, caused by the change in the perspectives of music therapists serving an ever-increasing variety of clients. I also assert that AAMT, although a smaller and less financially viable organization, emphasized creativity as the basis for clinical learning. I am thankful to AAMT for their support of the advanced methods during the period when the founders were not well received in other circles.

QUESTION SIX: DO YOU CONSIDER THIS METHOD TO BE A PART OF MUSIC THERAPY PRACTICE?

For me, this was probably the most potent of the questions I prepared for the experts. I believe that the answer to this question indicates the future viability of these four methods and hence, the future direction of music therapy. The experts, who represent the next generation of practitioners while also holding strong ties to the founders, helped me to formulate the answer. This is indeed the purpose for this final chapter, to discern the future of advanced music therapy practice in relation to the professional associations.

All the experts I interviewed responded that the four methods are now part of music therapy practice. According to one, "more and more students have become trainers and are spreading the news about the methods." No one believed that these methods were going to go away. The largest barrier to bringing these four methods fully into the music therapy fold is the fact that they are all taught outside of the universities, with the exception of a few universities in the US who offer Level I graduate classes in the Bonny Method and NR-MT and Gary Ansdell's program in the UK that combines NR-MT Level One training within a Master's degree curriculum. All music therapists in the US and UK pursue advanced methods training at a post-Master's level. To wit, music therapists usually pursue advanced training following their academic training.

Certain factors still impact the growth of advanced methods. It is of the utmost necessity that we depart from the expectation that Music Therapy must be studied within a university. None of these methods are taught in their entirety within a university. One respondent expressed this strongly:

> "I am not in favor of putting these methods into the Master's level [curriculum]. I am totally against that. How much can you teach at the Master's level? When you look at two years of a Master's program, you do not have a person who can do any of those [advanced] practices."

I do not predict that universities will welcome the advanced methods training programs into their curricula, as they do not seem to fit the purview of most academic programs. Hence, training will probably remain independent from academic training.

Another hindrance is that the cost of the training is competitive and does not result in a degree or license. In the US, entry into the field of music therapy is at Bachelor's level, and entry into advanced methods training is at post-Master's level. In the UK, entry into the field of music therapy is at Master's level. Since my role began as a music therapy academician in 1992, I have argued passionately for music therapy to move to Master's level of entry to practice. As the debate drags on, my frustration grows. I am convinced that the profession's movement to Master's level is essential for many reasons. However, that discussion goes beyond the purview of this book. I do contend that in order to perpetuate these four advanced methods of music therapy practice, music therapists must continue to develop the profundity of skills needed for deeper psychotherapeutic work.

Although most experts represented one method, a few were familiar with more than one. One respondent was critical of advanced methods training. She felt that they were not based on practice, theory, and research, and that to have an advanced method, you have to have all three. She continued that a founder may have written a book, for example, but did not conduct research. In another example, a founder may not have based the approach on strong theoretical foundations, but was a visionary. The respondent also believed that the training, even at post-Master's level, did not contain enough psychodynamic training in regard to highly vulnerable populations. She felt that the advanced methods institutes were not looking keenly enough at how the methods needed to change to survive in the future.

QUESTION SEVEN: OVERALL, WHAT DO YOU FORESEE FOR THE FUTURE OF THE ADVANCED METHODS?

The experts answered this question slowly and thoughtfully. Some were worried about the future of their chosen method. A few of the respondents who were trainers worried about the impact of their death on the future of the method. Other respondents were highly confident that the method would survive regardless.

One expert felt that having to practice the classical technique as it was taught by the founders may hold back the effectiveness of the method and was costing too much. Other respondents listed all of the changes they were trying to make, such as collaborating with other therapists and conducting additional research to ensure the method would continue. One expert proudly talked about all the training she was doing by Skype as a way to connect with students all over the world.

UNANSWERED QUESTIONS

This is where I choose to end my inquiry into the four advanced methods of music therapy practice: Analytical Music Therapy, the Bonny Method of Guided Imagery and Music, Nordoff-Robbins

Music Therapy, and Vocal Psychotherapy. I have attempted to understand these four methods via interviews with experts, publications, and observing music therapy sessions. This book has presented you with the history, theoretical underpinnings, training, techniques, and publications of each method. I have presented and attempted to answer a number of questions throughout this book. Now I leave these unanswered questions to ponder:

- What do you think the future of Analytical Music Therapy, the Bonny Method of Guided Imagery and Music, Nordoff-Robbins Music Therapy, and Vocal Psychotherapy will be?
- Will they survive in their present form? Or will they continue to change to match the needs of the constantly shifting healthcare market?
- Will the profession of music therapy in the US move to a Master's level of entry? If so, how might this impact these and other advanced methods of music therapy practice? If not, how might this impact these and other advanced methods of music therapy practice?
- Has the Master's level of entry in the UK impacted the development of the advanced methods of practice described in this book?
- If they survive, where should advanced methods be taught? Should universities assume responsibility for teaching advanced methods or should training programs remain independent of academic institutions?
- If these methods survive, should they continue in their traditional form, as introduced by the founders, or should the techniques be adapted for new client groups or clinical needs?
- If the advanced methods change considerably, as posed in the previous question, at what point would they become a new method?

When I first started this book, I thought of the four advanced methods as separate entities parallel to but separated from the profession, like a hedgerow of trees. My overriding question was whether these advanced methods would continue to operate independently from the music therapy profession or could somehow reach congruency within the profession. Through the process of writing this book, I have finally received my answer. *These advanced methods are now part of the music therapy profession.* They are forms of advanced music therapy practice. Even the Bonny Method is a form of advanced music therapy practice based on its founder, Helen Bonny, regardless of the fact that some of the practitioners and trainers are not music therapists. Because of the music therapy profession's propensity for change, the associations and the advanced methods have become interdependent yet separate entities. What came to my mind a few days ago was a metaphor for this new relationship: a beautiful black and white print entitled "*Two Trees II*" by Thomas Wood, an artist from the Pacific Northwest. I own this print; it sits on my study wall. I see two trees standing strongly side by side, with their roots intertwined and their branches touching. Overhead, a bird is flying toward whatever comes next.

APPENDICES

Appendix 4-A: Documents by Mary Priestley (*N*=24)

Year	Type of document	Source of document
1969	Conference report	Journal of British Music Therapy
1972	Article	Journal of British Music Therapy
1974	Conference report	Journal of British Music Therapy (co-written with Peter Wright)
1975	Article	Journal of British Music Therapy
1975	Book	St. Martin's Press, London
1976	Article	New Psychiatry
1976	Article	Nursing Times
1977	Article	Journal of British Music Therapy
1978	Article	Journal of British Music Therapy
1980	Article	British Journal of Projective Psychology
1984	Article	Journal of British Music Therapy
1985	Article	Journal of British Music Therapy
1987	Article	Music Therapy
1987	Article	Journal of British Music Therapy
1988	Conference paper	British Society for Music Therapy (BSMT)
1988	Article	European String Teachers' Association
1988	Article	Music Therapy
1989	Article	British Society for Music Therapy

Year	Type of document	Source of document
1989	Article	British Society for Music Therapy
1994	Book	Barcelona Publishers
1995	Chapter	Harwood Publishers
2002	Chapter	Analytical Music Therapy: Origin and Development (co-written with Johannes Th. Eschen)
n.d.	Article	British Society for Music Therapy
n.d.	Article	British Society for Music Therapy

Appendix 4-B: Publications about Analytical Music Therapy (AMT) (*N*=35)

Year	Author	Type of document	Title of publication
1987	K. Bruscia	Chapter	Analytical Music Therapy, in *Improvisational Models of Music Therapy*
1994	M. Langenberg, J. Frommer, and W. Tress	Article	A Qualitative Research Approach to Analytical Music Therapy in *Music Therapy*
1995	B. Scheiby	Chapter	Death and Rebirth Experiences in Music and Music Therapy, in *Listening, Playing, Creating*
1998	B. Scheiby	Chapter	Listen to the Music of the Unconscious: Using Counter-transference as a Compass in Analytical Music Therapy, in *Therapeutic Presence: Bridging Expression and Form*
1998	B. Scheiby	Chapter	The Role of Musical Counter-transference in AMT, in *The Dynamics of Music Psychotherapy*

Year	Author	Type of document	Title of publication
1999	B. Scheiby	Chapter	"Better Trying Than Crying": Analytical Music Therapy in a Medical Setting, in Applications of Music in *Medicine Vol. II: Theoretical and Clinical Perspectives*
1999	B. Scheiby	Chapter	Music as Symbolic Expression: An Introduction to Analytical Music Therapy in Beyond Talk Therapy, in *Beyond Talk Therapy: Using Movement and Expressive Techniques in Clinical Practice*
2001	B. Scheiby	Chapter	Forming an Identity as a Music Psychotherapist Through Analytical Music Therapy Supervision, in *Music Therapy Supervision*
2002	J. Th. Eschen	Chapter	Analytical Music Therapy: Introduction in *Analytical Music Therapy*
2002	S. Hadley	Chapter	Theoretical Bases of Analytical Music Therapy in *Analytical Music Therapy*
2002	B. Hesser	Chapter	Supervision of Music Therapy Students in a Music Therapy Graduate Training Programme in *Analytical Music Therapy*
2002	M. Jahn-Langenberg	Chapter	Some Considerations on the Treatment Techniques of Psychoanalytically Established Music Therapy in *Analytical Music Therapy*
2002	J. Kowski	Chapter	The Sound of Silence: The Use of Analytical Music Therapy Techniques with a Nonverbal Child in *Analytical Music Therapy*

Year	Author	Type of document	Title of publication
2002	W. Mahns	Chapter	The Psychodynamic Function of Music in Analytical Music Therapy with Children, in *Analytical Music Therapy*
2002	I. Pedersen	Chapter	Analytical Music Therapy with Adults in Mental Health and in Counseling Work, in *Analytical Music Therapy*
2002	I. Pedersen	Chapter	Analytically Oriented Music Therapy: The Priestley Model, in *Guide to Music Therapy: Theory, Clinical Practice, Research and Training*
2002	I. Pedersen	Chapter	Psychodynamic Movement: A Basic Training Methodology for Music Therapists, in *Analytical Music Therapy*
2002	I. Pedersen	Chapter	Self-Experience for Music Therapy Students: Experiential Training in Music Therapy as a Methodology: A Mandatory Part of the Music Therapy Programme at Aalborg, in *Analytical Music Therapy*
2002	C. Purdon	Chapter	The Role of Music in Analytical Music Therapy: Music as a Carrier of Stories, in *Analytical Music Therapy*
2002	B. Scheiby and B. Alsaham	Chapter	Improvisation as a Musical Healing Tool and Life Approach: Theoretical and Clinical Applications of Analytical Music Therapy Improvisation in a Short- and Long-term Rehabilitation Facility, in *Analytical Music Therapy*

Year	Author	Type of document	Title of publication
2004	L. Bunt	Article	Mary Priestley, Interviewed by Leslie Bunt, *Voices*
2005	B. Scheiby	Article	An Intersubjective Approach to Music Therapy, in *Music Therapy Perspectives*
2005	B. Scheiby	Chapter	"Dying Alive", in *Music Therapy at the End of Life*
2007	L. Eyre	Monograph	Changes in Images, Life Events, and Music in AMT
2007	J. Kowski	Chapter	"Can You Play with Me?" Dealing with Trauma, Grief and Loss Through Analytical Music Therapy and Play Therapy, in *Healing the Inner-City Child: Creative Arts Therapies with At-Risk Youth*
2009	S. Hadley	Article	Exploring Relationships Between Mary Priestley's Life and Work, in *Nordic Journal of Music Therapy*
2009	B. Scheiby	Article	Analytical Music Therapy and Regression [lecture from 4th World Congress of Music Therapy, March 29, 1983, Paris, France] in *Voices*
2010	B. Scheiby	Chapter	Analytical Music Therapy and Integrative Medicine, in *Music Therapy and Trauma: Bridging Theory and Clinical Practice*
2012	T. M. C. Auf der Heyde	Dissertation	Interpersonal Rhythms Disrupted by a History of Trauma
2012	M. Cooper	Dissertation	A Music Analysis of How Mary Priestley Implemented the Techniques She Used for Analytical Music Therapy

Year	Author	Type of document	Title of publication
2013	B. Abrams	Chapter	A Perspective on the Role of Personal Therapy in Analytical Music Therapy Training in Self-experiences, in *Music Therapy Education, Training, and Supervision*
2013	B. Scheiby	Chapter	Analytic Music Therapy for Pain Management and Reinforcement of Self-Directed Neuroplasticity, in *Music and Medicine: Integrative Models in Pain Medicine*
2013	B. Scheiby	Chapter	Insight Aquired through Analytical Music Therapy Supervision, in *Art Media in Psychotherapy Supervision: Insight and Vitality*
2014	H. Ahonen and A. M. Desideri	Article	Heroines' Journey: Emerging Story by Refugee Women During Group Analytical Music Therapy, *Voices*

Appendix 4-C: Themes of Writings about AMT by Authors Other Than Mary Priestley (*N*=35)

Theme	Number	Percentage of writings
Clinical Settings	8	23
Psychoanalytic Theory	8	23
Overview of AMT	4	11
Education and Supervision	3	9
Research and AMT	2	5
Other*	10	29

Note: * Death/Rebirth, Rehabilitation, Interview with Mary Priestley, Trauma, Priestley's Process, and Musical Analysis of Priestley's Techniques, Personal Experience with AMT.

Appendix 5-A: Documents Written by Helen Bonny (*N*=38)

Date	Author	Title	Publication/source
1965	M. Toombs, V. Walker, and H. Bonny	Dance therapy with retarded adolescents	*Journal of Music Therapy* 2, 115–117
1968	H. Bonny	Preferred loudness of recorded music of hospitalized psychiatric patients and hospital employees	*Journal of Music Therapy* 5, 44–52
1972	H. Bonny and W. Pahnke	The use of music in LSD music research	*Journal of Music Therapy* 9, 64–87
1973	H. Bonny and L. Savary	*Music and Your Mind: Listening with a New Consciousness*	Station Hill Press, NY: Barrytown
1974	H. Bonny and R. Tansill	Music, a Legal High	In G. Waldorf (ed.) *The Addictive Client*. Baltimore, MD: School of Social Work, University of Maryland
1975	H. Bonny	Music and consciousness	*Journal of Music Therapy* 12(3), 121–135
1975	H. Bonny	Music and Emotional Disturbance	Presented at Music Educators National Conference
1976	H. Bonny	Music and Psychotherapy	Dissertation
1977	J. Kellogg, M. MacRae, H. Bonny, and F. di Leo	The use of the mandala in psychological evaluation and treatment	*American Journal of Art Therapy 16*, 123–134

Date	Author	Title	Publication/source
1977	H. Bonny and J. Kellogg	Guided Imagery and Music and the Mandala: A Case Study	Proceedings of the Seventh Annual Conference of the American Art Therapy Association
1978	H. Bonny	Facilitating GIM Sessions	Monograph 1, Baltimore MD: ICM
1978	H. Bonny	The Role of Taped Music Programs in the GIM Process	Monograph 2, Baltimore, MD: ICM
1980	H. Bonny	*Music and Sound in Health*	In *Health for the Whole Person*. Boulder, CO: Westview Press
1980	H. Bonny	GIM Therapy: Past, Present, and Future Implications	Monograph 3, Baltimore, MD: ICM
1982	H. Bonny	An Informal Sharing of Ideas	Presented at Internal Symposium on Music Therapy, New York City
1983	H. Bonny	Cycles of Experience: Past, Present and Future	Presented at AAMT Conference, Philadelphia, PA
1983	H. Bonny	Music listening for intensive coronary care units: A pilot project	*Music Therapy 3(1)*
1983	H. Bonny	Music RX Manual: An Innovative Program Designed for the Hospital Setting	Salina, KS: Bonny Foundation
1984	H. Bonny	The Musical Lifeline: Present Perspectives and Future Possibilities	Proceedings of the 11th Annual Conference of CAMT 6
1984	H. Bonny	Music as an adjunct to anesthesia in operative procedures	*Journal of the American Association of Nurse Anesthetists 2(1)*
1984	H. Bonny	Prologue	*Music Therapy 4(1)*, 1–4

Date	Author	Title	Publication/source
1984	H. Bonny	Epilogue	*Music Therapy 4(1)*, 106–109
1985	H. Bonny	Music: The Language of Immediacy	Presented at National Conference of Art Therapies Association
1986	H. Bonny	Music and Healing	Presented at the American Holistic Medical Association Conference, Seattle, WA
1986	H. Bonny	Music and healing	*Music Therapy 6a(1)*, 3–12
1987	H. Bonny	Music: The language of immediacy	*Arts in Psychotherapy 14*, 255–261
1989	H. Bonny	Reaching Out by Reaching Within	Presented at 16th Annual Canadian Association for Music Therapy Conference, Ottawa, Ontario, CA
1989	H. Bonny	Sound as symbol: GIM in clinical practice	Music Therapy Perspectives: The CA Symposium on Clinical Practices 6, 7–10
1990	H. Bonny	Augment Your Creative Chord	Presented at Great Lakes National Association for Music Therapy Conference
1990	H. Bonny	Music and change	*Newsweek 4*, August 20, 5–10
1993	H. Bonny	Body listening: A new way to review GIM tapes	*Journal of the Association for Music and Imagery 2*, 3–13
1993	H. Bonny	Music in the Receptive Mode	Presented at Midwestern National Association for Music Therapy Conference, Lawrence, KS, March 19, 1993

Date	Author	Title	Publication/source
1994	H. Bonny	Twenty-one years later: A GIM update	*Music Therapy Perspectives: Psychiatric Music Therapy 12(2)*, 70–74
1996	F. Goldberg and H. Bonny	New directions in the Bonny Method of GIM	Music Therapy International Report, AAMT 10
1997	H. Bonny	Untitled manuscript	In J. Moreno (ed.) *Music Therapists of Our Time: Profiles in Creativity*, never published
1997	H. Bonny	The state of the art of music therapy	*The Arts in Psychotherapy 24 (1)*, 65–73
2002	H. Bonny	Collected Writings	*Music and Consciousness: The Evolution of Guided Imagery and Music*, Dallas, TX: Barcelona Publishing
n.d.	H. Bonny	Outline for edited book on GIM	Never published

Appendix 5-B: Documents Written in English about the Bonny Method of Guided Imagery and Music (N=181)

Date	Author	Title	Publication/source
1981	L. Summer	Guided imagery and music with the elderly	*Music Therapy, 1*, 39–42
1983	P. Nolan	The Use of GIM in the Clinical Assessment of Depression	Master's Thesis
1983	P. Nolan	Insight therapy: Guided Imagery and Music in a forensic psychiatric setting	*Music Therapy, 3*, 43–51

Date	Author	Title	Publication/source
1985	L. Summer	Imagery and music	*Journal of Mental Imagery 9(4)*, 83–90
1985	A. M. S. Kovach	Shamanism and GIM: A comparison	*Journal of Music Therapy, 23* (3), 154–165
1988	F. Goldberg, T. Hoss, and T. Chesna	Music and imagery as psychotherapy with a brain damaged patient: A case study	*Music Therapy Perspectives, 5*, 41–45
1988	L. Summer	*GIM in the Institutional Setting*	St. Louis, MO: Magnamusic-Baton
1989	F. Goldberg	Music psychotherapy in acute psychiatric inpatient and private practice settings	*Music Therapy Perspectives, 6*, 40–43
1990	S. Merritt	*Mind, Music and Imagery*	New York City: Plume Books
1990	R. McDonald	The Efficacy of GIM as a Strategy of Self-Concept and Blood-Pressure Change among Adults with Essential Hypertension	Dissertation
1990	C. McKinney	The effect of music on imagery	*Journal of Music Therapy, 27*, 34–46
1991	K. Bruscia	Modes of consciousness in GIM: A therapist's experience of the guiding process	In C. Kenny (ed.) *Listening, Playing Creating Essays on the Power of Sound*, Albany, NY: SUNY
1991	K. Bruscia	Embracing life with AIDS: Psychotherapy through GIM	In *Case Studies in Music Therapy*, Dallas, TX: Barcelona Publishing
1992	J. Borling	Perspectives on growth with a victim of abuse: A Guided Imagery and Music [GIM] case study	*Journal of the Association for Music and Imagery, 1*, 85–98
1992	C. Bush	Dreams, mandalas, and music imagery: Therapeutic uses in a case study	*Journal of the Association for Music and Imagery, 1*, 33–42

Date	Author	Title	Publication/source
1992	J. Dutcher	Tape analysis: Creativity I	*Journal of the Association for Music and Imagery, 1*, 107–118
1992	F. Goldberg	Images of emotion: The role of emotion in Guided Imagery and Music	*Journal of the Association for Music and Imagery, 1*, 5–18
1992	S. Hale	Wounded woman: The use of Guided Imagery and Music in recovering from a mastectomy	*Journal of the Association for Music and Imagery, 1*, 99–106
1992	K. Hanks	Music, affect and imagery: A cross-cultural exploration	*Journal of the Association for Music and Imagery, 1*, 19–32
1992	L. Summer	Music: An aesthetic elixir	*Journal of the Association for Music and Imagery, 1*, 43–54
1992	E. Pickett	Guided Imagery and Music (GIM) with a dually-diagnosed woman having multiple addictions	*Journal of the Association for Music and Imagery, 1*, 55–68
1992	R. Skaggs	Music as co-therapist: Creative resource for change	*Journal of the Association for Music and Imagery, 1*, 77–84
1992	S. Stokes	Letting the sound depths arise	*Journal of the Association for Music and Imagery, 1*, 69–76
1993	K. Lewis	Using Guided Imagery and Music to clarify and support relationship changes: A case study	*Journal of the Association for Music and Imagery, 2*, 87–98
1993	S. Merritt	The healing link: Guided Imagery and Music and the body/mind connection	*Journal of the Association for Music and Imagery, 2*, 14–28

Date	Author	Title	Publication/source
1993	C. McKinney	The case of Therese: Multidimensional growth through Guided Imagery and Music	*Journal of the Association for Music and Imagery*, 2, 99–110
1993	E. Pickett, & C. Sonnen	Guided Imagery and Music: A music therapy approach to multiple personality disorder	*Journal of the Association for Music and Imagery*, 2, 49–72
1993	A. Short	GIM during pregnancy: Anticipation and resolution	*Journal of the Association for Music and Imagery*, 2, 73–86
1993	Tasney	Beginning the healing of incest through Guided Imagery and Music: A Jungian perspective	*Journal of the Association for Music and Imagery*, 2, 35–48
1993	D. R. Vaux	GIM applied to the 50-minute hour	*Journal of the Association for Music and Imagery*, 2, 29–34
1993	V. Walker	Integrating Guided Imagery and Music with verbal psycho-Therapy: A case study	*Journal of the Association for Music and Imagery*, 2, 111–121
1994	R. L. Blake & S. Bishop	The Bonny Method of GIM in the treatment of PTSD for adult and adolescent survivors of trauma	*Music Therapy*, 12, 25
1994	R. L. Blake	Vietnam veterans with post traumatic stress disorder: Findings from a music and imagery project	*Journal of the Association for Music and Imagery*, 3, 5–17
1994	V. Clarkson	Learning through mistakes: Guided Imagery and Music with a client in a hypomanic episode	*Journal of the Association for Music and Imagery*, 3, 77–94

Date	Author	Title	Publication/source
1994	F. Goldberg	The Bonny Method of Guided Imagery and Music as individual and group treatment in a short-term psychiatric hospital	*Journal of the Association for Music and Imagery, 3,* 18–34
1994	F. Holligan	Guided Imagery and Music in a spiritual retreat	*Journal of the Association for Music and Imagery, 3,* 59–68
1994	F. Pickett	Awareness of body sensations and physical movement as part of the Guided Imagery and Music experience	*Journal of the Association for Music and Imagery, 3,* 95–103
1994	R. Skaggs	Conversations: An analysis of the music program	*Journal of the Association for Music and Imagery, 3,* 69–76
1994	M. Ventre	Guided Imagery and Music in process: The interweaving of the archetype of the mother, mandala, and music	*Music Therapy, 12,* 98–103
1994	M. Ventre	Healing the wounds of childhood abuse: A Guided Imagery and Music case study	*Music Therapy Perspectives, 12,* 98
1994	J. G. Weiss	Accessing the inner family through Guided Imagery and Music	*Journal of the Association for Music and Imagery, 3,* 49–58
1994	A. Wrangsjo	Psychoanalysis and Guided Imagery and Music: A comparison	*Journal of the Association for Music and Imagery, 3,* 35–48
1995	A. Lem	An Integrated Profile of BrainWave Activity and Structural Variability in the Study of Music and Music Imagery in Vivo.	Master's Thesis
1995	K. Bruscia	The many dimensions of transference	*Journal of the Association for Music and Imagery, 4,* 3–16

Date	Author	Title	Publication/source
1995	K. Bruscia	Manifestations of transference in Guided Imagery and Music	*Journal of the Association for Music and Imagery, 4,* 17–36
1995	C. Bush	*Healing Imagery and Music: Pathways to the Inner Self.*	Portland, OR: Rudra Press
1995	M. Clark	The hero's myth in Guided Imagery and Music therapy	*Journal of the Association for Music and Imagery, 4,* 49–66
1995	V. Clarkson	Adapting a Guided Imagery and Music series for a nonverbal man with autism	*Journal of the Association for Music and Imagery, 4,* 121–138
1995	S. Merritt and S. Schulberg	Guided Imagery and Music and collective grief: Facing the shadow of the Holocaust	*Journal of the Association for Music and Imagery, 4,* 103–120
1995	C. H. McKinney, M. Antoni, A. Kumar, and M. Kumar	The effects of Guided Imagery and Music on depression and beta-endorphin levels in healthy adults: A pilot study	*Journal of the Association for Music and Imagery, 4,* 67–78
1995	C. H. McKinney and F. Tims	Differential effects of selected classical music on the imagery of high and low imagers: Two studies	*Journal of Music Therapy, 32,* 22–45
1995	B. Pickett	Guided imagery and music: A technique for healing trauma	*Journal of the Association for Music and Imagery, 4,* 93–102
1995	L. Summer	Melding musical and psychological processes: The therapeutic musical space	*Journal of the Association for Music and Imagery, 4,* 37–48
1995	B. Wrangsjo and D. Korlin	Guided Imagery and Music as a psychotherapeutic method in psychiatry	*Journal of the Association for Music and Imagery, 4,* 79–92

Date	Author	Title	Publication/source
1996	D. M. Beck	Listening with open ears	*Journal of the Association for Music and Imagery*, 5, 25–36
1996	E. Pickett	Guided Imagery and Music in head trauma rehabilitation	*Journal of the Association for Music and Imagery*, 5, 51–20
1996	M. Roy	Guided Imagery and Music group experiences with adolescent girls in a high school setting	*Journal of the Association for Music and Imagery*, 5, 61–74
1996	A. Short	Jungian archetypes in Guided Imagery and Music therapy: Approaching the client's fairytale	*Journal of the Association for Music and Imagery*, 5, 37–50
1996	R. Skaggs	Literature review: The Bonny Method of Guided Imagery and Music	*Journal of the Association for Music and Imagery*, 5, 75–104
1996	B. Smith	Uncovering and healing hidden wounds: Using Guided Imagery and Music to resolve complication and disenfranchised grief	*Journal of the Association for Music and Imagery*, 5, 13–24
1996	L. Toomey	Literature review of Guided Imagery and Music	[Unpublished]
1996	G. Villaincourt	Therapy for the therapist	*Journal of the Association for Music and Imagery*, 5, 105–116
1997	McKinney, et. al	Effects of Guided Imagery and Music on mood and cortisol in healthy adults	*Health Psychology*, 16, 390–400
1998	J. Booth	The Paradise program: A new music program for Guided Imagery and Music	*Journal of the Association for Music and Imagery*, 6, 15–36

Date	Author	Title	Publication/source
1998	K. Bruscia	Modes of consciousness in Guided Imagery and Music	*The Dynamics of Music Psychotherapy* (pp. 491–526)
1998	M. Clark	The Bonny Method of Guided Imagery and Music and spiritual development	*Journal of the Association for Music and Imagery, 6,* 55–62
1998	V. Clarkson	Spiritual insights of a Guided Imagery and Music client with autism	*Journal of the Association for Music and Imagery, 6,* 87–104
1998	K. Lewis	The Bonny Method of Guided Imagery and Music: Matrix for transpersonal experience	*Journal of the Association for Music and Imagery, 6,* 63–85
1998	J. Marr	Guided Imagery and Music at the end of life: Case studies in palliative care	*Journal of the Association for Music and Imagery, 6,* 37–54
1998	M. McIvor	Heroic journeys: Experience of a Maori group with the Bonny Method	*Journal of the Association for Music and Imagery, 6,* 105–118
1998	S. Wesley	Music, Jung, and making meaning	*Journal of the Association for Music and Imagery, 6,* 3–14
1998	L. Summer	*Guided Imagery and Music in the Institutional Setting*	St. Louis: Magnamusic-Baton
1997	L. Summer	Considering the future of music therapy	*The Arts in Psychotherapy* 24, 75–80
1999	R. Buell	Emerging through music: A journey towards wholeness with Guided Imagery and Music	In J. Hibben (ed.) *Inside Music Therapy: Client Experiences,* New Braunfels, TX: Barcelona Publishers

Date	Author	Title	Publication/source
1999	T. Caughman and J. Caughman	Tools of rediscovery: A year of Guided Imagery and Music	In J. Hibben (ed.) *Inside Music Therapy: Client Experiences*, New Braunfels, TX: Barcelona Publishers
1999	D. Erdonmez-Grocke	Pivotal moments in Guided Imagery and Music	In J. Hibben (ed.) *Inside Music Therapy: Client Experiences*, New Braunfels, TX: Barcelona Publishers
1999	D. Erdonmez-Grocke	The music which underpins Imagery and Music	In T. Wigram and J. DeBacker *Clinical Applications of Music Therapy in Psychiatry.* London: Jessica Kingsley Publishers, pp. 197–210
1999	C. Izenberg-Grzeda	Experiencing the music in Guided Imagery and Music	In J. Hibben (ed.) *Inside Music Therapy: Client Experiences*, New Braunfels, TX: Barcelona Publishers
1999	M. Neilsen and T. Moe	Chaos, crisis, development, cosmos	In J. Hibben (ed.) *Inside Music Therapy: Client Experiences*, New Braunfels, TX: Barcelona Publishers
1999	A. Newell	Dealing with physical illness: GIM and the search for self	In J. Hibben (ed.) *Inside Music Therapy: Client Experiences*, New Braunfels, TX: Barcelona Publishers
1999	C. Schulberg	Out of the ashes: Transforming despair into hope with music and imagery	In J. Hibben (ed.) *Inside Music Therapy: Client Experiences*, New Braunfels, TX: Barcelona Publishers
1999	M. Ventre	A tape from Lilly	In J. Hibben (ed.) *Inside Music Therapy: Client Experiences*, New Braunfels, TX: Barcelona Publishers

Date	Author	Title	Publication/source
2000	L. O. Bonde	Metaphor and narrative in Guided Imagery and Music.	*Journal of the Association for Music and Imagery, 7,* 59–76
2000	D. Brooks	Anima manifestations of men using Guided Imagery and Music: A case study	*Journal of the Association for Music and Imagery, 7,* 77–87
2000.	K. Bruscia	A scale for assessing responsiveness to Guided Imagery and Music	*Journal of the Association for Music and Imagery, 7,* 1–7
2000	L. Bunt	Transformational processes in Guided Imagery and Music	*Journal of the Association for Music and Imagery, 7,* 44–58
2000	D. Burns	The effect of classical music on the absorption and control of mental imagery	*Journal of the Association for Music and Imagery, 7,* 34–43
2000	J. Marr	The Effects of Imagery Sequence in the BM-GIM	Master's Thesis
2000	A. Meadows	The validity and reliability of the *Guided imagery and responsiveness scale*	*Journal of the Association for Music and Imagery, 7,* 8–33
2000	T. Moe, A. Roesen, and Raben	Restitutional factors in Group Music Therapy with Psychiatric Patients based on a Modification of Guided Imagery and Music	*Nordic Journal 9,* 165–179
2000	L. Ole Bonde	Metaphor and narrative in Guided Imagery and Music	*Journal of the Association for Music and Imagery, 7,* 59–76
2001	J. Band, S. Quilter, and G. Miller	The influence of selected music and inductions on mental imagery: Implications for practitioners of Guided Imagery and Music	*Journal of the Association for Music and Imagery, 8,* 13–34

Date	Author	Title	Publication/source
2001	D. M. Beck	Guided Imagery and Music guide as spiritual director	*Journal of the Association for Music and Imagery, 8,* 75–88
2001	D. Burns	The effect of BM-GIM on the mood and life quality of cancer patients	*Journal of Music Therapy, 38,* 51–65
2001	M. Carlsson	Kundalini and the Bonny Method of Guided Imagery and music	*Journal of the Association for Music and Imagery, 8,* 35–56
2001	V. Clarkson	Awareness meditation practice: Applications to guiding and supervising	*Journal of the Association for Music and Imagery, 8,* 1–12
2001	E. Jacobi & G. Eisenberg	The efficacy of the Bonny Method of Guided Imagery and Music in the treatment of rheumatoid arthritis	*Journal of the Association for Music and Imagery, 8,* 57–74
2002	B. Abrams	Definitions of transpersonal Guided Imagery and Music experiences.	*Nordic Journal 11,* 103–126
2002	B. Abrams	Method of analyzing music programs used in the Bonny Method	In K. Bruscia and D. Grocke (eds) *Guided Imagery and Music: The Bonny Method and Beyond,* New Braunfels, TX: Barcelona Publishers
2002	B. Abrams	Transpersonal dimensions of the Bonny Method	In K. Bruscia and D. Grocke (eds) *Guided Imagery and Music: The Bonny Method and Beyond,* New Braunfels, TX: Barcelona Publishers
2002	D. Brooks	Supervision strategies for the Bonny Method of Guided Imagery and Music (BM-GIM)	In K. Bruscia and D. Grocke (eds) *Guided Imagery and Music: The Bonny Method and Beyond,* New Braunfels, TX: Barcelona Publishers

Date	Author	Title	Publication/source
2002	D. Burns	Guided Imagery and Movement in the treatment of individuals with chronic illness	In K. Bruscia and D. Grocke (eds) *Guided Imagery and Music: The Bonny Method and Beyond*, New Braunfels, TX: Barcelona Publishers
2002	K. Bruscia	The boundaries of Guided Imagery and Music and the Bonny Method	In K. Bruscia and D. Grocke (eds) *Guided Imagery and Music: The Bonny Method and Beyond*, New Braunfels, TX: Barcelona Publishers
2002	K. Bruscia	Client assessment in the Bonny Method of Guided Imagery and Music	In K. Bruscia and D. Grocke (eds) *Guided Imagery and Music: The Bonny Method and Beyond*, New Braunfels, TX: Barcelona Publishers
2002	K. Bruscia	Developments in music programming for the Bonny Method	In K. Bruscia and D. Grocke (eds) *Guided Imagery and Music: The Bonny Method and Beyond*, New Braunfels, TX: Barcelona Publishers
2002	K. Bruscia	A psychodynamic orientation to the Bonny Method	In K. Bruscia and D. Grocke (eds) *Guided Imagery and Music: The Bonny Method and Beyond*, New Braunfels, TX: Barcelona Publishers
2002	N. Cohen	Ethical considerations in Guided Imagery and Music	In K. Bruscia and D. Grocke (eds) *Guided Imagery and Music: The Bonny Method and Beyond*, New Braunfels, TX: Barcelona Publishers
2002	V. Clarkson	Combining Gestalt dreamwork and the Bonny Method	In K. Bruscia and D. Grocke (eds) *Guided Imagery and Music: The Bonny Method and Beyond*, New Braunfels, TX: Barcelona Publishers

Date	Author	Title	Publication/source
2002	F. Goldberg	A holographic field theory model of the Bonny Method of Guided Imagery and Music	In K. Bruscia and D. Grocke (eds) *Guided Imagery and Music: The Bonny Method and Beyond*, New Braunfels, TX: Barcelona Publishers
2002	D. Grocke	The evolution of Bonny's music programs	In K. Bruscia and D. Grocke (eds) *Guided Imagery and Music: The Bonny Method and Beyond*, New Braunfels, TX: Barcelona Publishers
2002	D. Grocke	The Bonny music programs	In K. Bruscia and D. Grocke (eds) *Guided Imagery and Music: The Bonny Method and Beyond*, New Braunfels, TX: Barcelona Publishers
2002	D. Grocke	International advances in the Bonny Method	In K. Bruscia and D. Grocke (eds) *Guided Imagery and Music: The Bonny Method and Beyond*, New Braunfels, TX: Barcelona Publishers
2002	D. Grocke	Qualitative research in Guided Imagery and Music	In K. Bruscia and D. Grocke (eds) *Guided Imagery and Music: The Bonny Method and Beyond*, New Braunfels, TX: Barcelona Publishers
2002	R. Kasayka	A spiritual orientation to the Bonny Method: To walk the mystical path on practical feet	In K. Bruscia and D. Grocke (eds) *Guided Imagery and Music: The Bonny Method and Beyond*, New Braunfels, TX: Barcelona Publishers
2002	D. Körlin and B. Wrangsjö	Treatment effects of GIM therapy	*Nordic Journal 11*, 3–15

Date	Author	Title	Publication/source
2002	D. Körlin	A neuropsychological theory of traumatic imagery in the Bonny Method of Guided Imagery and Music	In K. Bruscia and D. Grocke (eds) *Guided Imagery and Music: The Bonny Method and Beyond*, New Braunfels, TX: Barcelona Publishers
2002	A. Meadows	Gender implications in therapists' constructs of their clients	*Nordic Journal 11*, 127–141
2002	A. Meadows	Psychotherapeutic applications	In K. Bruscia and D. Grocke (eds) *Guided Imagery and Music: The Bonny Method and Beyond*, New Braunfels, TX: Barcelona Publishers
2002	A. Meadows	Distinctions between the Bonny Method of Guided Imagery and Music and other imagery techniques	In K. Bruscia and D. Grocke (eds) *Guided Imagery and Music: The Bonny Method and Beyond*, New Braunfels, TX: Barcelona Publishers
2002	A. McKinney	Quantitative research in Guided Imagery and Music: A review	In K. Bruscia and D. Grocke (eds) *Guided Imagery and Music: The Bonny Method and Beyond*, New Braunfels, TX: Barcelona Publishers
2002	T. Moe	Restitutional factors in receptive group music therapy inspired by Guided Imagery and Music	*Nordic Journal 11*, 152–166
2002	T. Perilli	A theory of metaphor in the Bonny Method of Guided Imagery and Music	In K. Bruscia and D. Grocke (eds) *Guided Imagery and Music: The Bonny Method and Beyond*, New Braunfels, TX: Barcelona Publishers

Date	Author	Title	Publication/source
2002	E. Pickett	A history of the literature on Guided Imagery and Music	In K. Bruscia and D. Grocke (eds) *Guided Imagery and Music: The Bonny Method and Beyond*, New Braunfels, TX: Barcelona Publishers
2002	A. Short	Guided Imagery and Music in medical care	In K. Bruscia and D. Grocke (eds) *Guided Imagery and Music: The Bonny Method and Beyond*, New Braunfels, TX: Barcelona Publishers
2002	L. Summer	Group music and imagery therapy: Emergent receptive techniques in *Music Therapy* practice	In K. Bruscia and D. Grocke (eds) *Guided Imagery and Music: The Bonny Method and Beyond*, New Braunfels, TX: Barcelona Publishers
2002	M. Ventre	The individual form of the Bonny Method of Guided Imagery and Music (BMGIM)	In K. Bruscia and D. Grocke (eds) *Guided Imagery and Music: The Bonny Method and Beyond*, New Braunfels, TX: Barcelona Publishers
2002	S. Wesley	Guided Imagery and Music with children and adolescents	In K. Bruscia and D. Grocke (eds) *Guided Imagery and Music: The Bonny Method and Beyond*, New Braunfels, TX: Barcelona Publishers
2003	N. Cohen	Musical choices: An interview with Helen Lindquist Bonny	*Journal of the Association for Music and Imagery, 9*, 1–26
2003	N. Hahna and J. Borling	The Bonny Method of Guided Imagery and Music (GIM) with intimate partner violence	*Journal of the Association for Music and Imagery, 9*, 41–58
2003	K. Martenson-Blom	Guided Imagery and Music in supervision	*Journal of the Association for Music and Imagery, 9*, 98–118

Date	Author	Title	Publication/source
2003	L. Moffit and A. Hall	"New grown with pleasant pain" (Keats): Recovering from sexual abuse with the use of the Bonny Method of Guided Imagery and Music and the use of poetry	*Journal of the Association for Music and Imagery*, 9, 59–78
2003	M.T. Rankin	Audio divina: Introducing a contemplative practice for contemporary times	*Journal of the Association for Music and Imagery*, 9, 79–98
2003	W. Richards	Navigation within consciousness: Insights from four decades of psychotherapy research with imagery, music, and entheogens	*Journal of the Association for Music and Imagery*, 9, 27–40
2004	E. Abbott	Client experiences with the music in the Bonny Method of Guided Imagery and Music	In A. Meadows (ed.) *Qualitative Inquiries in Music Therapy*, Vol. II, New Braunfels, TX: Barcelona Publishers
2004	L. Ole Bonde	The Bonny Method of Guided Imagery and Music with Cancer Survivors: A Psycho-Social Study with Focus on the Influence of the Bonny Method of Guided Images and Music on Mood and Quality of Life.	Dissertation
2005	B. Abrams and R. Kasayka	Music imaging for persons at the end of life	In J. Loewy and C. Dileo (eds) *Music Therapy at the End of Life*, Cherry Hill, NJ: Jeffrey Books

Date	Author	Title	Publication/source
2005	D. M. Beck	Recapturing a vision to become fully human: The Bonny Method as a servant source in discovering the authentic self	*Journal of the Association for Music and Imagery*, 10, 45–54
2005	J. Booth	Music, drawing, and narrative: An adaptation of the Bonny Method of Guided Imagery and Music	*Journal of the Association for Music and Imagery*, 10, 55–74
2005	L. Cadrin	Dying well: The Bonny Method of Guided Imagery and Music at the end of life	*Journal of the Association for Music and Imagery*, 10, 1–26
2005	V. Clarkson	Enhancing Bonny Method sessions with subtle energy healing	*Journal of the Association for Music and Imagery*, 10, 27–44
2005.	D. E. Grocke	The role of the therapist in BMGIM	*Music Therapy Perspectives*, 23, 36–44
2005	A. Scott	Cultural dimensions in music and imagery: Archetype and ethnicity on GIM practice	*Journal of the Association for Music and Imagery*, 10, 75–90
2007	E. Abbott	Facilitating Guided Imagery and Music: What therapists intend, experience and do	*Journal of the Association for Music and Imagery*, 11, 1–20
2007	D. Körlin	Music breathing, breath grounding, and modulation of the Bonny Method of Guided Imagery and Music	*Journal of the Association for Music and Imagery*, 11, 79–109
2007	K. Kirkland	Suffering and the sublime: A case study of music, metaphor, and meaning	*Journal of the Association for Music and Imagery*, 11, 21–38

Date	Author	Title	Publication/source
2007	R. Martin	The Effect of a Series of Guided Imagery and Music Sessions on Music Performance Anxiety	Master's Thesis
2007	L. Ole Bonde	Imagery, metaphor, and perceived outcomes in six cancer survivors' Bonny Method of Guided Imagery and Music therapy	In A. Meadows (ed.) *Qualitative Inquiries in Music Therapy*, Vol. III, New Braunfels, TX: Barcelona Publishers
2007	L. Powell	An adaption of the Bonny Method of Guided Imagery and Music for public schools	*Journal of the Association for Music and Imagery*, 11, 65–78
2007	D. Scott	Individual differences in response to the Bonny Method of Guided Imagery and Music	*Journal of the Association for Music and Imagery*, 11, 39–63
2007	M. Zanders	Metaphors clients use to explain their experiences in BM-GIM	In S. Hadley (ed.) *Qualitative Inquiries in Music Therapy*, Vol. IV, New Braunfels, TX: Barcelona Publishers
2009	V. Clarkson	Mandala analysis: A clinical case study	*Journal of the Association for Music and Imagery*, 12, 75–93
2009	M. Hearns	Journey beyond abuse: Healing through music and imagery	*Journal of the Association for Music and Imagery*, 12, 47–59
2009	B. Mi-Hyun	Am I a shaman? Transformation of a Korean Guided Imagery and Music Fellow's and a traditional healer's consciousness through music	*Journal of the Association for Music and Imagery*, 12, 61–73

Date	Author	Title	Publication/source
2009	M. Ryan	Holotropic breathwork and the Bonny Method: The co-evolution of two transpersonal therapeutic modalities	*Journal of the Association for Music and Imagery, 12*, 95–117
2009	L. Summer	Client Perspectives of the Music in Guided Imagery and Music	Dissertation
2009	G. Trondalen	Exploring the rucksack of sadness: Focused time-limited Bonny Method of Guided Imagery and Music with a female executive	*Journal of the Association for Music and Imagery, 12*, 1–20
2009	M. Viega	Body listening as a method of understanding a music program used in the Bonny Method of Guided Imagery and Music	*Journal of the Association for Music and Imagery, 12*, 21–45
2010	K. Blom	Transpersonal-spiritual BMGIM experiences and the process of surrender	*Nordic Journal, 20*, 185–203
2010	F. Goldberg and L. Mitran	The central tenets of the Bonny Method of Guided Imagery and Music	*Voices, 10*, DOI: http://dx.doi.org/10.15845/voices.v10i3.438
2010	A. Meadows	The evolution of Guided Imagery and Music programming	*Voices 10*, DOI: http://dx.doi.org/10.15845/voices.v10i3.497
2010	D. Grocke	An overview of research in the Bonny Method of Guided Imagery and Music	*Voices 10*, DOI: http://dx.doi.org/10.15845/voices.v10i3.340
2010	M. F. Lin, M. C. Hsu, H. J. Chang, et. al.	Pivotal Moments and changes in the Bonny Method of Guided Imager and Music for patients with depression	*Journal of Clinical Nursing, 19*, 1139–1148

Date	Author	Title	Publication/source
2010	B. Muller	Guided Imagery and Music: A Survey of Current Practices	Dissertation
2010	D. Short, H. Gibb, & C. Holmes	Integrating words, images, and text in BM-GIM: Finding connections through semiotic intertextuality	*Nordic Journal*, DOI: 10.1080/08098 131003764031
2010	Various	Authors Commemorative volume for Helen Bonny	*Voices, 10*, DOI: http://dx.doi.org/10.15845/voices.v10i3
2011	D. M. Beck	Music mirroring the sounds of the soul: A listening source for self-appraisal	*Journal of the Association for Music and Imagery, 13*, 99–110
2011	B. Davis	The Bonny Method and shamanic journeying: Pathways to living with higher consciousness	*Journal of the Association for Music and Imagery, 13*, 45–55
2011	Y. Illcheva	Dreamwork in the Bonny Method of Guided Imagery and Music: GIM as a dreamwork vessel	*Journal of the Association for Music and Imagery, 13*, 57–75
2011	T. Moe	Group Guided Imagery and Music therapy for inpatients with substance abuse disorder	*Journal of the Association for Music and Imagery, 13*, 77–98
2011	G. G. Perelli	Integration process in the Bonny Method and music and imagery	*Journal of the Association for Music and Imagery, 13*, 23–44
2011	E. T. Sema	Separation and mourning: A Bonny Method of Guided Imagery and Music case study	*Journal of the Association for Music and Imagery, 13*, 1–22

Date	Author	Title	Publication/source
2013	A. Heiderscheit	Guided Imagery and Music: Deprivation and its contribution to pain in eating disorders	In J. Mondanaro and G. Sara (eds) *Music and Medicine: Integrative Models in the Treatment of Pain*, New York: Satchnote Press
2013	N. Jackson	Backed into a corner: The use of Guided Imagery and Music in the care of a woman with chronic pain	In J. Mondanaro and G. Sara (eds) *Music and Medicine: Integrative Models in the Treatment of Pain*, New York: Satchnote Press
2014	M. Clark	A new synthesis model of the Bonny Method of Guided Imagery and Music	*Journal of the Association for Music and Imagery, 14,* 1–22
2014	V. Clarkson	Seeking the inner father: Integrating grief through Guided Imagery and Music	*Journal of the Association for Music and Imagery, 14,* 23–38
2014	A. Clements-Cortes	Breaking free: Healing physical, verbal, and sexual abuse through the Bonny Method of Guided Imagery	*Journal of the Association for Music and Imagery, 14,* 39–60
2014	B. Muller	Variations in GIM: Taking a Closer Look	New Brautels, TX: Barcelona Publishers
2014	A. Nadata	The depiction of a hero's journey in Bonny Method of Guided Imagery and Music Sessions	*Journal of the Association for Music and Imagery, 14,* 61–74
2014	S. Stokes-Stearns	The music of *Paradox*: Harmonizing shadow and music	*Journal of the Association for Music and Imagery, 14,* 75–104
2014	R. Yawney	The integration of the Bonny Method of GIM And client-centered verbal psychotherapy in treating a substance use disorder	*Journal of the Association for Music and Imagery, 14,* 105–123

Appendix 6-A: Documents Written by Paul Nordoff, Clive Robbins, and Co-Writers (*N*=27)

Date	Author	Title	Publication/source
1961	Nordoff and Robbins	The Juniper music therapy project at Devereux schools	*The Devereux Dial*, Devereux Foundation
1964	Nordoff and Robbins	Music therapy and personality change in autistic children	*Journal of the American Institute of Homeopathy 57*
1965	Nordoff and Robbins	Improvised music for autistic children	*Music Journal 23*
1966	Nordoff and Robbins	The scope of music therapy for handicapped children	*Music in Education 31*
1967	Nordoff and Robbins	Musical activities for handicapped children	*Music Journal 25*
1968	Nordoff and Robbins	Improvised Music as Therapy for Autistic Children	In E.T. Gaston (ed.) *Music in Therapy*. London: Macmillan
1968	Nordoff and Robbins	*The Book of Children's Play Songs*	Bryn Mawr, PA: Theodore Presser
1971	Nordoff and Robbins	*Music Therapy in Special Education*	New York: John Day Books in Special Education
1971	Nordoff and Robbins	*Therapy in Music for Handicapped Children*	London: Victor Gollancz Ltd
1974	Nordoff	Instruction on Improvisation	Presentations and recordings used with NR-MT students; 19 lectures, 10 hours: unpublished
1974	Nordoff	Talks on Music	In P. Robbins and C. Robbins (eds) Presentations and recordings used with NR-MT students

Date	Author	Title	Publication/source
1977	Nordoff and Robbins	*Creative Music Therapy: Individualized Treatment for the Handicapped Child*	New York: John Day Books in Special Education
1980	Robbins and Ca. Robbins	*Music for the Hearing Impaired and Other Special Groups*	St. Louis: MMB Music
1981	Ca. Robbins and Robbins	Reaching the Music Child Within the Deaf Child	Proceedings of the 8th Annual Conference of the Canadian Association for Music Therapy
1987	Ca. Robbins and Robbins	Creative Music Therapy	Proceedings of the 13th Annual Conference of the Australian Music Therapy Association
1987	Ca. Robbins and Robbins	Realizing the Musical Potential Inborn in the Hearing Impaired	Proceedings of the 13th Annual Conference of the Australian Music Therapy Association
1988	Nordoff	*The Whole Tone* Series	London: Nordoff-Robbins Music Therapy Centre Series 9, Number 1
1988	Ca. Robbins and Robbins	A visit to South Africa	*Journal of the Australian Music Therapy Association 11*
1991	M. Forinash and Robbins	A time paradigm: Time as a multilevel phenomenon in music therapy	*Music Therapy 10(1)*
1991	Robbins and Ca. Robbins	Creative music therapy in bringing order, change and communicativeness to the life of a brain-injured adolescent	In K. Bruscia (ed.) *Case Studies in Music Therapy,*. Gilsum, NH: Barcelona Publishers

Date	Author	Title	Publication/source
1991	Robbins and Ca. Robbins	Self-communications in creative music therapy	In K. Bruscia (ed.) *Case Studies in Music Therapy*, Gilsum, NH: Barcelona Publishers
1993	Robbins	The creative processes are universal	In M. Heal and T. Wigram (eds) *Music Therapy in Health and Education*, London: Jessica Kingsley Publishers
1997	Robbins	*What a Wonderful Song Her Life Sang: An Anthology of Appreciation for Carol Robbins*	New York: The International Trust for Nordoff-Robbins Music Therapy
1998	Robbins	Introduction to the study of Edward	*Nordic Journal of Music Therapy 7(1)*
1998	Nordoff and Robbins	Edward	*Nordic Journal of Music Therapy 7(1)*
1998	Nordoff	*Healing Heritage: Paul Nordoff Exploring the Tonal Language of Music* (reissued)	Gilsum, NH: Barcelona Publishers
2005	Robbins	*A Journey into Creative Music Therapy*: Volume IV of the NR-MT Monograph Series	Gilsum, NH: Barcelona Publishers

Note: *Nordoff = Paul Nordoff; Robbins = Clive Robbins; Robbins, Ca. = Carol Robbins.

Appendix 6-B: Documents Written in English About Creative Music Therapy or NR-MT (*N*=42)

Date	Author	Title	Publication/source
1987	K. Bruscia	Creative music therapy	In *Improvisational Models of Music Therapy*, Springfield, IL: C. C. Thomas Publisher Ltd
1992	M. Forinash	A phenomenological analysis of the Nordoff-Robbins approach to music therapy: The lived experience	*Music Therapy 11(1)*, 120–141
1994	M. S. Ritholz and A. Turry	Journey by train	*Music Therapy 12(2)*
1995	K. Aigen	An aesthetic foundation of clinical theory: An underlying basis of CMT	In C. Kenny (eds) *Listening, Playing, Creating: Essays on the Power of Sound*, New York: SUNY Press
1995	D. Aldridge, D. Gustorff and L. Neugebauer	A preliminary study of creative music therapy in the treatment of children with developmental delay	*The Arts in Psychotherapy 22(3)*, 189–205
1995	G. Ansdell	*Music for Life: Aspects of Creative Music Therapy with Adult Clients*	London: Jessica Kingsley Publishers
1997	K. Aigen	*How We Are in Music: One Year with an Adolescent Creative Music Therapy Group:* Volume II of the NR-MT Monograph Series	St. Louis, MO: MMB Music
1998	K. Aigen	*Paths of Development in Nordoff-Robbins Music Therapy*	Gilsum, NH: Barcelona Publishers

Date	Author	Title	Publication/source
1998	A. Turry	Transference and countertransference in Nordoff-Robbins Music Therapy	In K. Bruscia (ed.) *The Dynamics of Music Psychotherapy*, Gilsum, NH: Barcelona Publishers
1999	M. Logis and A. Turry	Singing my way through it: Facing the cancer, darkness, and fear	In J. Hibben (ed.) *Inside Music Therapy: Client Experiences*, New Braunfels, TX: Barcelona Publishers
1999	A. Turry and A. E. Turry	Creative song improvisations for children with cancer	In C. Dileo (ed) *Music Therapy and Medicine*, Cherry Hill, NJ: Jeffrey Books.
1999	M. S. Ritholz and C. Robbins	*Themes for Therapy*	New York: Carl Fischer Music
2001	A. Turry	Supervision in NR-MT training program	In M. Forinash (ed.) *Music Therapy Supervision*, Gilsum, NH: Barcelona Publishing
2002	T. Tyler	In the music prison: The story of Pablo	In J. Sutton (ed) *Music, Music Therapy, and Trauma*, London: Jessica Kingsley Publishers.
2003	M. S. Ritholz and C. Robbins	*More Themes for Therapy*	New York: Carl Fischer Music
2003	A. Turry and D. Marcus	Using the NR approach to music therapy with adults diagnosed with autism	In D. Weiner and L. Oxford, *Action Therapy for Families and Groups*, Washington, DC: American Psychological Association

Date	Author	Title	Publication/source
2005	K. Aigen	*Being in Music: Foundations of Nordoff-Robbins Music Therapy Volume I of the NR-MT Monograph Series*	Gilsum, NH: Barcelona Publishers
2005	A. Turry and D. Marcus	Teamwork: Therapist and co-therapist	*Music Therapy Perspectives 23(1)*, 53–69
2006	L. Forrest	Singing, playing, and storytelling: Creative music experiences in community pediatric palliative care	*Journal of Palliative Care 22(3)*
2007	J. Fachner	Co-therapists in Nordoff/Robbins Music Therapy	*Music Therapy Today 8(1)*
2007	F. Simpson	*Every Note Counts: The Story of Nordoff-Robbins Music Therapy*	London: James and James
2008	A.A. Darrow	Nordoff-Robbins music therapy	Introduction to Approaches in Music Therapy
2008	K. Stachyra	Nordoff-Robbins music therapy	*Voices 8(3)*
2009	A. Turry	Integrating musical and psychological thinking: The relationship between music and words in clinically improvised songs	*Music and Medicine 1*
2009	K. Aigen	Verticality and containment in song and improvisation: An application of schema theory to Nordoff-Robbins Music Therapy	*Journal of Music Therapy 46(3)*

Date	Author	Title	Publication/source
2009	F. Simpson	*The Nordoff-Robbins Adventure: Fifty Years of Creative Music Therapy*	London: James and James
2010	G. Ansdell and M. Pavlicevic	Practicing "gentle empiricism": The Nordoff-Robbins research heritage	*Music Therapy Perspectives 28*
2010	M. L. Cooper	Clinical-musical responses of Nordoff-Robbins music Therapists: The process of clinical improvisation	In S. Hadley (ed.) *Qualitative Inquiries in Music Therapy*, Vol. V, New Braunfels, TX: Barcelona Publishers
2010	M. L. Hartley, A. Turry and P. Raghavan	The role of music and music therapy in aphasia rehabilitation	*Music and Medicine 2*
2010	D. M. Kim	Towards musical individuation: Korean female music therapists' experiences in the Nordoff-Robbins Music Therapy certification program	*The Arts in Psychotherapy 37*
2010	R. Verney and G. Ansdell	*Conversations on Nordoff-Robbins Music Therapy:* Volume V of the NR-MT Monograph Series	Gilsum, NH: Barcelona Publishers
2010	S. Sorel	Presenting Carly and Elliott: Exploring roles and relationships in a mother–son dyad in Nordoff-Robbins Music Therapy	In S. Hadley (ed.) *Qualitative Inquiries in Music Therapy*, Vol. V, New Braunfels, TX: Barcelona Publishers
2011	M. Logis	Facing the dread and desolation of cancer through music therapy	*Music and Medicine 3(1)*

Date	Author	Title	Publication/source
2012	Various	Various	*Music Therapy Approaches: Tribute to Clive Robbins and Special Music Education 4(1)*
2012	Various	Tribute to Clive Robbins	*Voices 12*
2013	M. M. P. Acosta	Improvised singing: A Nordoff-Robbins based vocal music therapy intervention in the treatment of pain	In J. Mondanaro and G. Sara (eds) *Music and Medicine: Integrative Models in the Treatment of Pain*, New York: Satchnote Press
2013	J. C. Birnbaum	*Healing Childhood Trauma Through Music and Play*: Volume VI of the NR-MT Monograph Series	Gilsum, NH: Barcelona. Publishers
2013	F. B. Haslbeck	The interactive potential of Creative Music Therapy with premature infants and their parents: A qualitative study	*Nordic Journal 23(1)*
2014	K. Aigen	Music-centered dimensions of Nordoff-Robbins Music Therapy	*Music Therapy Perspectives 32(1)*
2014	J. C. Birnbaum	Intersubjectivity and Nordoff-Robbins Music Therapy	*Music Therapy Perspectives 32(1)*
2014	N. Guerrero	From history to contemporary: Nordoff-Robbins Music Therapy in collaborative interdisciplinary rehabilitation	*Music Therapy Perspectives 32(1)*
2014	M. Ritholz	The primacy of music and music resources in Nordoff-Robbins Music Therapy	*Music Therapy Perspectives 32(1)*

BIBLIOGRAPHY

Abrams, B. (2002) 'Definitions of transpersonal BMGIM experience.' *Nordic Journal of Music Therapy 11*(2), 103–126.

Abrams, B. (2013) 'A Perspective on the Role of Personal Therapy in Analytical Music Therapy Training.' In K. Bruscia (ed.) *Self Experiences in Music Therapy Education, Training, and Supervision.* New Braunfels, TX: Barcelona Publishers.

Aigen, K. (1998) *Paths of Development in Nordoff-Robbins Music Therapy.* Gilsum, NH: Barcelona Publishers.

Aigen, K. (2005a) *Being in Music: Foundations of NR-MT. 1.* The Nordoff-Robbins Music Therapy Monograph Series. New Braunfels, TX: Barcelona Publishers.

Aigen, K. (2005b) *Music-Centered Music Therapy.* New Braunfels, TX: Barcelona Publishers.

Aigen, K. (2014) *The Study of Music Therapy: Current Issues and Concepts.* New York: Routledge.

Ainlay, G.W. (1948) 'The Place of Music in Military Hospitals.' In D. M. and M. Schoen (eds) *Music and Medicine.* New York: Henry Schuman.

Altshuler, I. (1941) 'The part of music in resocialization of mental patients.' *Occupational Therapy and Rehabilitation 20*, 75–86.

Altshuler, I. (February, 1945) 'The past, present, and future of musical therapy.' *Educational Music Magazine*, 16–17, 53–54.

AMI (Association for Music and Imagery) (2015a) *Interactive Directory of GIM Practitioners.* Accessed on June 16, 2015 at http://ami-bonnymethod.org/resources/directory.

AMI (2015b) *Home: About.* Accessed on June 16, 2015 at http://ami-bonnymethod.org/about.

AMI (2001 rev.) *Education Standards and Procedures for The Bonny Method of GIM.* Author.

AMTA (2006) *Advisory on Levels of Practice.* Silver Spring, MD: Author.

AMTA (2007a) *Advisory on Specialized Training.* Silver Spring, MD: Author.

AMTA (2007b) *Policy of the use of Acronyms.* Silver Spring, MD: Author.

AMTA (2010) *Master's Level Entry: Core Considerations.* Silver Spring, MD: Author.

AMTA (2011) *Master's Level Entry: Moving Forward.* Silver Spring, MD: Author.

AMTA (rev. 2013) *Professional Competencies.* Silver Spring, MD: Author.

AMTA (2014) *What is Music Therapy?* Accessed on June 20, 2014 at www.musictherapy.org/about/musictherapy.

AMTA (rev. 2014) *Code of Ethics.* Silver Spring, MD: Author.

AMTA (2015) *Music Therapy Perspectives.* Accessed on June 16, 2015 at www.musictherapy.org/research/pubs.

AMTA (rev. 2015a) *Standards for Education and Clinical Training.* Silver Spring, MD: Author.

AMTA (rev. 2015b) *Standards of Clinical Practice.* Silver Spring, MD: Author.

AMTA (rev. 2016a) *By-Laws.* Silver Spring, MD: Author.

AMTA (rev. 2016b) *Advanced Competencies.* Silver Spring, MD: Author.

AMTA and CBMT (2015) *Scope of Music Therapy Practice.* Silver Spring, MD: Author.

Ansdell, G. (1995) *Music for Life: Aspects of Creative Music Therapy with Adult Clients.* London: Jessica Kingsley Publishers.

Assagioli, R. (1965) *Psychosynthesis: A Manual of Principles and Techniques.* New York: Viking Press.

Austin, D. (1999) 'Vocal Improvisation in Analytically Oriented Music Therapy with Adults.' In T. Wigram and J. de Backer (eds) *Clinical Applications of Music Therapy in Psychiatry* (pp.141–157). London: Jessica Kingsley Publishers.

Austin, D. (2001) 'In search of the self: The use of vocal holding techniques with adults traumatized as children.' *Music Therapy Perspectives 19*(1), 22–30.

Austin, D. (2004) 'When Words Sing and Music Speaks: A Qualitative Study of In Depth Music Psychotherapy with Adults.' Doctoral dissertation, New York University.

Austin, D. (2007) 'Vocal Psychotherapy.' In B. Crowe (ed.) *Effective Clinical Practice in Music Therapy: Music Therapy for Children, Adolescents, and Adults with Mental Disorders* (pp.76–93). Silver Spring, MD: American Music Therapy Association.

Austin, D. (2008) *The Theory and Practice of Vocal Psychotherapy: Songs of the Self.* London: Jessica Kingsley Publishers.

Austin, D. (2011). 'Foreword.' In F. Baker & S. Uhlig (eds) *Voicework in Music Therapy: Research and Practice* (pp. 13-17). London: Jessica Kingsley Publishers.

Austin, D. (2016) *Vocal Psychotherapy: Free Associative Singing.* Accessed on September 11, 2016 at https://youtu.be/IkJja3RgUHg.

Beck, D. M. (2005) 'Recapturing a vision to become fully human: The Bonny Method as a servant source in discovering the authentic self.' *Journal of the Association for Music and Imagery 10*, 45–54.

Birge, E. B. (1966). *History of Public School Music in the United States.* Washington, DC: MENC.

Bond, A. H. (2008) *Margaret Mahler.* New York: McFarland & Co.

Bonny, H. (1975) 'Music and consciousness.' *Journal of Music Therapy* 12(3), 121–135.

Bonny, H. (1978) *Facilitating GIM Sessions: GIM Monograph #1*. Baltimore, MD: ICM Books.

Bonny, H. L. (1978) *The Role of Taped Music Programs in the GIM Process: GIM Monograph #2*. Baltimore, MD: ICM Books.

Bonny, H. (1994) 'Twenty-one years later: A GIM update.' *Music Therapy Perspectives: Psychiatric Music Therapy* (ed. F. Goldberg) 12(2), 70–74.

Bonny, H. (1997) 'The art of music therapy.' *The Arts in Psychotherapy* 24(1), 65–73.

Bonny, H. (2002) 'Autobiographical Essay.' In L. Summer (ed.) *Music and Consciousness: The Evolution of Guided Imagery and Music*. Gilsum, NH: Barcelona Publishers.

Bonny, H. L. and Latteier, C. (1983) *Music Rx Manual: An innovative program designed for the hospital setting*. Salina, Kansas: The Bonny Foundation.

Bonny, H. L. and Savary, L. M. (1974) *Music and Your Mind*. Barrytown, NY: Station Hill Press.

Boxberger, R. (1963) 'An historical study of the National Association for Music Therapy.' Doctoral dissertation, University of Kansas, Lawrence.

Bruscia, K. (1987) *Improvisational Models of Music Therapy*. Springfield, IL: Charles C. Thomas.

Bruscia, K. (1996) *Music for the Imagination: Rationale, Implications and Guidelines for Its Use in Guided Imagery and Music*. Santa Cruz, CA: AMI.

Bruscia, K. (1998) *Defining Music Therapy* (2nd edn). New Braunfels, TX: Barcelona Publishers.

Bruscia, K. (2002) 'Foreword.' In B. Stige, *Culture-Centered Music Therapy* (pp. xiii-xviii). Gilsum, NH: Barcelona Publishers.

Bruscia, K. (ed.) (2012) *Readings on Music Therapy Theory*. Gilsum, NH: Barcelona Publishers.

Bruscia, K. (2014) *Defining Music Therapy* (3rd edn). New Braunfels, TX: Barcelona Publishers.

Bruscia, K. and Grocke, D. E. (eds) (2002) *Guided Imagery and Music: The Bonny Method and Beyond* (pp.563–591). Gilsum, NH: Barcelona Publishers.

Bruscia, K., Hesser, B. and Hillman Boxill, E. (1981) 'Essential competencies for the practice of music therapy.' *Music Therapy* 1, 43–49.

Bunt, L. (2004) 'Mary Priestley interviewed by Leslie Bunt.' *Voices* 4(2).

Bunt, L. (2015) 'The integration of art and science in music therapy training: Some challenges in the UK.' In K. Goodman (ed.) *International Perspectives in Music Therapy Education and Training: Adapting to a Changing World*. Springfield, IL: Charles C Thomas.

Bunt, L. and Hoskyns, S. (eds) (2002) *The Handbook of Music Therapy*. Hove: Brunner-Routledge.

Bunt, L. and Stige, B. (2014) *Music Therapy: An Art Beyond Words* (2nd edn). London: Routledge.

Bush, C. (1999) *Healing Imagery and Music: Paths to the Inner Self.* New York. Sterling.

Cadrin, L. (2005) 'Dying well: The Bonny Method of GIM at end of life.' *Journal of the Association for Music and Imagery 10,* 1–25.

CBMT (Certification Board for Music Therapists) (1985) *Examination Content Outline.* Downingtown, PA: Author.

CBMT (2001) *Code of Professional Practice.* Downingtown, PA: Author.

Charboneau, E. A., Gordon, B. and Green, J. P. (2008) 'Music Therapy.' In *Encyclopedia of Music in Canada.* Accessed on April 1, 2008 at www.thecanadianencyclopedia.com/index.cfm?PgNm=TCE&Params=U1ARTU0002520.

Chen, G., Elisha, E., Timor, U. and Ronel, N. (2012) 'Parents' perceptions of their adolescent sons' recovery in a therapeutic community for addicted clients.' *International Journal of Offender Therapy and Comparative Criminology 57*(11), 1417–1436.

Clarkson, V. (2005) 'Enhancing Bonny Method sessions with subtle energy healing.' *Journal of the Association for Music and Imagery 10,* 27–43.

Cohen, N. (2004) 'Musical choices: An interview with Helen Lindquist Bonny.' *Journal of the Association for Music and Imagery 9,* 1–26.

Cooper, M. L. (2012) 'A musical analysis of how Mary Priestley implemented the techniques she developed for analytical music therapy.' Doctoral dissertation, Temple University, Philadelphia, PA.

Darrow, A. A. (ed.) (2008) *Introduction to Approaches in Music Therapy* (2nd edn). Silver Spring, MD: American Music Therapy Association.

Darrow, A. A. and Heller, G. N. (1985) 'Early advocates of music education for the hearing impaired: William Wolcott Turner and David Ely Bartlett.' *Journal of Research in Music Education 33,* 269–279.

Davis, W. (1987) 'Music therapy in nineteenth-century America.' *Journal of Music Therapy 19,* 76–87.

Davis, W. B. (1988) "Music Therapy in Victorian England." *Journal of British Music Therapy, 2*(1), 10–17.

Davis, W. and Gfeller, K. E. (2002) 'Music Therapy: A Historical Perspective.' In W. B. Davis, K. E. Gfeller and M. H. Thaut (eds) *An Introduction to Music Therapy: Theory and Practice* (2nd edn) (pp.15–34). New York: McGraw-Hill Higher Education.

Davis, W. B., Gfeller, K. E. and Thaut, M. H. (1999) *An Introduction to Music Therapy: Theory and Practice.* New York: McGraw-Hill.

De Leon, G. (2000) *The Therapeutic Community: Theory, Model and Method.* New York: Springer Publishing Company.

de l'Etoile, S. (2000) 'The history of the undergraduate curriculum in music therapy.' *Journal of Music Therapy 37,* 51–71.

Dictionary.com (2014a) 'Model'. Accessed on 4 February 2014 at www.dictionary.com/browse/model?s=t.

Dictionary.com (2014b) 'Theory'. Accessed on 4 February 2014 at www.dictionary.com/browse/theory?s=t.

Dodds, M. (dir.) (1987) *Music and The Shadow*.

Doerner, N. M. (2015) F5 [Computer Software]. Retrieved from http://audiotranskription.de

Dictionary.com (2016) 'Scientific Method'. Accessed on 20 July 2017 at www.dictionary.reference.com/browse/scientific+method.

Elliott, W. (1996) *Tying Rocks to Clouds: Meetings and Conversations with Wise and Spiritual People* (rev. edn.). New York: Image Books.

Eschen, J. Th. (ed.) (2002) *Analytical Music Therapy*. London: Jessica Kingsley Publishers.

Eyre, L. (2007) 'Changes in Images, Life Events and Music in Analytical Music Therapy. A Reconstruction of Mary Priestley's Case Study of "Curtis." In A. Meadows (ed.) *Qualitative Inquiries in Music Therapy: A Monograph Series* (Vol. 3, pp.1–30). Gilsum, NH: Barcelona Publishers.

French, S. (1994a) 'Models.' In R. J. Corsini (ed.) *Encyclopedia of Psychology* (Vol. 2, pp.421–422). New York: John Wiley & Sons.

French, S. (1994b) 'Models in science.' In R. J. Corsini (ed.) *Encyclopedia of Psychology* (Vol. 2, pp.622–623). New York: John Wiley & Sons.

Freud, S. (1938) *An Outline of Psychoanalysis*. New York: Norton.

Gaston, E. T. (1968) 'Man and music.' In E. T. Gaston (ed.) *Music in Therapy* (pp.7–29). New York: Collier Macmillan Ltd.

Gibbons, A. C. and Heller, G. (1985) 'Music therapy in Handel's England: Browne's Musica Medicina 1729.' *College Music Symposium 25*, 59–72.

Goldberg, F. S. (1992). Images of emotion: The role of emotion in Guided Imagery and Music. *Journal of the Association for Music and Imagery, 1*, 5-17.

Goldberg, F. S. (1995) 'Bonny Method of Guided Imagery.' In T. Wigram, B. Saperston, and R. West (eds) *The Art and Science of Music Therapy: A Handbook* (pp.112–128). Abingdon: Routledge.

Goldberg, F. S. and Dimiceli-Mitran, L. (2010) 'The central tenets of the Bonny Method of GIM: Consciousness and the integration of psychotherapy and spirituality.' *Voices 10*(3).

Goodman, K. (2011) *Music Therapy Education and Training: From Theory to Practice*. Springfield, IL: Charles C. Thomas.

Grocke, D. E. (2002) 'The Bonny Method Programs.' In K. E. Bruscia and D. E. Grocke (eds) *Guided Imagery and Music: The Bonny Method and Beyond* (pp.99–133). Gilsum, NH: Barcelona Publishers.

Hadley, S. (2001) 'Exploring relationships between Mary Priestley's life and work.' *Nordic Journal of Music Therapy 10*(2), 37–41.

Haig, B. D. (2010) 'Models.' In N. J. Salkind (ed.) *Encyclopedia of Research Design* (Vol. 2, pp.826–830). Thousand Oaks, CA: Sage.

Hammersley, M. (2004) 'Theory.' In M. Lewis-Beck, A. Bryman and T. Liao (eds) *The Sage Encyclopedia of Social Science Research Methods* (p.1123). London: Sage Publications.

Hanson-Abromeit, D. (2015) 'A conceptual methodology to define the therapeutic function in music.' *Music Therapy Perspectives 33*(1), 25–38.

HCPC (2013) *Standards of Proficiency: Arts Therapists.* Author.

HCPC (Health and Care Professions Council) (2016a) *Standards of Conduct, Performance and Ethics.* Author.

HCPC (2017) *Standards of Education and Training Guidance.* Author. Accessed on May 16, 2017 at www.hcpc-uk.co.uk/publications/standards/index.asp?id=195.

Heller, G. N. (1987) 'Ideas, initiatives, and implementations: Music therapy in America, 1789–1848.' *Journal of Music Therapy 24,* 35–46.

Hillman Boxill, E. (1985) *Music Therapy for the Developmentally Disabled.* Bethesda, MD: Aspen Systems Corporation.

Horden, P. (ed.) (2000) *Music as Medicine: The History of Music Therapy Since Antiquity.* Aldershot: Ashgate Publishing.

Jacobson, E. (1938) *Progressive Relaxation.* Chicago, IL: University of Chicago Press.

Jung, C.G. (1951) *Fundamental Questions of Psychotherapy.* Trans. R. F. C. Hull. Princeton, NJ: Princeton University Press.

Keiser, L. H. (1986) *Conscious Listening: An Annotated Guide to the ICM Taped Music Programs.* Port Townsend, WA: Institute for Consciousness and Music.

Kenny, K. (2012) *Music and Life in the Field of Play: An Anthology.* Gilsum, NH: Barcelona Publishers.

Keyes, L. (1973) *Toning: The Creative Power of the Voice.* Marina del Rey, CA: DeVorss.

Kirkland, K. (2009) 'Suffering and the subline: A case study of music, metaphor and meaning. *Journal of the Association of Music and Imagery 11,* 21–28.

Körlin, D. (2009) 'Music breathing, breath grounding, and modulation of the Bonny Method of Guided Imagery and Music (BMGIM) theory, method, and consecutive cases.' *Journal of the Association for Music and Imagery 11,* 79–109.

Kowski, J. (2007) 'Can You Play with Me? Dealing with Trauma, Grief and Loss through Analytical Music Therapy and Play Therapy.' In V. A. Camilleri (ed.) *Healing the Inner City Child: Creative Arts Therapies with At-Risk-Youth,* pp.1–31). London: Jessica Kingsley Publishers.

Leuner, H. (1984) *Guided Affective Imagery.* Stuttgart, Germany: Thieme Medical Publishers.

Maibom, H. L. (2010) 'Theory theory.' *Encyclopedia of Research Design* (Vol. 2, pp.995–997). Thousand Oaks, CA: Sage.

Meadows, T. (2010) 'The evolution of GIM programming.' *Voices 10* (3).

Melzack, R. and Wall, P. (1982) *The Challenge of Pain.* Harmondsworth: Penguin Books.

Merriam, A. P. (1964) *The Anthropology of Music.* Evanston, IL: Northwestern University Press.

Merriam Webster (2014a) 'Method'. Accessed on 4 February 2014 at https://www.merriam-webster.com/dictionary/method.

Merriam Webster (2014b) 'Model'. Accessed on 4 February 2014 at https://www.merriam-webster.com/dictionary/model.

Merriam Webster (2014c) 'Theory'. Accessed on 4 February 2014 at https://www.merriam-webster.com/dictionary/theory.

Merriam Webster (2015) 'Strategy'. Accessed on 4 February 2014 at https://www.merriam-webster.com/dictionary/strategy.

Merritt, S. (1990) *Mind, Music and Imagery.* New York: Plume.

Michel, D. E. and Pinson, J. (2005) *Music Therapy in Principle and Practice.* Springfield, IL: Charles C. Thomas.

Muller, B. (2014) *Variations in Guided Imagery and Music: Taking a Closer Look.* New Braunfels, TX: Barcelona Publishers.

NAMT (1993) *NAMT Educational Competencies.* Silver Spring, MD: Author.

NAMT (1996) *Professional Competencies.* Silver Spring, MD: Author.

NOCA (National Organization for Competency Assurance) (2004) *Standards for the Accreditation of Certification Programs.* Author.

Nordoff, P. and Robbins, C. (1962) *The First Book of Children's Play Songs.* Bryn Mahr, PA: Theodore Presser.

Nordoff, P. and Robbins, C. (1977) *Creative Music Therapy: Individualized Treatment for the Handicapped Child.* New York: John Day Books in Special Education.

Nordoff, P. and Robbins, C. (1998) "Edward." *Nordic Journal of Music Therapy, 7,* 57–64.

Nordoff-Robbins Center for Music Therapy (2015) 'Training Programs.' Accessed on September 7, 2015 at http://steinhardt.nyu.edu/music/nordoff/training.

Nordoff-Robbins Centre London (2011) 'Master of Music Therapy (Nordoff-Robbins): Music, Health, Society.' Accessed on September 7, 2015 at www.nordoff-robbins.org.uk/our-centres-and-units.

Nordoff-Robbins Centre, London (2015) 'Train to Become a Music Therapist.' Accessed on September 7, 2015 at www.nordoff-robbins.org.uk/training.

Online Etymology Dictionary (2014a) 'Method'. Accessed on 4 February 2014 at www.etymonline.com/index.php?allowed_in_frame=0&search=theory.

Online Etymology Dictionary (2014b) 'Theory'. Accessed on 4 February 2014 at www.etymonline.com/index.php?allowed_in_frame=0&search=theory.

Parry, D. (Dir.) (1976) *The Music Child* [film]. Cambridge, MD: David Parry Productions.

Preston-Roberts, P. (2011) 'An interview with Dr. Diane Austin.' *Voices 11* (1).

Priestley, M. (1965) *Going Abroad.* London: Harper Collins.

Priestley, M. (1975) *Music Therapy in Action.* London: Constable.

Priestley, M. (1994) *Essays on Analytical Music Therapy.* Phoenixville, PA: Barcelona Publishers.

QSR International (2016) NVivo for Mac. Retrieved from http://www.qsrinternational.com.

Robbins, C. (1997) *What a Wonderful Song her Life Sang. An anthology of appreciation for Carol Robbins.* New York: International Trust for Nordoff-Robbins Music Therapy.

Robbins, C. (2005) *A Journey into Creative Music Therapy* (Vol. 4). *The Nordoff-Robbins Music Therapy Monograph Series.* New Braunfels, TX: Barcelona Publishers.

Robbins, C. and Robbins, C. (1981) *Music for the Hearing Impaired and Other Special Groups.* St. Louis, MO: MMB Music.

Russo, F. (1994) 'Models in science.' In R. J. Corsini (ed.) *Encyclopedia of Psychology* (Vol. 2, pp.623–625). New York: John Wiley & Sons.

Ruud, E. (1980) *Music Therapy and Its Relationship to Current Treatment Theories.* St. Louis, MO: Magnamusic Baton.

Scheiby, B. B. (1999) 'Music as Symbolic Expression: An Introduction to Analytical Music Therapy.' In D. J. Wiener (ed.) *Beyond Talk Therapy: Using Movement and Expressive Techniques in Clinical Practice* (pp.263–285). Washington, DC: APA Books.

Scheiby, B. B. (2010) 'Analytical Music Therapy and Integrative Medicine: The Impact of Medical Trauma on the Psyche.' In K. Stewart (ed.) *Music Therapy and Trauma: Bridging Theory and Clinical Practice* (pp.74–87). New York: Satchnote.

Scheiby, B. B. (2013) 'Opnaaelse af indsigt gennem analytisk musikterapi (AMT) supervision. [Insight acquired through analytical music therapy (AMT) supervision].' In I.N. Pedersen (ed.) *Art Media in Psychotherapy Supervision: Insight and Vitality.* Aalborg: Aalborg Universitetsforlag.

Scheiby, B. B. and Montello, L. (1994) 'Introduction to Psychodynamic Peer Supervision in Music Therapy: "Dancing with the Wolves" in the Client-Therapist Relationship.' In *Connections: Integrating Our Work and Play: Conference Proceedings of the Annual Conference of the American Association for Music Therapy* (pp.217–223).

Schmidt Peters, J. (1987) *Music Therapy: An Introduction.* Springfield, IL: Charles C. Thomas.

Sears, W. (1968) 'Processes in music therapy.' In E. Thayer Gaston (ed.) *Music in Therapy* (pp.30–44). New York: Macmillan.

Shakespeare, W. (1974) *The Tragedy of Romeo and Juliet*. In *The Riverside Shakespeare* (pp.1055–1099). Boston, MA: Houghton Mifflin Company.

Simpson, F. (2007) *Every Note Counts*. London: James & James.

Simpson, F. (2009) *The Nordoff-Robbins Adventure: Fifty Years of Creative Music Therapy*. London: James & James.

Stam, J. J. (2010a) "Theory." In N. J. Salkind (ed.) *Encyclopedia of Research Design* (Vol. 3, pp.1498–1502). Thousand Oaks, CA: Sage.

Stam, J. J. (2010b) "Method." In N. J. Salkind (ed.) *Encyclopedia of Research Design* (Vol. 3, pp.1325–1329). Thousand Oaks, CA: Sage.

Stige, B. (2002) *Culture-Centered Music Therapy*. Gilsum, NH: Barcelona Publishers.

Stige, B. (2015) 'The practice turn in music therapy theory.' *Music Therapy Perspectives 33*(1), 3–11.

Stokes, S. J. (1992) 'Letting the sound depths arise.' *Journal of the Association for Music and Imagery* 69–76.

Summer, L. (1997) 'Considering the future of music therapy.' *The Arts in Psychotherapy 24*(1), 75–80.

Taylor, D. B. (1981) 'Music in general hospital treatment from 1900–1950.' *Journal of Music Therapy 18*, 62–73.

Trondalen, G. (2009) 'Exploring the rucksack of sadness: Focused time-limited Bonny Method of Guided Imagery and Music with a female executive.' *Journal of the Association for Music and Imagery 12*, 1–20.

Tyler, H. M. (2000). 'The music therapy profession in modern Great Britain.' In P. Horden (ed.), *Music as medicine: The history of music therapy since antiquity* (pp.375-393). Aldershot, UK: Ashgate Publishing.

van Atta, K. (1980) *An Account of the Events Surrounding the Origin of Friends Hospital and a Brief Description of the Early Years of Friends Asylum 1817–1820*. Accessed on November 5, 2005 at www.friendshospitalonline.org

Van de Wall, W. (1936) *Music in Institutions*. New York: Russell Sage Foundation.

Ventre, M. and McKinney, C. H. (2015) 'The Bonny Method of Guided Imagery and Music.' In B. L. Wheeler (ed.) *Music Therapy Handbook* (pp.196–205). New York: Guilford Press.

Wartofsky, M. (1979) *Models: Representation and the Scientific Understanding*. Dordrecht, the Netherlands: Reidel.

Watts, T. D. (1980) 'Theories of aging: The difference in orientations.' *Journal of Music Therapy 17*, 84–89.

Wheeler, B. L. (2012) 'Introduction to the 9th World Congress of Music Therapy.' *Voices 12*(1), 1–2.

Wigram, T., Nygaard Pedersen, I. and Bonde, L. O. (2002) *A Comprehensive Guide to Music Therapy*. London: Jessica Kingsley Publishers.

Winnicott, D. W. (1971) *Playing and Reality*. London: Routledge.

Wright, P. and Priestley, M. (1972) 'Analytical music therapy.' *British Journal of Music Therapy 3*(2), 20–24.

SUBJECT INDEX

accessing unconscious technique 86–7
Advanced Certified Music Therapist (ACMT) 34–5
advanced methods of music therapy practice
  change in relationship with method
    amendments 177
    new populations 178–9
    personal reconstruction 175–6
    question to experts 71
    relationship with music 176
    responses from experts 175–9
    roots 177
  changes in professional music therapy association' attitudes towards method
    question to experts 71
    responses from experts 185–7
  in context 167–8
  defining 'advanced' 67–9
  formative process for 68
  future of advanced methods
    question to experts 71
    responses from experts 192
  intentions to create new music therapy approach
    question to experts 71
    responses from experts 179–84
  meaning of 'advanced' 65–7
  method as part of music therapy practice
    question to experts 72
    responses from experts 190–2
  method teaching about music therapy
    question to experts 71
    response from experts 173–4
  problem with definitions 65–7
  questions about current practice and training 70–1
  questions about founders 69–70
  questions to experts 71–2
    responses 168–87, 190–2
    unanswered 192–3

reasons for methods resonating
  challenge 171
  imagery 170
  music 169–70
  question to experts 71
  receiving method 168–9
  relationships 172–3
  responses from experts 168–73
  self-discovery 170–1
  tree analogy 189, 194
  see also Analytical Music Therapy (AMT); Bonny Method of Guided Imagery and Music (BMGIM); Nordoff-Robbins Music Therapy; Vocal Psychotherapy (VP)
aesthetic shaping 140–1
affirmations/celebrations 87
Alvin, Juliette 50–1, 79, 136, 179, 181
amendments 177
American Association for Music Therapy (AAMT) 32–6, 40, 43, 109, 136, 182, 190
American Music Therapy Association (AMTA)
  competencies 39–40
  function 36
  general education and training 38–9
  internship 40
  levels of education 41
  membership and employees 36–7
  official documents 37–8, 68
  openness to potential of music therapy as form of psychotherapy 109–10
  post-unification 36–41
  unification 35–6, 43
AMT see Analytical Music Therapy (AMT)
AMTA see American Music Therapy Association (AMTA)
Analytical Music Therapy (AMT)
  acceptance of 185
  as advanced method of music therapy 69
  concern about future 93–4

— 242 —

SUBJECT INDEX

educational requirements 65
experience of receiving 81–2, 168
functions of improvisation 81
method 80–2
as model of music therapy 63
observing sessions 88–90
Priestley
  as initiator of 76, 80
  recording sessions 85, 169
  writings on 91–2, 163
psychodynamic foundations 82
resistance 84
roots 177
techniques
  accessing unconscious 86–7
  consciousness probing 86
  ego strengthening 87–8
  improvised music 81, 83, 85–6
training 90–1, 94
transference and countertransference in 84
writings by other authors 92–3
Anderton, Margaret 25–6
Association for Music and Imagery (AMI) 101, 114–18
Association of Professional Music Therapists (APMT) 50–1, 53
Austin, Diane
adulthood 151–2
on change in music therapy profession 186
early years 150
emphasizing observation of vocal behaviors 152–5
focus primarily on traditionally able persons 178
intention to create new music therapy approach 183–4
meeting with 149
on training 158–60
in video 156
wounded healer 172
writings 160–1, 163, 172
Austin Vocal Psychotherapist (AVPT) 160
awareness and response 140–1

Bartlett, Ely 23–4
behaviorism 189–90
bioenergetics 175
Blumer, George 24
BMGIM *see* Bonny Method of Guided Imagery and Music (BMGIM)
board certification 38, 40–1, 142–3
Board Certified (BC) 35
Bonny, Helen
AMTA honoring 109–10
benefits of music 104
career summary 105–6

cut-log diagram of consciousness 107
early years 96–9
egg-shaped diagram of psychosynthesis 106–7
encouraging students 169
experimentation with relaxation techniques 110
friendship with 95–6
on importance of training 115
influences on 106–8
intention to create new music therapy approach 182
as mother 99–101
music programs emulating drug effects 105–6, 178
and music therapy 103–4
rejection by members of NAMT 109, 185
violin experience 101–3
writings by 119–21, 127, 163
Bonny Method of Guided Imagery and Music (BMGIM)
defining GIM 108–10
educational requirements 65
as form of advanced music therapy practice 69, 194
method 104–6
music programs 113–15
new uses of 178–9
techniques
  induction 111–12
  music 112
  postlude 113
  prelude 111
  relaxation 110
theoretical foundations 106–8
training 115–18, 190–1
writings
  by Helen Bonny 119–21, 127, 163
  by other authors 121–7, 163
breath 150, 153
British Association for Music Therapy (BAMT) 53
British Society for Music Therapy (BSMT) 50–1, 53, 136
Browne, Richard 46–7

central nervous system (CNS) 26–7
Certification Board for Music Therapists (CBMT) 34–6, 41–2
Certified Music Therapist (CMT) 34–5
challenge 171
consciousness, cut-log diagram of 107
consciousness probing technique 86, 89
Corning, James Leonard 24
countertransference 84, 155, 160, 172, 179
CPCM (Council for Professions Complementary to Medicine) 53

— 243 —

depth 174
dream intracommunication 87
dream resolution 87

Edison, Thomas 25
education
AMTA
  general 38–9
  levels of 41
  in United Kingdom 53–5
ego strengthening technique 87–8
engagement 140–1
essence statements 155
European Association for Music and Imagery (EAMI) 117
exploring relationships 87

free associative singing 155–8, 160, 172
Freud, Sigmund
free association technique 155
influence on Helen Bonny 107
influence on Mary Priestley 82–3, 92, 179
Friends Asylum 23

Gatewood, Esther 26–7
GIM *see* Bonny Method of Guided Imagery and Music (BMGIM)
Goldie Leigh Hospital 51, 136, 142
group clinical improvisation 139
guided imagery 86
Guild of St. Cecilia 47–9
Guildhall School of Music and Drama 50–2, 54, 79, 93, 136, 179–80

Handel's England 45–7
Harford, Frederick Kill 47–9
Health and Care Professions Council (HCPC) 53–5, 144
Health Professions Council (HPC) 52–3
history of music therapy
in United Kingdom 45–55
in United States 21–43
holding 86–7, 89
hospitals
changes in UK music therapy practice 47–50
changes in US music therapy practice 24–9, 189
Goldie Leigh 51, 136, 142
reasons for use of music in 49
treatment models 49

Ilsen, Isa Maud 26
imagery 170
indigenous techniques 139–40
indigenous theory 61–2
internship

AMTA 40
Diane Austin 151
investigating emotional investment 86, 89
Irvin Can Beat the Drum 140–2
"Iso Maneuver" 28

Jung, Carl
influence on Diane Austin 151–2, 172
influence on Helen Bonny 107–8
influence on Mary Priestley 82, 179

Kane, Evan O'Neill 25, 48
knowledge, skills and abilities (KSAs) 34–5

Levels of Practice (LOP) 37–8, 41, 68
Lowen, Alexander 175, 179
LSD (lysergic acid diethylamide) 104–5, 113, 178

Maryland Psychiatric Research Center (MPRC) 104–5, 110, 182
Mason, Lowell 23
Medicina Musica 45–7
method
advanced 65–72
definitions 59
linkage with Shakespeare's rose 57
music therapy 64–5
origin of term 64
relation with theory and model 58
scientific 64
milieu therapy 27–8
mindfulness-based stress reduction (MBSR) 175–6
model
definition 59
explanations 62
linkage with theory and method 58
music therapy 62–3
music
benefits of 104
in BMGIM 112, 169–70, 176
as core to therapy 169–70
relationship with 176
music-centeredness 82, 173–4
Music Child, The 129–30
Music Educators National Conference (MENC) 30
music programs
BMGIM 113–15
emulating effects of drugs 105–6, 178
Music Teachers National Association (MTNA) 29–31
Music Therapist-Board Certified (MT-BC) 35, 41–2
music therapy

and Helen Bonny 103–4
history in United Kingdom
  19th century 47–9
  20th century 49–51
  growth in courses 51–2
  in Handel's England 45–7
  music therapy as career 52–3
  training and education 53–5
history in United States
  before 1900 21–4
  from 1900 to 1940 25–8
  growth spurt 43
  need for training standards 29–30
  professional associations 31–43
method 57–9, 64–72
model 58–9, 62–3
theory 58–62
myths 87, 107

NAMT *see* National Association for Music Therapy (NAMT)
National Association for Music Therapy (NAMT)
  awarding of own designations 35
  Clive Robbins and Paul Nordoff 186
  criticisms of 32–3
  development 31–2
  Diane Austin 184
  early goals 42–3
  Helen Bonny 109, 182, 185
  illustration of mindset 103–4, 134
  lack of standardization across programs 39–40
  origins 31, 42
  unification 32, 34–6, 43, 109, 190
National Association of Schools of Music (NASM) 39
National Commission on Health Certifying Agencies (NCHCA) 35, 41
National Health Service (NHS) 53
National Institute of Mental Health (NIMH) 135
National Music Council (NMC) 30
National Organization for Competency Assurance (NOCA) 35, 41–2
National Therapeutic Society of New York 25, 48
natural sounds 150, 153
new populations 178–9
non-directivity 140–1
Nordoff, Paul
  challenging clients 171
  and Clive Robbins
    in Europe 136–7
    meeting 133–5
    in United States 135–6
  death of 137
  early years 131–2

intention to create new music therapy approach 182–3
  in *Irwin Can Beat the Drum* 141
  as music therapy pioneer 51
  relations with NAMT 186
  writings 144–6
Nordoff-Robbins Music Therapy
  as advanced method of music therapy 69
  educational requirements 65
  and *The Music Child* 129–30
  name of approach 137–8
  new course at Roehampton 51
  purity of music 169
  seeds sown for 131
  techniques
    group clinical improvisation 139
    indigenous 139–40
    Irvin Can Beat the Drum 140–2
  training 54, 66, 143–4, 191
  UK programs 52
  use with people with traumatic brain injuries 178
  working with music 172–3
  writings
    by Nordoff and Robbins 144–6
    by other authors 146–7
NRMT/NR-MT *see* Nordoff-Robbins Music Therapy

pain control 26–7
patterns of significance 88
personal reconstruction 175–6
phonographs 25, 48
post-graduate, multiple meanings of 66
Priestley, Mary
  adulthood 78–9
  bioenergetics 175
  early years 76–7
  impact on therapeutic milieu 82
  influence on Diane Austin 151
  as initiator of AMT 76, 80
  intention to create new music therapy approach 179–81, 183
  mentors 82–3
  music therapy training 79
  recording sessions 85, 169
  resistance 84, 179
  role of psychoanalysis 80, 82–3, 178–80
  and training 79, 179–81, 183
  transference and countertransference 84, 179
  Wikipedia entry 75–6
  working with 168–9
  writings on AMT 91–2, 163
professional associations (US) 31–43
Professionals Supplementary to Medicine Act (PSMA) 52–3
programmed regression 88

psychiatry 27–8, 92, 151, 178, 185
psychoanalysis 80, 82–3, 178–80
psychosynthesis 106–7

reality rehearsal 87
Registered Music Therapist (RMT) 31, 35
relationships 172–3
resistance 84, 89–90, 179
Robbins, Clive
  autobiographical narrative 138
  as captivating speaker 130
  challenging clients 171
  early years 132–3, 142
  intention to create new music therapy approach 182–3
  in *Irwin Can Beat the Drum* 141
  as music therapy pioneer 51
  and Paul Nordoff
    in Europe 136–7
    meeting 133–5
    in United States 135–6
  relations with NAMT 186
  writings 144–6
  roots 177
Rush, Benjamin 22–3

scientific method 47, 64
scientific revolution 47–8
self-discovery 170–1
Seymour, Harriet Ayer 26
Society for Music Therapy and Remedial Music 49–50
somatic communication 86
speaking voice 150, 153
splitting 86
Streeter, Elaine 51
sub-verbal communication 88
suicide 88
supportive music coactivity 140–1

theory
  definitions 58
  explanations 59–60
  indigenous 61–2
  linkage with method and model 58
  music therapy 60–1
  theoretical foundations of BMGIM 106–8
therapeutic community (TC) 64
toning 150, 154
training
  AMT 90–1, 94
  AMTA 38–9
  BMGIM 115–18, 190–1
  drawbacks to 191–2
  and Mary Priestley 79, 179–81, 183
  need for standards in 29–30

Nordoff-Robbins Music Therapy 54, 66, 143–4, 191
semantics 66
  in UK universities 51–2, 54–5, 65–6, 191
  in United Kingdom 51–5
  in US universities 25–6, 30–2, 40, 42, 129, 190–1
Vocal Psychotherapy 118, 158–60
transference 84, 155, 179
Turner, William Wolcott 23–4
Turry, Alan 131, 137–8, 142
two trees 189, 194

United Kingdom
  history of music therapy in 45–55, 136
  semantics 65–6
United States
  history of music therapy in 21–43
  Nordoff and Robbins in 135–6
  semantics 65–6
universities
  AMT training in 94
  limitations in training 191
  music therapy training in UK 51–2, 54–5, 65–6, 191
  music therapy training in US 25–6, 30–2, 40, 42, 129, 190–1
  question of responsibility for teaching advanced methods 193
University of West England 52, 54–5
Urban Federation of Music Therapists (UFMT) 32–3

Vescelius, Eva 25, 48
violin experience 101–3
vocal grounding 154–5
vocal holding 154–5, 160
vocal improvisation 150, 154
vocal mirroring 155
Vocal Psychotherapy (VP)
  as advanced method of music therapy 69, 149
  educational requirements 65, 158–9
  learning from other methods 163
  observing free associative singing session 156–8
  primary instrument 169
  techniques 150, 152–5
  training 118, 158–60
  writings
    by Diane Austin 160–1, 163, 172
    by other authors 162
  youth of method 149–50, 162

Whittaker, James 24
wholeness 87
wounded healer 172

AUTHOR INDEX

Abrams, B. 80–2, 84, 107–8
Aigen, K. 61–2, 131, 133–7, 174
Ainlay, G. W. 29
Altshuler, I. 28, 30
AMI (Association for Music and Imagery) 115–16, 118
AMTA (American Music Therapy Association) 32, 36–41, 68
Ansdell, G. 136, 138, 142
Assagioli, R. 106
Austin, D. 150–5, 159–60, 172, 184

Beck, D. M. 109
Birge, E. B. 23
Bond, A. H. 154–5
Bonde, L. O. 49, 63
Bonny, H. L. 94, 97–8, 102–5, 107–9, 111, 113, 115, 119–21, 163
Boxberger, R. 21–2, 26, 29–31
Bruscia, K. 34, 57–8, 61–3, 65, 67–8, 114, 125, 138
Bunt, L. 21, 29, 48–53, 60, 77, 80
Bush, C. 125

Cadrin, L. 109
CBMT (Certification Board for Music Therapists) 34–5, 37
Charboneau, E. A. 49–50
Chen, G. 64
Clarkson, V. 109
Cohen, N. S. 96–8, 102
Cooper, M. L. 86

Darrow, A. A. 24, 57
Davis, W. B. 22–7, 30–1, 48, 103
De Leon, G. 64–5
de l'Etoile, S. 25, 30–2
Dictionary.com 58–9, 64
Dimiceli-Mitran, L. 107–8
Dodds, M. 83
Doerner, N. M. 167

Elliott, W. 167–8
Eschen, J. Th. 93
Eyre, L. 85

French, S. 62
Freud, S. 155

Gaston, E. T. 30, 60, 129
Gfeller, K. E. 22, 27, 103
Gibbons, A. C. 46–7
Goldberg, F. S. 107–8, 170
Goodman, K. 50–1, 53
Gordon, B. 49–50
Green, J. P. 49–50
Grocke, D. E. 114, 125

Hadley, S. 76, 79–80, 82–4
Haig, B. D. 62
Hammersley, M. 59
Hanson-Abromeit, D. 60
HCPC (Health and Care Professions Council) 53–4
Heller, G. N. 22, 24, 46–7
Hesser, B. 34
Hillman Boxill, E. 27–9, 31–2, 34
Horden, P. 22–3, 25
Hoskyns, S. 53

Jacobson, E. 110–11
Jung, C. G. 172

Keiser, L. H. 106
Kenny, K. 60–1
Keyes, L. 154
Körlin, D. 109
Kowski, J. 86

Latteier, C. 106
Leuner, H. 110

Maibom, H. L. 60
McKinney, C. H. 106

Meadows, T. 104–5
Melzack, R. 27
Merriam, A. P. 26
Merriam Webster 58–9, 67
Merritt, S. 125
Michel, D. E. 27, 30, 34
Montello, L. 84
Muller, B. 125

NAMT (National Association for Music Therapy) 34, 40
NOCA (National Organization for Competency Assurance) 42
Nordoff, P. 138, 141, 145–6
Nordoff-Robbins Center for Music Therapy 142
Nordoff-Robbins Centre, London 144

Online Etymology Dictionary 58–9

Parry, D. 130
Pedersen, I. N. 49, 63, 94
Pinson, J. 27, 34
Preston-Roberts, P. 150–2, 154
Priestley, M. 78, 83–9, 181

QSR International 167

Robbins, Clive 131–5, 137–8, 141, 145–6, 186
Robbins, Carol 137

Russo, F. 62
Ruud, E. 60–1

Savary, L. M. 105, 119–20, 163
Scheiby, B. B. 81–5, 90–1, 93–4
Schmidt Peters, J. 25–6, 28, 30, 33–4
Sears, W. 60
Shakespeare, W. 57
Simpson, F. 131–5
Stam, J. J. 59, 64
Stige, B. 21, 29, 48–50, 60–1
Stokes, S. J. 108
Summer, L. 109, 125

Taylor, D. B. 25–8, 32
Thaut, M. H. 22
Trondalen, G. 107
Tyler, H. M. 47–50

van Atta, K. 23
Van de Wall, W. 28
Ventre, M. 106

Wall, P. 27
Wartofsky, M. 62–3
Watts, T. D. 60
Wheeler, B. L. 138
Wigram, T. 49, 63
Winnicott, D. W. 154
Wright, P. 85

CPI Antony Rowe
Eastbourne, UK
March 21, 2023